MW00737182

From Microfinance to Small Business Finance
The Business Case for Private Capital Investments

From Microfinance to Small Business Finance

The Business Case for Private Capital Investments

Edited by

Benoit Leleux
Stephan Schmidheiny Professor of Entrepreneurship and Finance, IMD, Switzerland

Dinos Constantinou
Managing Director, Global Microfinance Group, Switzerland

with the assistance of
Mope Ogunsulire

First published 2007 by
PALGRAVE MACMILLAN
Houndmills, Basingstoke, Hampshire RG21 6XS and
175 Fifth Avenue, New York, N.Y. 10010
Companies and representatives throughout the world

PALGRAVE MACMILLAN is the global academic imprint of the Palgrave
Macmillan division of St. Martin's Press, LLC and of Palgrave Macmillan Ltd.
Macmillan® is a registered trademark in the United States, United Kingdom
and other countries. Palgrave is a registered trademark in the European
Union and other countries.

ISBN-13: 978-0-230-01979-9   hardback
ISBN-10: 0-230-01979-X   hardback

This book is printed on paper suitable for recycling and made from fully
managed and sustained forest sources. Logging, pulping and manufacturing
processes are expected to conform to the environmental regulations of the
country of origin.

A catalogue record for this book is available from the British Library.

A catalog record for this book is available from the Library of Congress.

10   9   8   7   6   5   4   3   2
16   15   14   13   12   11   10   09   08

Printed and bound in Great Britain by
Antony Rowe Ltd, Chippenham and Eastbourne

Contents

List of Figures

List of Tables

Foreword

This publication, like the conference it records, reflects a growing interest in microfinance and small business finance on the part of the private sector. I believe that the move of the private sector into microfinance shows promise of transforming the field and significantly broadening the impact of microfinance on the lives of poor people.

In some sense, microfinance has been around forever: Moneylenders in India, saving and loan associations of various sorts and revolving credit schemes in Africa and Latin America have existed for centuries. They were expensive – particularly the moneylenders – but they did provide poor people with some access to financing for their business activities.

Despite the long history of microfinance in some form, development professionals only started focusing on it about 15 years ago, when the evidence began to accumulate that the depth and the reach of financial sectors matter enormously to the growth process and the development process.

Then came the question, "What about the impact of microfinance?" We had no answer until recently, but now the body of evidence on microfinance is growing, and it has convinced me. I am sure that in 20 years' time, the evidence will be as strong on the importance of microfinance to development and to helping poor people out of poverty, as it is now on the overall role of finance in development.

There are recent studies in the World Bank that show that the reach of financial institutions into poorer areas affects growth. There are micro-studies that I find even more persuasive: In particular, Professor Robert Townsend of the University of Chicago has, for nearly a decade, followed a group of villages in Thailand and watched how access to finance in that area has affected the individuals who were able to borrow. Through this kind of study, you can see people who had access to finance beginning to move out of poverty and create small and medium-size enterprises.

I suspect there are two reasons for the involvement of all of the participants in the Private Capital Symposium from which this publication emerged: Firstly, we are interested in investing and in helping others decide to invest; and secondly, we believe that this form of investment makes a contribution to improving the lives of other people. This is an investment that can actually help people achieve their own potential. And the more we can spread that message, and that activity, the better.

There are business people making money from microfinance and small business finance in developing countries – ICICI in India, Compartamos in Mexico, and many others. To encourage private investment from industrialized countries, we need to demonstrate that there is a real business case for microfinance and small business finance – and the success of these companies goes a long way in that direction.

Many microfinance institutions have been constrained because they have not taken on the traditional banking role of accepting deposits. There has been a focus on the lending side, although poor people also want to save. But if these institutions can take deposits as well as lend, they will have their own financing sources. This makes a significant contribution to the business case.

We also need to establish better routes for private capital from the industrialized world to invest in microfinance institutions. Although there are private equity funds interested in microfinance, we lack a well-developed brokerage system. When I was with Citigroup, I saw that private bank clients wanted to find places to invest, and I saw people on the commercial side helping them.

My experience with Citigroup shows that there are many ways for a major international financial institution to partner with microfinance institutions. The first is to provide microfinance institutions with capital, raised in local capital markets or even in international capital markets. Citigroup has also taken loans onto its books that were originally lent by microfinance institutions. I found it very touching to see these loan documents, such as one describing a loan for a hundred dollars to a person who had successfully repaid nine previous loans.

Citigroup, in cooperation with companies in other countries, has also developed insurance products for poor people. The remittance field is another area where, in collaboration with local institutions that have widespread branch networks, an institution from the industrialized countries can contribute significantly to reducing the cost of financing for poor people. And, of course, there is the demand from poor people for savings opportunities.

Finally, large international institutions can help train microfinance institutions in developing countries. There are many opportunities for this type of support.

All these areas of collaboration between microfinance institutions and international private sector banks are still developing. Financial brokerage services develop when there is both demand and supply. I can see that demand is growing. On the other side, there are companies that need financing. But it is not yet easy to invest in microfinance institutions.

There are several reasons why international financial institutions should partner with existing microfinance institutions in developing countries, rather than going directly to the market themselves. One reason is the high transaction cost per customer: This is a labor-intensive business. Another is that, owing to the nature of the microfinance customer base, borrowers often lack credit records. In many countries, there are also regulatory issues that complicate the microfinance market.

Also, it might be dangerous, in terms of public relations, for an international company to be seen to be making high profit margins off poor people, and companies such as Citigroup will not put themselves in that position. But the truth is that very high rates of return have been earned in this market. That is a sign that there is room for more competition and room to compete the rates of return down.

If we look forward five or ten years and project out current trends, we can see how some of the current obstacles will be resolved. First of all, the ability to collect information and to store it has already changed drastically. For example, I visited a branch of BRI in rural Indonesia in 1997, and there they were sitting at their computers, registering the loans on a system connected into Jakarta. Projecting that out, we will have much better records on both savers and borrowers, and the rates of return they can earn.

As more tracking data becomes available, we will find that some percentage of people who take out microfinance loans eventually go on to create small businesses. Following their customers, some microfinance institutions will move up the scale, to become lenders to small enterprises.

I believe that in the coming year we will see a much greater ability to move through the regular capital markets – whether in the industrialized countries or in the developing countries – to invest in a variety of microfinance institutions. These institutions will become more standardized and more capable of providing the sort of information that will enable investors to judge them.

At present, there is enormous interest in this area. Five to ten years from now, it may be a more competitive environment for microfinance institutions. Professionalism is growing both on the side of the providers of microfinance in developing countries, and on the side of the providers of finance in both developing and industrialized countries.

I believe that this industry will develop significantly, although it will always account for only a small share of the global value of financial assets. But more important than the industry's size is its impact: Microfinance can do a great deal to help people out of poverty. My own early skepticism about microfinance was cured when I actually visited microfinance projects in the field, and saw how much good small amounts of financing can do for people. I look forward to watching the industry grow and make a significant contribution to reducing poverty.

STANLEY FISCHER
Governor, Bank of Israel

Preface 1

Geneva is a city that regularly demonstrates its concern for world affairs. It is home to some of the most important multilateral institutions that provide assistance to populations in need. One can think of the ICRC, the UNHCR and the WHO, to name just a few.

Geneva is known for hosting many high-level meetings on topics that significantly impact on world matters and contribute to the future of developing countries.

Geneva is also a leading world financial center, with a strong emphasis on investments (140 banks, $1.2 trillion in assets under management). It is therefore not surprising that Geneva was for two days, in October 2005, the capital of microfinance, providing a platform for bankers, investors and many organizations active in microfinance to discuss the future of this promising asset class, coinciding with the UN International Year of Microcredit 2005.

Geneva has strong credentials in microfinance, thanks in particular to some brilliant forerunners active at UNCTAD who began to give thought to mobilizing private capital on behalf of microfinance institutions.

It was in Geneva that the first private investment fund in microfinance was launched, the *Dexia Micro-Credit Fund*, domiciled in Luxemburg, but designed from head to toe in Geneva and managed by the Geneva-based company *BlueOrchard*.

It was also in Geneva that the *MIX Market* was launched, to act not only as a global reference on the performance of MFIs, but above all as an investment tool for mobilizing private capital.

There are several reasons why investors are beginning to find the idea of investing in microfinance quite attractive:

- volatility is low
- risks are well managed through broad diversification
- investments are de-correlated from the macroeconomic environment and from the financial markets
- there is a growing demand for asset classes, or a sub-segment of asset classes, that offer absolute returns.

However, financial advisers and investment managers remain resistant to private investment in microfinance. We must remember that they are the trustees of assets placed in their hands by a third party, and therefore their fiduciary duty obliges them to invest in financial instruments that combine good returns with the best guarantees of preservation of capital, as well as adequate liquidity and transparency.

One of the aims of this symposium was to combat preconceived ideas among financial intermediaries, who may believe that microfinance is:

- not a fully-fledged asset class
- neither a high-yield bond nor an emerging market equity investment
- subject to lack of control, of due diligence, of marketability and liquidity
- a form of charity
- subject to currency risk.

We believe the symposium achieved its goal, and that the financial intermediaries in attendance became convinced that it is not only the privilege of multilateral institutions like the IFC or the EBRD, and some pioneer investors, to invest in microfinance.

This publication, which summarizes the presentations and discussions during the symposium, will reach a much wider circle, and we hope it will convince readers across the financial sector of the scale of the opportunity for private investment in microfinance.

The Geneva Financial Center is proud to have actively co-organized and co-funded the Geneva Private Capital Symposium, contributing to making microfinance "mainstream."

I wish to thank the other sponsors of the symposium, and especially the Geneva-based financial institutions that made this event possible: Credit Suisse, Deutsche Bank, Lombard Odier Darier Hentsch & Cie, Pictet & Cie, Dexia Asset Management and the Cantonal Bank of Geneva.

IVAN PICTET
Chairman, Geneva Financial Center
www.geneva-finance.ch

Preface 2

Real World. Real Learning®

IMD is one of the world's leading business schools, with over 50 years' experience in developing the leadership capabilities of international business executives at every stage of their careers. The majority of program participants come from medium to large corporations and all have an international orientation to their businesses.

IMD faculty members, as geographically diverse as the participants the institution attracts, are recognized world authorities in their fields. They divide their time between teaching, carrying out research and acting as consultants to major companies in many industries. This ensures that they remain firmly on top of the latest developments in managerial practice. Faculty draw on this experience to create a particularly effective learning environment that is highly conducive to tackling critical issues facing businesses today and tomorrow.

IMD is truly international. Every year some 8000 executives, representing more than 90 nationalities, attend more than 20 open enrollment Executive Development Programs (including the top-rated, intensive one-year full-time MBA program and Executive MBA programs) as well as company-specific Partnership Programs. English is the working language at IMD, though no single business approach or cultural background dominates. There are currently more than 55 000 Alumni based in over 140 countries and more than 40 Alumni clubs worldwide.

IMD Research & Development – Real World. Real Learning®

IMD brings pertinent, cutting-edge research into the classroom in the shortest possible time, keeping its programs up-to-date. Its research embodies its "Real World. Real Learning" philosophy and remains relevant by working closely with its clients and the more than 180 multinational companies that make up its Learning Network. IMD programs are constantly updated by faculty's timely, practical research. IMD's goal is to conduct state-of-the-art research as well as develop relevant real-world material. Currently, over 80 research projects are under way, each led by one or several faculty members. The school follows the following key principles to achieve its research mission:

- Focus research on practical challenges facing companies today.
- Translate insights into relevant output and materials to be used in the classroom.
- Constantly and deeply involve faculty and leading executives from around the world.
- Use the "live audience" to define new directions to explore.

IMD also runs a number of specific research centers:

World Competitiveness Center

This center of excellence produces the World Competitiveness Yearbook (WCY) amongst other products and services. The WCY is the world's most renowned and comprehensive annual report on the competitiveness of nations, ranking as well as analysing how a nation's environment creates and sustains the competitiveness of enterprises.

Forum for Corporate Sustainability Management

Corporations participate in the Forum to build a sustainable business advantage through social and environmental strategic action. The member companies are also partners and business associates of IMD.

IMD – Lombard Odier Darier Hentsch Family Business Research Center

Building on expertise gained over 18 years, the center provides cutting-edge educational programs to family businesses all over the world. The research center serves the needs of family firms by authoring original case studies, articles and books on subjects critical to family business success.

Preface 3

Geneva Financial Center

The Geneva Financial Center (hereafter the Center) is the trade association of the Geneva financial community, promoting its development.

Geneva is well known as the ultimate reference in the Private banking industry. This reputation is based on generations of experience accumulated by the 140 banks present in Geneva and the hundreds of independent asset managers, as well as by the skills of the 30 000 people that compose the Geneva financial community.

Geneva is also a leading worldwide platform in the commodities trading and financing business.

Structured as a foundation, the Center is a forum of ideas and actions. Its board is composed of top representatives of the Geneva financial community: large banks, foreign-owned banks, private bankers, cantonal banks, independent asset managers, accounting firms, law firms and insurance companies.

The Center follows developments affecting the local scene, acting on the business environment or providing public comments depending on the circumstances. It regularly organizes events, such as the Microfinance symposium in October 2005, which it is proud to have co-organized with the CASIN (the Centre for Applied Studies in International Negotiations).

The Center is a member of the Swiss Bankers Association, and participates in its public affairs commission.

The Center is also active on the training side, ensuring that local financial institutions enjoy a highly trained workforce. It therefore plays a central role between the Geneva banks and the various schools and institutes specializing in financial training. With the assistance of local partners, we define the requirements (i.e., "*référentiels*") for specific banking skills and are actively involved in setting up new training programs (such as *compliance*, or *risk management*, to take recent examples). Our specific web site on training matters gives more details on this activity: www.edubank.ch.

Thanks to our small but dedicated staff, we endeavor to develop activities that:

- are complementary to those of the front-line actors of the Geneva financial scene
- provide assistance to the local banking community and are value-added driven to the financial community
- reinforce Geneva's reputation as a significant and respected financial center.

On our web site, www.geneva-finance.ch, you will also find many links and information to the Swiss and Geneva financial scene, as well as useful tips for visitors and newcomers to Geneva.

STEVE BERNARD
Managing Director, Geneva Financial Center

Preface 4

C A S I N
The Centre for Applied Studies in International Negotiations

This book represents a learning journey to uncover an emerging investment opportunity: micro and small business finance. It examines the evolving concept of microfinance, presents the size, nature and growth potential of the industry's demand for private capital, introduces the current suppliers of private capital and makes a comparative analysis of currently used microfinance business models. The book dispels prejudices and should serve as a guide to potential investors interested in innovations in capital finance. In all these objectives, it follows closely the spirit of the international symposium held in Geneva in October 2005, Investing Private Capital in Micro & Small Business Finance.

The symposium resulted from a pretext – the United Nations' designation of 2005 as the International Year of Microcredit – and an opportunity, the genuine interest of Financial Geneva to seriously examine microfinance as a business proposal. CASIN – which for years has recognized the significant role and potential of microfinance – seized the occasion and laid itself down as a bridge between the financial experts and the microfinance champions from the field. Our objective was to showcase today's leading investment vehicles and business models in micro and small business finance and appeal to the financial community, from institutional to "field" investors, to explore this emerging asset class. By so doing, we felt that Geneva, a global financial hub and a center of major international organizations, would offer a lasting contribution to the UN Year of Microcredit 2005.

This book is the completion of this objective. Its purpose is to make it easier for potential investors to commit to the microfinance industry. Micro and small business finance are fast-growing segments of the financial industry, opening the door to a whole range of financial products for fund managers and private investors worldwide. The industry is becoming more market-driven and structured. As a result, it is receiving larger volumes of private capital. Microfinance is slowly becoming mainstream finance.

The focus of this book expands beyond microcredit and addresses microfinance. The terms are not interchangeable, as the scope of microfinance includes financial services other than loans, such as microsavings and microinsurance. Furthermore, small business finance is also tackled. The latter was an issue of debate. Some feel that what applies to microfinance is not valid for small business finance and therefore that one should concentrate exclusively on microfinance. We believe otherwise, as we see a continuum between micro and small business finance.

This book is structured around four core issues, the demand for private capital in micro and small business finance, introduced by Vijay Mahajan; leading approaches and successful business models in micro and small business, discussed by Benoît Leleux and Dinos Constantinou and others; the sources of private capital flowing into the industry, analysed by Marc de Sousa Shields and others; the critical factors and enabling framework conditions for private investment in micro and small business finance, presented by Kathryn Imboden.

We would like this book to be a first stage in a learning journey that will convince more investors to discover microfinance as an emerging business paradigm that benefits all stakeholders.

JEAN F. FREYMOND
Director, CASIN

XIMENA ESCOBAR DE NOGALES
Deputy Director and Senior Economic Counsellor, CASIN

CASIN was established in 1979 as a learning platform. It is engaged in:

- Capacity Building of leaders from governments, business and civil society in international governance, diplomacy, negotiation and conflict management, as well as in development and trade issues.
- Problem and conflict solving through dialogue and facilitation.
- Research and coaching to assist policy and decision-makers, negotiators and senior managers in their search for policy options.

CASIN initiated the action-oriented Geneva Private Capital Symposium in 2004. This platform is designed for the private sector to expand knowledge on development challenges, share experiences, network and uncover economic opportunities to serve underserved markets, thus securing a more inclusive market economy.

The Geneva Private Capital Symposium is a bridge between the corporate world, the public sector, international organizations and civil society.

As a Symposium Architect, CASIN designs, together with its business partners, event content and structure to deliver high-impact learning. CASIN also strives to facilitate successful interaction between the private sector and civil society.

Acknowledgements

An endeavor such as this one inevitably implies a team effort. The Symposium and its proceedings would not have been possible without the intellectual guidance and leadership of Benoît Leleux and Jean F. Freymond. We would not have gone far without Ivan Pictet's personal commitment, his vision and his capacity to bring on board key financial players, starting with the Geneva Financial Centre. Steve Bernard's commitment was central in mobilizing crucial support to realizing the Symposium. Finally, Ximena Escobar de Nogales, played a major part in conceptualizing the project and pulling the right strings to keep the whole venture together.

Other mentors, in particular, Jean Philippe de Schrevel, Dinos Constantinou, Melchior de Muralt, Christina Barrineau and Cédric Lombard, contributed considerably to the success of this project, be it by sharing their knowledge of the industry, assisting in shaping the event, including in its very early stages when different projects were proposed by establishing vital contacts or providing moral support.

The Symposium was co-organized by CASIN and the Geneva Financial Center, to the staff of which goes our deep appreciation. A special tribute is to be paid to Catherine Carrera, Lisa Lundby and Gertrude Monnet for their most professional engagement and to Julian K. Lee and Albert Diversé who devoted endless passion and dedication to make the Symposium happen.

Our gratitude also goes to the authors of the papers, Suvalaxmi Chakraborty, Dinos Constantinou, Christoph Freytag, Hanns-Michael Hoelz, Kathryn Imboden, Benoît Leleux, Vijay Mahajan, Sanjay Sinha, Marc De Sousa Shields, Damian Von Stauffenberg and Michael Steidl. Equally we wish to thank the Symposium speakers and contributors and in particular Kofi Annan, Stanley Fischer, Tom Easton and Alexandre de Lesseps.

The Symposium and publication of this book would not have been possible without the support of financial institutions, most of which are already engaged in microfinance, as well as the Swiss State Secretariat for Economic Affairs (SECO), and the Swiss Agency for Development and Corporation (SDC), which on the occasion of the UN Year of Microcredit did much to promote microfinance.

Finally, the book materialized thanks to Anna Brown's dedication to make it happen.

Sponsors

Credit Suisse

Deutsche Bank

Swiss Agency for Development and Cooperation (SDC)

SECO (Swiss State Secretariat for Economic Affairs)

Pictet

LODH

BCGE

Dexia

Geneva Financial Centre

This book has been produced with the participation of the Geneva Financial Center (GFC) and The Centre for Applied Studies in International Negotiations (CASIN). We thank them both wholeheartedly for the organization of the 2005 event, basis of the present book, and thank the GFC for its financial support.

Academic support for the conference and this book was provided by IMD – International Institute for Management Development.

Abbreviations

ADB	Asian Development Bank
ADR	American Depositary Receipts
AFD	Agence Française de Développement
AG	Aktiengesellschaft (stock corporation incorporated in Germany)
BIS	Bank of International Settlements
C1/GBL	Category 1–Global Business Licensed Company (offshore company incorporated in Mauritius)
CGAP	Consultative Group to Assist the Poor
CIS	Commonwealth of Independent States
CSO	Central Statistical Office (India)
EBRD	European Bank for Reconstruction and Development
EIB	European Investment Bank
FINCA	Foundation for International Community Assistance
FMO	Netherlands Development Finance Company
GmbH	Gesellschaft mit beschränkter Haftung (limited liability company incorporated in Germany)
GMG	Global Microfinance Group SA
I&P	Investisseur et Partenaire pour le Développement
IDB	Inter-American Development Bank
IDBI	Industrial Development Bank of India
IFC	International Finance Corporation
IFCI	Industrial Finance Corporation of India
IFI	International Financial Institution
IMI	Internationale Micro Investitionen
IPC	Internationale Projekt Consult GmbH
IPC-PC	IPC-ProCredit
IRDP	Integrated Rural Development Programme (India), see SGSY
JLG	Joint Liability Group
KfW	Kreditanstalt für Wiederaufbau
LF-H	La Fayette-Horus
M-CRIL	Micro-Credit Ratings International
MDGs	Millennium Development Goals
ME	Microenterprise
MF	Microfinance

MFCM	Microfinance Capital Markets Update
MFI	Microfinance Institution
MIS	Management Information System
MIX	Microfinance Information eXchange
MSE	Micro and Small Enterprises
MSME	Micro, Small and Medium Enterprises
NABARD	National Bank for Agricultural and Rural Development (India)
NBFC	Non-Banking Financial Company
NBFI	Non-Banking Financial Institutions
NEF	National Equity Fund (India)
NGO	Non-Governmental Organization
NYSE	New York Stock Exchange
OI	Opportunity International
OPIC	Overseas Private Investment Corporation
PAR	Portfolio at Risk
PB	Partner Bank
PCH	ProCredit Holding
PE	Private Equity
ROA	Return on Assets
ROE	Return on Equity
RSBF	Russia Small Business Fund
SA	Société par Actions (stock corporation incorporated in French-speaking Switzerland)
SARL	Société par Actions à Responsabilité Limitée (limited company incorporated in France)
SAS	Société par Actions Simplifiée ("simplified" stock company incorporated in France – not suitable for public listing)
SBFI	Small Business Finance Institution
SBIC	Small Business Investment Corporation
SGSY	Swarnajayanti Gram Swarojgar Yojana
SHG	Self Help Group
SIDBI	Small Industries Development Bank of India
SME	Small and Medium-Sized Enterprises
TA	Technical Assistance
TOR	Terms of Reference
UMLP	Ukraine Micro Loan Program
UN	United Nations
VC	Venture Capital

Glossary

American Depositary Receipt – A negotiable certificate issued by a US bank representing a specific number of shares of a foreign company traded on a US stock exchange.

Bankable – The term "bankable" refers to individuals and enterprises that are in a position to benefit from financial services, by generating income to repay loans, building savings or accumulating assets.

Debt/Equity ratio – A measure of a company's financial leverage calculated by dividing long-term debt (or total liabilities) by stockholder equity. It indicates what proportion of equity and debt the company is using to finance its assets.

Downscaling – Building MSE lending capacity within existing commercial banks by setting up micro lending departments within the banks.

Financial intermediation – The process whereby intermediaries borrow from consumers or savers, and lend to companies or others that need resources for investment. For example, banks are financial intermediaries that take in money as deposits and other financial products and pay it out as mortgages and other types of loans.

Financial self-sufficiency – The degree to which an MFI covers its costs if receiving no subsidies at all. Please refer to Appendix 2 for a detailed explanation of the calculation of this term.

Gearing – The amount of debt used to finance a firm's assets, or the use of various financial instruments or borrowed capital to increase the potential return of an investment.

Investment fund – A firm that invests the pooled funds of retail investors – for a fee – in line with stated investment objectives.

Junk bond – A bond with a speculative credit rating of BB (Standard & Poor's) or BA (Moody's) or lower. Junk or high-yield bonds offer investors higher yields than bonds of financially sound companies.

Leverage – Same as Gearing.

Micro loans – Loans to micro enterprises.

Micro-credit – Micro-credit is the provision of credit services to low-income entrepreneurs, and is sometimes used to refer to the actual micro-loan.

Microenterprise – There is no single, internationally accepted definition of the term micro-enterprise, and no single definition has been used in this volume. Micro, small and medium enterprises have different characteristics, and are variously defined in different countries and organizations based on criteria such as sales or number of employees. The following are the commonly used definitions in the major markets of Latin America, Europe and Asia, but please also refer to Chapter 1 for an outline of definitions used around the world.

Latin America – A microenterprise is a small-scale business in the informal sector, employing less than five people, and may be based out of the home. Examples include small retail kiosks, sewing workshops and market stalls.[1] The Inter-American Development Bank defines, as a rule of thumb, a microenterprise to be a business with 10 employees or less and total assets of less than US$20 000, excluding those in professional sectors such as medical and legal practices.[2]

Europe – The European Commission defines a microenterprise as having 0 to nine employees and a turnover of less than €2 million per its recommendation C (2003) 1422 of 6 May 2003. The European Bank for Reconstruction and Development generally considers that a micro-enterprise has financing needs of US$10 000 or less and employs up to 10 people.[3]

Asia – The Asian Development Bank defines microenterprises as non-crop enterprises (excluding professionals and high-technology firms) employing less than ten workers, including the owner-operator and family workers.[4]

Microfinance – In this book, the term is used to denote both micro and small business finance i.e. the provision of credit products and other financial services to micro and small businesses.

Microfinance institution – A regulated, or non-regulated, financial institution lending to micro, small and medium enterprises (MSMEs) and individuals, mainly in emerging economies, who typically do not have access to financial services from the formal banking sector.

Microfinance network – The term microfinance "network" is used by the Microfinance Information eXchange to denote adherence, affiliation or outright ownership of a number of microfinance institutions to over-arching organizations.

Millennium Development Goals – The eight Millennium Development Goals (MDGs) are a set of time-bound and measurable targets for combating poverty, hunger, disease, illiteracy, environmental degradation and discrimination against women. World leaders and the world's leading development institutions agreed, at the United Nations Millennium Summit in September 2000, to: (1) eradicate extreme poverty and hunger, (2) achieve universal primary education, (3) promote gender equality and empower women, (4) reduce child mortality, (5) improve maternal health, (6) combat HIV/AIDS, malaria and other diseases, (7) ensure environmental sustainability, and (8) develop a global partnership for development.

PAR > 1 day – The percentage of the portfolio affected by arrears of more than one day.

Portfolio-at-Risk – Portfolio-at-risk measures the percentage of the portfolio that is past due – that is, the value of all loans outstanding that have one or more installments of principal in arrears – by more than a certain number of days. This includes the entire unpaid principal balance, including both the past due and future installments, but excluding accrued interest and any loans that have been restructured or rescheduled. It is calculated as the total outstanding balance of loans past due divided by the active portfolio. Portfolio-at-risk is usually divided into categories according to the amount of time passed since the first missed principal installment.

Refinancing – This is an extension or increase (or both) in the amount of existing debt, such as happens when a business or person revises their debt repayment schedule, or replaces an older loan with a new loan offering better terms.

Small enterprises – Enterprises with typically fewer than 50 employees.

Small loans – Loans to small enterprises.

Social investing (social investment fund) – Also known as ethical investing or socially conscious investing. Choosing to invest in companies that operate ethically, provide social benefits and are sensitive to the environment.

Specialty MFI funds – Investment fund set up specifically to invest in microfinance institutions.

Upscaling – The evolution of a microfinance institution into a full financial institution.

Notes

1 Derived from the ACCIÓN Glossary of Terms. ACCIÓN International. http://www.accion.org/micro_glossary.asp (accessed 31 October 2006).
2 Taken from Inter-American Development Bank. *Microenterprise Development Strategy: No. MIC 103*. Washington, D.C.: IDB, 1997.
3 European Bank for Reconstruction and Development. *Small Business: EBRD Sector Factsheet*. London: EBRD, 2006.
4 Asian Development Bank. *Microenterprise Development: Not By Credit Alone*. Manila: ADB, 1997.

Notes on Contributors

Suvalaxmi Chakraborty is leading the rural and agri business of ICICI Bank, which has achieved three-fold growth in the last two years, reaching out to rural population across 200 districts of the country. She has crafted the rural strategy emphasizing sectoral approach and customization of financial solutions to large corporations, agri small and medium enterprises and to rural retail customers. She has spearheaded development of rural retail products including crop loans and farm equipment loans to farmers, commodity based loans and working capital facility to traders, microfinancial services to low-income households and private banking services to rural rich. She has been responsible for building the rural business model through a technology backed hybrid distribution channel, a combination of branch and non-branch channels such as credit access centers, kiosks, Micro Finance Institution partners and Business Correspondents. She has also up robust credit processes and risk management systems to ensure an optimum risk return model of the rural business. She leads the rural marketing and branding initiatives aimed towards creating a strong brand identity in rural areas.

Ms. Chakraborty joined ICICI in 1989 and successively worked in the project finance, financial accounting systems, treasury, Internet banking and corporate banking divisions. Prior to her engagement with ICICI, she audited large Indian and transnational companies for Pricewaterhouse Coopers. She currently represents ICICI Bank on the standing committee on Agro Business of Indian Banks' Association and Agriculture Council of Confederation of Indian Industries. She has represented ICICI on the board of Clearing Corporation of India and headed the Risk Management working committee in Indian Association of Corporate Treasurers and CFOs (INACT). She has also previously served as Director on the Board of Fixed Income Money Markets and Derivatives Association (FIMMDA). Ms. Chakraborty holds a B.Com (Hons) and has completed professional programs in Financial Investment Technology at Berkeley's Haas School of Business and in Leading Change and Organizational Renewal at Stanford's Graduate School of Business.

Dinos Constantinou has 12 years experience in banking, microfinance and management consulting. He began his professional career in corporate credit and international banking with Barclays Bank in Paris and

Dresdner Bank in Frankfurt. Joining Internationale Projekt Consult (IPC) in 1995, he went on to lead major long-term micro and small business credit projects for the EBRD and IADB in Russia and Ecuador, respectively. From 2000 to 2002, he worked as a strategy consultant with Gemini Consulting and Cell Consulting. He returned to microfinance in late 2002 with the idea of launching an institution to finance micro and small businesses in post-crisis Argentina. Together with a group of purely private investors, he founded Global Microfinance Group SA in Lausanne, Switzerland and Argentina Microfinanzas SA, the first for-profit MFI in Argentina in 2004. Dinos holds a BSc with First Class Honours in Economics from the University of Bristol, as well as an MA in European Economic Studies from the College of Europe and an MBA from the IMD Switzerland. He speaks eight languages, including English, Spanish, German, Russian and French.

Christoph Freytag is Managing Director of IPC GmbH with responsibility for supervising several financial institution-building projects in Eastern Europe and the former Soviet Union. He previously served as CEO of ProCredit Banks in Serbia (2003–4) and Bulgaria (2001–3), having headed the team responsible for establishing the latter institution. He was assigned to Russia for five years, working initially as a bank adviser with the EBRD Russia Small Business Fund in various cities and later serving as Deputy Chairman of KMB Bank. Under his management all three banks became respected market leaders in micro and small business lending in their markets. Mr Freytag is a certified commercial banker and holds a *cum laude* degree in economics from the University of Frankfurt. Before joining IPC in 1995 he worked within the corporate/international division of a major German bank, where he was involved in the planning of subsidiaries/acquisitions of banks in Eastern Europe and South America, performing market studies, financial projections and financial due diligence work. Mr Freytag is married and has three children.

Hanns Michael Hölz after completing an apprenticeship at Deutsche Bank and thereafter successfully studying Business Management at the University of Mannheim, joined Badische Kommunale Landesbank Mannheim (Head of the Board of Management's Office). Since 1986 he has been working for the Deutsche Bank Group.

As Global Head he takes responsibility for Deutsche Bank's Corporate Citizenship (Co-Head Corporate Social Responsibility), Sustainable Development (Group Compliance Officer for Sustainability Management System) and Sport.

He is a Board Member of several Deutsche Bank organizations, e.g. Deutsche Bank Americas Foundation and Deutsche Bank Africa Foundation and others. His responsibilities include representing Deutsche Bank in national and international committees, e.g. UN Global Compact (Member of Kofi Annan's former Advisory Council), Member of the Board of Global Reporting Initiative and World Business Council for Sustainable Development. Additionally, he is a Committee Member of the German Sport Aid Foundation and the National Anti-Doping Agency.

He has dedicated the last 15 years to promoting corporate citizenship with the last 10 years almost solely dedicated to shaping the debate on sustainable development – both within and outside of Deutsche Bank. His efforts are focused on communicating the new sustainability paradigm and setting into motion the changes necessary to achieve it. Some of his activities include:

- Chairman UNEP FI (2000–5), co-author of UNEP declaration "A statement by banks on the environment and sustainable development".
- Chairman of The Bellagio Forum for Sustainable Development.
- Member of Board of Directors Global Reporting Initiative.
- Member of Board Econsense, Forum of Sustainable Development, Co-chair of the Econsense Association.
- Director Peace Parks Foundation.

His major activities include, in particular, promoting the concept of microfinance to enable families to rise from poverty and create opportunities for self-employment as well as his commitment within the Deutsche Bank Africa Foundation. The Foundation works on the premise that sustainable progress and peace can only be achieved through parallel development of the underlying social, economic and ecological conditions. In 2003 he was honored with the BAUM Environment Award.

Kathryn Imboden has worked in the field of economic development for over 30 years, for the Swiss Agency for Development and Cooperation (SDC), the OECD Development Centre, the Club du Sahel and the US Treasury Department. From 1986 to 2001, she was with SDC in Bern, during which time she was responsible for SDC's economic work (macroeconomics and financial sector). Ms Imboden chaired the Executive Committee of the Consultative Group to assist the Poorest (CGAP) from 1999 to 2001. She served as Policy Change Manager at Women's World Banking (WWB) from 2001–4. Ms Imboden joined UNCDF in July 2004 as Senior Policy Adviser. She has been responsible for piloting a multi-stakeholder consultation process leading to the preparation of a forth-coming "Blue Book on Building Inclusive Financial Sectors," in the context of the 2005 International Year of Microcredit. A citizen of Switzerland and the US, she has a BA in Economics from Mount Holyoke College and a Diploma from the Institut d'études politiques in Paris.

Benoît F. Leleux is the Stephan Schmidheiny Professor of Entrepreneurship and Finance at IMD, where he is Director of the MBA Program and Director of Research & Development. His areas of special interest are venture capital and private equity, combining expertise in entrepreneurship and growth management. Dr Leleux directs the Chief Executive Organization (CEO) Seminars and the MBA start-up projects. He was previously Visiting Professor of Entrepreneurship at INSEAD and director of the 3i VentureLab and Associate Professor and Zubillaga Chair in Finance and Entrepreneurship at Babson College, Wellesley, MA (USA) from 1994 to 1999. He obtained his PhD at INSEAD, specializing in corporate finance and venture capital. His experience includes four years of corporate venturing in South East Asia for a major agribusiness conglomerate. He is active in a number of private equity funds, as well as numerous start-up companies in Europe and the US, either as director, investor, and/or adviser.

Recent research papers look at the private equity investment behaviors of the largest family offices in Europe, drivers of the risk attitudes of major investors in private equity, pitfalls of equity-for-service arrangements, how corporate investors learn in their venturing efforts. He is the author of "A European Casebook on Entrepreneurship and New Ventures" with David Molian. He holds an MSc in agricultural engineering and an MA in education from the Université Catholique de Louvain (Belgium), and an MBA from Virginia Polytechnic Institute and State University. He was a fellow of the Sasakawa Young Leaders Program in Japan and the College for Advanced Studies in Management (CIM) in Brussels.

His works have earned some distinguished awards, including the 1996 Best Paper Award in international finance at the FMA conference in New York and the 1996 Best Paper Award at the Academy of Entrepreneurial Finance. His teaching cases have repeatedly won both EFMD European Case Writing Awards and ECCH European Case Awards.

Vijay Mahajan is a graduate of the Indian Institute of Technology, Delhi, 1970–75, the Indian Institute of Management, Ahmedabad, 1979–81, and was a mid-career fellow at the Woodrow Wilson School of

Public International Affairs, Princeton University, USA, 1988–89, where he studied economic development policy.

After IIT, Vijay worked in Philips India as a marketing executive for four years, before going to IIM-Ahmedabad. His urge to work for rural development, which was seeded in his student days at the IIT, was strengthened during the extensive travel he did in poorer eastern India while with Philips. Thus, by the time he went to IIM-A, he had decided to work in development and used his two years not only to do a number of courses related to management of economic and social development but also to learn from the experiences of IIM-A Professors Ravi Matthai and Ranjit Gupta, the founders of IIM-A's Jawaja Rural Development project.

Graduating from IIM-A in 1981, Vijay started working in the rural development field in Bihar, the poorest state of eastern India. In 1983, he established an NGO, PRADAN (Professional Assistance for Development Action). By 2006, PRADAN worked with over 100 000 poor households, promoting livelihoods and community institutions. PRADAN's work is highly regarded by the NGO community, the government and also by young professionals, over 300 of whom work in it at the grassroots, with some of India's poorest people.

Moving on from PRADAN in 1991, in search of a scalable, mainstream approach to livelihood promotion, Vijay carried out various consulting assignments related to rural livelihoods from 1991–95, for the World Bank, SDC and NABARD. Vijay co-authored the book *The Forgotten Sector: Non-Farm Employment and Enterprises in Rural India*, and since then has published over 50 articles on microfinance, livelihoods and development.

In 1995, Vijay conceptualized BASIX as a new generation livelihood promotion institution and it was set up in mid-1996. To April 2006, when Vijay stepped aside as its CEO, BASIX had helped support over 250 000 livelihoods of poor households in the agriculture, allied and non-farm sectors by extending micro-credit worth over INR 545 crore (US$125 million). BASIX goes well beyond micro-credit to offer a "triad" of livelihood promotion services including savings and insurance services, agricultural/business development services and institutional development services to rural producers and their groups.

While building BASIX as a livelihood promotion agency, Vijay has been active in the field of policy analysis and advocacy. He is a member of the national Committee on Financial Inclusion, established by the Government of India, the National Microfinance Equity and Development Fund and the Insurance Regulatory and Development Authority (IRDA) of India. He serves on the Boards of the global Consultative Group to

Assist the Poor (CGAP) and the Development Finance Forum and major Indian development organizations – BASIX, PRADAN, ASSEFA, Gram Vikas and the Development Support Centre and of educational institutions – the Indian Institute of Forest Management and Institute of Rural Management, Anand (IRMA).

In 2002, Vijay was selected as one of the 60 "Outstanding Social Entrepreneurs" of the world, by the Schwab Foundation, set up by the founder of the World Economic Forum (WEF), Davos. In this capacity, he attended the WEF 2003 and 2004 and was a speaker in a number of sessions in Davos. In 2003, Vijay received the Distinguished Alumnus Award from the IIT, Delhi.

Vijay is married to Savita, who is Assistant Dean, Indian School of Business, Hyderabad, and they have a son, Chirag and a daughter, Chandni.

Mope Ogunsulire was a research associate at IMD International, Lausanne until June 2006, focusing on corporate strategy, entrepreneurship and energy. She wrote several case studies on the strategic challenges facing companies in emerging markets, including Russia and South Africa. Prior to joining IMD in 2004, she worked in development finance as an investment officer with the International Finance Corporation (IFC, the private sector lending arm of the World Bank). From 1998-2003, she structured and executed project finance transactions and arranged loan syndications for IFC clients in Latin America, Africa and Asia. In addition, she managed a portfolio of debt and equity assets, as well as managing relationships with syndicate banks. Before joining the World Bank, she worked for several years in construction project management and structural engineering design, focusing on water, power and transport infrastructure projects both in the private sector and with the Environment Agency, UK. She holds a BSc (Hons) in civil engineering from the University of Lagos, and an MBA from IMD, Switzerland.

Sanjay Sinha is Managing Director of Micro-Credit Ratings International Limited (MCRIL) – a company established specifically to carry out professional assessments (ratings) of MFIs and provide other services designed to promote the flow of investments into the microfinance sector. He has over 27 years of development consulting experience in South and Southeast Asia. He has specialized in the sector of livelihood activities including sub-sectoral analyses of activities of relevance to poor people of the region, micro-enterprise promotion and BDS, agriculture and livestock production as well as forestry in addition to microfinance.

Sanjay Sinha has an MPhil in Economics from Oxford University, UK. In 1983, he co-founded EDA Rural Systems, which is now one of the premier microfinance and livelihoods consulting companies in Asia. Over the past 22 years, EDA has worked for all the major development institutions active in Asia. The idea of M-CRIL emerged out of EDA's experience with MFIs and from undertaking policy studies in the field of microfinance.

Marc de Sousa Shields is a Partner with Enterprising Solutions Global Consulting, an international development consulting firm specializing in enterprising solutions for social, environmental and economically sustainable development. Marc's work in sustainable development focuses on social and environmental investment, microfinance and small and medium sized business development in developing countries. Marc has led a number of innovative projects, including several focusing on MFI finance, social investment in emerging markets, microfinance and housing, and commercial bank downscaling to microfinance. Marc was co-founder and the Executive Director of the Social Investment Organization in Canada, treasurer of a community credit union, Director of Social Investment at a national bank, and co-founder of the Morelos Forum, an international think tank on global social investment issues. Marc is the research director and author of "Financing MFIs: A Context to the Transitions to Private Capital". See www.esglobal.com for a list of select publications and presentations.

Damian von Stauffenberg is founder and CEO of MicroRate, the premier rating agency for MFIs with offices in Washington, Lima and Johannesburg. Mr von Stauffenberg worked at the World Bank and its private sector affiliate, the International Finance Corporation from 1970 to 1995. Since retiring from the IFC, he has dedicated himself to helping microfinance institutions gain access to commercial funding. Positions he held in the past include member of the Board and Chairman of the Investment Committee of Profund, a US$23 million equity fund for Latin American micro-enterprise lenders; Chairman of the Board and Treasurer of Seed Capital Development Fund, Ltd; and member of the Executive Committee and Board of the Latin American Challenge Investment Fund and of Microvest, two loan funds that pioneered the concept of funding microfinance through market instruments. He was the Chairman of the World Bank's Staff Association and a member of the World Bank Group's Pension Finance Committee. Mr von Stauffenberg is a German national who lives in the United States.

Michael Steidl has more than 10 years of experience providing consulting services to microfinance institutions and sectors in 25 countries in Latin America, the Caribbean, Asia, Eastern Europe and Africa. He worked for International Projekt Consult (IPC) between 1996 and 1999 and as an independent consultant from 1999 to 2002. Since then, he has been the Managing Director of Micro Service Consult, a German consulting firm. Mr Steidl's experience includes the provision of technical assistance in strategy development and implementation, product design and credit technology to some of the leading microfinance institutions. This close relationship with institutions has allowed him to gain insight into the needs and demand of MFIs for capital from different sources. As consultant to international organizations such as the IADB and the Kreditanstalt für Wiederaufbau (KfW), Mr Steidl has also gained an in-depth knowledge of the interests and institutional constraints of providers of public money to microfinance. This variety of practical experience allows Mr. Steidl to look at the problems of the provision of capital to microfinance institutions from various angles.

1
Introduction

Benoît Leleux, Dinos Constantinou and Mope Ogunsulire

Various authors have already set out the purpose of the conference, and its achievements, in the prefaces to this book. It is therefore not our purpose here to revisit this, but instead to give the reader a broad overview of the papers presented, and some of the fundamental discussions that took place during the conference. These confirmed that microfinance cannot, and should not, remain the preserve of social enterprise alone. Subsidized funding will not last forever, so the only path to sustainability is to move microfinance into the commercial domain, i.e. a specialized segment of the financial world. The best institutions have already recognized this, and grown into full financial institutions by adopting a for-profit approach. The latter is the only way to attract and mobilize, for the long term, significant private capital, and the conference confirmed the increasing appetite within private capital for microfinance investment opportunities. Investors want large, fast-growing markets, competent and professional management, reasonable pricing and ventures with strong, sustainable and competitive advantage.

Microfinance is already large; with profits as an objective, it could be huge and growing faster. Increasing inflows of private capital are encouraging more professional management. The market is still at an early stage of development, and as such offers opportunities for substantial returns to the early birds. Microfinance must commercialize to realize its full potential; only then will it be able to satisfy the needs of developing nations. A for-profit microfinance industry will offer significant opportunities for the private investor willing to venture into this field of considerable social and economic importance.

The book is organized in five parts, excluding this Introduction, that very much track the key microfinance dimensions as well as the structure of the October 2005 event. Part I introduces the market for microfinancing,

1

looking at the demand side of the overall industry, and considering some of the drivers of this demand. In Part II, we move from the macro- to the micro-level to consider the individual actors operating in the market, especially the microfinance institutions (MFIs) through which funds flow to the end borrowers. The focus is on understanding the various business systems, their genesis and modus operandi. Switching from demand to supply, but remaining at the micro-level, Part III gives an overview and some case studies on private capital in microfinance. In Parts IV and V, we return to the macro level to consider, first, the structural factors governing the actions of all players in this market, and finally, to examine the overall performance of the industry in a number of regions and how such performance can be assessed.

The changing reality of microfinance

In October 2006, the Norwegian Nobel Committee awarded the Peace Prize to Muhammad Yunus, and the microfinance institution he founded, Grameen Bank. The prize award further raised the global profile of microfinance, following close on the UN designation the previous year, of 2005 as the International Year of Microcredit. There seems little doubt that microfinance is now firmly entrenched on the global radar screen.

Yet, the image remains largely one of "doing good"; microfinance remains firmly within the confines of charity or philanthropy to many. There is no doubt that microfinance is rooted in a desire to help the poor and underprivileged. In a speech to the Commonwealth in 2003, Yunus said:

> I became involved in the poverty issue not as a policymaker or a researcher. I became involved because poverty was all around me. I could not turn my eyes away from it.

In the mid-1970s, faced with a local bank's unwillingness to lend to the poor – considering them not creditworthy – Yunus decided to act as guarantor for their loans. They always paid their dues. Yet he continued to face difficulties in expanding lending through existing banks. In 1983, Yunus created Grameen Bank, a bank for the poor that would give loans without collateral. About the same time that Yunus was backing loans to Bangladeshi poor, ACCION was making its first small loans to micro- enterprises in Recife, Brazil. Originally begun in 1961 as a community development effort to help the poor help themselves, ACCION moved to microlending in 1973. After a decade of working with the poorest in

Latin America, ACCION realized its projects[1] did not tackle the main cause of urban poverty: lack of economic opportunity. It started giving microloans to the many urban poor who were running tiny informal businesses, but who remained trapped in poverty, as most of their profits were lost to the prohibitively high interest rates levied by local loan sharks. Then in 1981 Interdisciplinäre Projekt Consult GmbH (IPC) was founded, and later went on to revolutionize the industry with the development of its micro-lending "technology", which focused on individual, rather than group, lending. Early microcredit programs had been based on solidarity group lending in which every member of a group guaranteed the repayment of all the members. In spite of early opposition, others (including some ACCION affiliates) have since adopted its approach.[2] IPC first worked in Peru, setting up a system of municipal banks based on the German *Sparkassen* (savings bank) model. It used the word "technology" to denote its broader approach and methodology developed to bring credit to the microentrepreneur.

With such antecedents, it is not surprising that many continue to regard microfinance as primarily a powerful tool for poverty alleviation:

> For many years now, I have been impressed by the power of a simple, small loan to those for whom fate and circumstance have resulted in disadvantage. Maintaining people's integrity and showing them trust, whilst facilitating a way for them to rebuild their own lives is such a meaningful way of alleviating poverty.
>
> Her Majesty Queen Rania Al-Abdullah of the Hashemite Kingdom of Jordan, Emissary for the International Year of Microcredit 2005 and FINCA International Board Member

Indeed, microfinance is an important component for meeting the United Nations' Millennium Development Goals for 2015, with the Millennium Declaration calling for "microfinance projects which meet local community priorities".

But by considering only this aspect, we fail to do justice to the reality of microfinance today. In addition, keeping microfinance purely within the domain of development finance puts off private investors. As Ivan Pictet points out in his Preface to this volume, financial advisers and investment managers act as trustees of assets and operate under a fiduciary obligation. They must seek investments that combine good returns and guarantee capital preservation, liquidity and transparency. Put simply, private investors and their intermediaries cannot afford charity, and ultimately neither can microfinance as an industry. Profitability is, after all, the best guarantee of sustainability. While some private individuals invest in microfinance, much more money is managed by third parties – in Geneva alone, 140 banks have $1 trillion in assets under management.[3] It is therefore clearly important to address any erroneous preconceived notions prevailing among the investment community.

The reluctance of financial intermediaries to commit funds to microfinance may be rooted in several fears: the perception that microfinance is a form of charity, subject to currency risks, lacks even basic controls in general, is subject to poor oversight, has low marketability and even lower liquidity and that it is not a "proper" asset class for portfolio diversification. But how much truth is there in these assertions?

Many of these fears are indeed realistic, but effective ways already exist in the market to address them. Some of the concerns are simply not true. Microfinance is not charity. First, microfinance encompasses more than microcredit. It also consists of other financial services, including deposits, payments and insurance, many of which are a source of revenue for MFIs. Secondly, microcredits are loans, not grants. They are fully repayable, and successful MFIs boast very high repayment rates that compare favorably to other commercial credits. ProCredit Holdings, a global grouping of microfinance banks, reports loan losses of less than 0.5 percent per year; a level significantly lower than many Western European banks according to the company. Its PAR > 30[4] is 1.3 percent. In Chapter 8, Hanns-Michael Hölz compares the 1.5 percent average default rate[5] in a sample of 124 MFIs with 4 percent for US "A" rated borrowers, and 5.3 percent for high-yield corporate debt (or "junk bonds"). Finally, many of the most successful MFIs have transformed into formal financial institutions that have continued to operate successfully for three decades or more. As Michael Steidl reports later in this book (Chapter 6), ten of the largest MFIs reporting to the Microfinance Information Exchange have a five-year average return on equity (ROE) of 19.6 percent, while four of the group generated ROEs of 30 percent and more over the same period.[6] Nevertheless, as noted elsewhere in this book, the number of fully commercial MFIs remains limited and the majority are not commercially viable.

MFIs that have made the move into formal institutions are subject to the same regulatory oversight as all other national financial intermediaries. In addition, regulated local banks and finance companies also operate in the sector by "downscaling" to serve microenterprises. Liquidity remains an issue, but microfinance today offers structured investment opportunities that can certainly be considered as valid (albeit alternative) assets.

Examples include specialty microfinance vehicles and securitizations of microfinance portfolios – some securitizations have been sold to commercial investors such as pension funds, mutual funds and foundations. There is also a growing use of corporate bonds, often backed by a multilateral agency guarantee. Although MFI shares themselves are often illiquid, exit options are available to equity investors. These include buy-outs by strategic investors – such as large microfinance players like IPC, specialized funds and some mainstream banks – and selling the equity back to the community served by the MFI.

Finally, private investors today conducting due diligence on potential investments can draw on an increasing number of ratings offered by several independent agencies that rate MFIs. Standard financial measures are also emerging, that are widely accepted in the industry, and which may be used to gauge the performance and profitability of institutions (see Appendix 2).

While charitable and public money have been the catalysts for microfinance, commercial capital can, and indeed has to some extent, played a role in developing the market so that the industry has grown increasingly market-driven and developed the structures to operate profitably. But more must be done, for there is little doubt that significant amounts of commercial private money will be needed to fully realize the global potential of microfinance. The Geneva Microfinance Symposium 2005 represented an early step on the way towards stimulating more private sector investment interest in the sector.

Microfinance demand is big and growing fast

The first thing that strikes the new arrival to microfinance is the wide range in estimates of market size. Within this volume alone, estimates range from $45 billion[7] to $1000 billon.[8] Much depends on the definition of microenterprise. Estimates of demand sometimes also include financing for small, in addition to micro, enterprises. However, although the estimates may vary widely, the numbers are huge. McKinsey[9] estimates that only 10 percent of this market is currently being served, yet microfinance is today already a $10–30 billion industry. Growth is also impressive, with the industry estimated to be growing at 15–30 percent per annum.[10] In Chapter 2, Vijay Mahajan takes a closer look at the make up of demand and what is driving the growth in demand. One important factor is the large number of microenterprises – perhaps as many as 500 million worldwide – among which the demand for formal financial services (including capital) remains unmet.

Microfinance can be a powerful tool in poverty alleviation, hence the strong demand seen among microenterprises. Although initial studies show that it can also have a positive impact on employment, methodological issues have made it difficult to obtain empirical statistical evidence. As Mahajan notes in Chapter 2, some early work does however indicate some employment effects. Microloans below $100 rarely create new jobs. Between $100 and $1000, a small proportion of micro-loans create jobs and promote small trade. Nonetheless, both types of loans do improve the social situation of the borrower. Only loans above $5000, however, contribute to economic growth by enabling investment and increasing productivity.

Poverty alleviation and job creation are among the "social returns" sought by microfinance investors, which compensate for the relatively lower financial returns. Although MFIs can be profitable, returns to investors are low by commercial standards. Mahajan reports debt returns of approximately 2 percent and equity returns of 5 percent. Microfinance has been able to leverage such "social capital", but by only about 4 percent. CGAP estimates that in 2005 $655 million of foreign direct investment (FDI) was available to MFIs and small business finance institutions (SBFIs), of which less than 10 percent was private commercial capital. A further $1 billion was available in loans and grants. Hence, for every $100 of "social capital" mobilized by microfinance, it leveraged on average just $4 of commercial capital.[11]

One of the factors hindering the fulfillment of demand is the lack of absorptive capacity. There are currently not enough MFIs and SBFIs that qualify to receive financial support. Greater effort is therefore needed to build capacity in the sector from the bottom up. Another factor is that market coverage is skewed, with just 10 percent of microfinance FDI going to the world's regions in which 90 percent of the poorest live. Investment tends to be concentrated in Latin America and Eastern Europe.

Private investors interested in meeting this huge demand will have an important role to play. Socially conscious investors are needed to provide equity funding, and should be ready to take risks and accept initially lower returns. Profits will eventually rise, but in the meantime, there will certainly be the "social returns" mentioned above.

Microfinance funding: From public to private investment

In his Preface, Ivan Pictet notes several reasons why microfinance is becoming increasingly attractive to private investors. Volatility is low, risks are managed through broad diversification, investments may be uncorrelated or counter-cyclical to the general macroeconomic environment and the financial markets, and there is a growing demand for assets, or sub-segments of asset classes, that offer absolute returns. In addition, the market is growing more structured and transparent and offering more and more structured investment vehicles. Hence, its attractiveness continues to grow such that, in recent years, we have seen microfinance beginning to access private commercial capital in addition to savings and donor funding.

In Chapter 6, Michael Steidl traces the progress of private commercial investment in microfinance through a series of structured investment vehicles. The industry initially began with public money from development agencies and non-profit organizations, which provided capital to highly motivated local entrepreneurs. At first, the focus was on social, rather than financial, returns. With time, this has evolved into an acknowledgement that sustainability demands both. Foreseeing that subsidized funds would one day dry up – and they would therefore require commercial capital – MFIs began to behave more like for-profit organizations. That quasi-commercial approach led to the evolution, often termed the "upscaling" of the most successful MFIs into full-fledged financial institutions. As we saw earlier, some of these successful MFIs are very profitable ventures, with ROEs ranging up to 30 percent. But they remain rare: Steidl estimates that for every MFI that has achieved institutional and commercial viability, 50–100 have not. Many institutions, however, continue to survive on donor funding as the sector is not yet wholly market-driven.

Nevertheless, the profitability of the top performers did not go unnoticed. By the 1990s, the first private investment into microfinance began. But in the beginning this was limited to industry insiders and usually leveraged by public funds. As things evolved to the next stage in the late-1990s, development agencies played an important role in the creation of structured investment opportunities to attract conventional, non-microfinance, investors. Most have taken the form of specialty investment funds, of which there are three types (see Table 1.1).[12] Some private players also created microfinance funds. In Chapter 8, Hanns Michael-Hölz discusses Deutsche Bank's Microcredit Development Fund, launched in 1997, as well as the bank's wider involvement in microfinance.

July 2004 saw the emergence of an organized corporate bond market for microfinance institutions. Some were asset-backed securitizations of MFI portfolios, some backed by partial guarantees from a multilateral agency but a few were guaranteed by the MFI's financial strength alone. Most were sold to institutional investors, although brokers, foundations

Table 1.1 Three types of microfinance investment funds

Type of fund	Characteristics
Microfinance development funds	• Emphasize development rather than financial return. • Offer favorable financing and sometimes subsidized technical assistance.
Quasi-commercial microfinance investment funds *e.g. ProCredit, Profund*	• Clearly defined financial objectives. • Clear development mission.
Commercial microfinance investment funds *e.g. Dexia Micro-Credit, Micro Vest I, Triodos Fair Share fund*	• Target mainly mainstream financial investors.

Table 1.2 Examples of microfinance bond issues

• *July 2002* – IFC backed US$10 million Mexican Peso bond issue for Compartamos. Guaranteed by MFI strength, not loan portfolio. S&P mxA + rating.
• *July 2004* – First international securitization of MFI portfolio by Blue Orchard and Developing World Markets. US$40 million 7-year, fixed-rate notes; three subordinated and one OPIC-backed senior debt series. Investors included pension and mutual funds, foundations and individuals.
• *2005* – US$52 million Colombian Peso bond issue for WWB Cali. Duff & Phelps Colombia AA + rating. Investors included brokers, pension funds, financial institutions and individuals.

and individuals have participated too. But such financing still accounts for only a tiny part of total funding, with less than 2 percent of global funding supplied by the 10 successful financings described in Chapter 6. Nevertheless, more efficient investment structures are coming up and existing structure are achieving both economies of scale and greater standardization and transparency. Hence, early microfinance investment vehicles are now integrating further into the mainstream capital market. (See Table 1.2 for examples of microfinance bond issues.)

Evolutionary changes and challenges as microfinance goes mainstream

Transparency within the industry is increasing as private money flows in. Further pressure comes from supervisory authorities as more MFIs formalize and upscale into formal regulated financial institutions. Downscaling is also contributing to the increasing commercialization within the sector. As has happened in other financial market sectors, independent third parties have emerged to provide objective assessments of profitability and performance. In Chapters 10 and 11, two of the leading microfinance rating agencies provide some insight into the industry's key measurement metrics, and they review specific examples from Latin America, Africa and Asia. Finally, the industry has started to develop standardized measures for measuring the performance of MFIs.

However, important obstacles stand in the way before microfinance can be fully integrated into mainstream financial markets. Foremost among these are the attitude and size of MFIs. With a strong commitment to their institutional mission, MFIs are sometimes reluctant to act as normal businesses, distributing dividends and participating in anonymous share trading and mergers and acquisitions. Further, many MFIs remain too small to generate economies of scale or provide efficient services to investors, and they will remain outside the reach of the investor.

In addition to attitude and size, microfinance also faces several other challenges in its transition from public to private capital. Marc de Sousa Shields presents some of these in Chapter 7: access to savings, pricing and limited availability of debt and equity capital.

Savings are a critical means of accessing cheaper capital, thus reducing borrowing costs, but collecting enough to fuel growth is difficult for even large and successful MFIs. Few, if any, have reached the ideal deposit-to-loan funding ratio for small financial institutions of 90–95 percent. MFIs face several problems in attracting savings: lack of appropriate regulation, lack of management capacity, cost of start up and greater competition from commercial banks.

Pricing drives MFI appetite for debt. Although commercial bank debt is available to well-performing MFIs, most prefer to use capital from retained earnings, national development banks or international specialty funds because of pricing. Few MFIs have good liability management strategies, and development agency capital is just sufficient to keep MFIs from creating their own private capital networks.

Although it is true that commercial debt is available to well performing MFIs, such capital as is available is uneven among regions – concentrated, as noted earlier, in Latin America and Eastern Europe – and highly limited in most countries. Commercial lenders do not understand microfinance and are often constrained by reserve requirements that make lending to MFIs too expensive. Hence, they usually require strong guarantees. Microfinance institutions have found ways to meet collateral requirements, ranging from international loans to development agency guarantees. As we saw earlier, some MFIs have successfully raised debt through bond issues or securitizations. But restrictive national regulations, transaction costs that are too high relative to available funding and issue amounts too small to attract private interest, can be a bar to these methods. Debt capital is also increasingly available from specialty funds, but drawn from private sources only to a limited degree. This is because much private funding comes subsidized by the investor or government; few institutional investors can subsidize investment. Overall, what debt funding is available goes to a few large MFIs.

Turning to equity capital, we find that 80 percent of it, like debt capital, is subsidized or provided by development agencies.[13] There is no doubt that development agencies, like specialty funds, are important catalysts for leveraging commercial capital for microfinance and enabling the transition to private capital. But MFIs continue to use development capital even after they are able to access private capital. Thus, even profitable, regulated enterprises still draw on such capital with the result that most of the sector's high-risk capital is concentrated in a few large MFIs to the detriment of the smaller emerging institutions who need it most. In addition, as with debt, this influx of subsidized capital has negative consequences, such as preventing MFIs from developing private capital ties and a general crowding out of private capital from the market. The concentration of capital pushes the sector in pursuit of the wrong goal, i.e. creating large financial institutions rather than catalyzing new, fast-growing MFIs, which can then be sold to the larger institutions. Further, the continuing involvement of NGOs and development agencies can sometimes hinder the selling to larger institutions. The effect is to deny the sector some of the profit maximization and exit motivation that drives venture capital. So, there is clearly a role here for private investors to play in helping shift the focus of donors to capacity building. Finally, vis-à-vis local equity funding, little is available and so the sector is mostly owned by NGOs with some minority participation by specialty funds. Private ownership is however increasing, notably in Mexico and the Philippines. In general, much of the sector's equity comes from public funds, with several factors inhibiting private interest in microfinance equity: Illiquid shares, a "social" image and limited or no dividend payments.

Better understanding of MFIs critical to sound investment

Despite the above difficulties, there is an increasing appetite within the private and public sector for investment opportunities in microfinance, corresponding to the great unmet demand. And ever more sound investment vehicles for channeling that money into the sector. But as noted earlier, there are not enough institutions able to absorb the funds. Damian von Stauffenberg, in Chapter 10, sets out the resulting problem:

> the market is being squeezed for good investment opportunities. A market that is already not very large. With too much money chasing too few opportunities, mistakes will be made as caution is thrown to the wind.
> Damian von Stauffenberg, MicroRate, USA

An understanding of the current universe of institutions is therefore important for sound investment decisions. In Part II of this volume, we briefly consider the existing universe of MFIs. Leleux and Constantinou first consider the microfinance institution builders – examining their evolution and operation and suggesting a typology of microfinance business models (see Figure 1.1). They conclude that MFIs on the ground seem to be converging to similar operating, revenue, funding and organizational strategies. Further, they conclude that three main models have emerged so far: the tight network, the public–private banking group and the private equity/venture capital model. Freytag and Chakraborty go

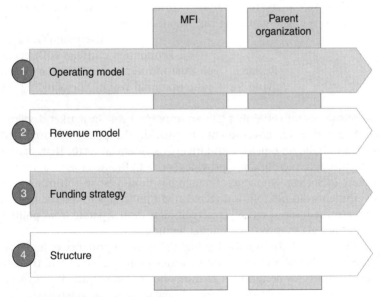

Note: MFI = Microfinance institution

Figure 1.1 Typology of microfinance business models

on to focus on specific examples of MFIs using several case studies. In particular, the downscaling model pioneered by the Inter-American Development Bank (IDB) about 20 years ago, and several models that evolved in ICICI Bank in India.

Building inclusive policy frameworks

As more private capital flows into microfinance, the nature of the industry will undoubtedly change. We have seen some of those changes in the sections above. But the core purpose of microfinance – the provision of financial services to the poor – will not change. In other words, microfinance is a key factor in building the inclusive financial sectors necessary so that all can participate in and contribute to national economic growth.

> People, poor and rich, need reliable financing so that their ideas can be brought together with assets to generate long-run sustainable growth. The two key ingredients to a well-functioning market economy are competition and access, competition so that performance keeps improving and access so that everyone has a chance to participate and nobody's talents are wasted. In the coming Year of Microcredit, we will focus on access to finance, for after all, people, poor and rich, need reliable financing so that their ideas can be brought together with assets to generate long-run sustainable growth.
>
> Raghuram G. Rajan
> Economic Counselor & Director,
> Research Department, International Monetary Fund
> Adviser for the International Year of Microcredit 2005

The private sector certainly plays an important role in market development. But it is for governments to provide the policy environment needed to build an efficient, and inclusive, financial sector that, particularly through microfinance, provides access to financial services for the poorest in society. And microfinance has done best in settings where governments did not follow directed credit policies, allowed the market to determine interest rates, kept credit allocation separate from politics and did not get involved with direct lending.[14]

In Chapter 9, Kathryn Imboden highlights the importance of financial inclusion, sets out a vision of an inclusive financial sector and the key considerations for designing a sound policy environment. She suggests a common vision, independent of national differences: to have multiple financial institutions collectively offering appropriate services to all parts

Table 1.3   Microfinance policy issues and strategic options

- Degree, and quality, of government intervention in the financial sector.
- Achievement of affordable and sustainable interest rates.
- Consumer protection.
- Government promotion of diverse institutions, within its supervisory capacity.
- Explicit inclusion of increasing access within regulatory and supervisory goals.
- The creation of access-friendly financial infrastructure.
- Above all, building access into overall financial sector policy.

of society, characterized by access for all to a full range of services, sound institutions and financial and institutional stability. To achieve this, certain conditions are key: the right to fair treatment, an acceptance of different models (for example, private, non-profit, public, public/private) transparency of financial policy interventions, good public sector governance and a well-functioning legal system. In addition, there must be macroeconomic stability, pro-poor growth policies and an openness to progress and change. As governments seek to establish a policy framework, certain issues and strategic options must be considered (see Table 1.3). In the end, effective financial inclusion is achieved by all stakeholders working well together to ensure that appropriate strategies are designed, and these are in turn developed into effective policy.

Conclusion

The lack of absorptive MFI capacity notwithstanding, microfinance has all the ingredients necessary to become an attractive market for private investments as various papers in this volume show:

- Huge demand.
- Fast growth.
- Profitable institutions with returns enhanced by social components.
- Returns potentially uncorrelated to mainstream markets and other asset classes.
- A growing array of standard investment instruments, some offering interesting liquidity and marketability characteristics.
- Increasing transparency, enforced by rating agencies.

The market's attractiveness can only grow as the further influx of private capital forces further evolution. Furthermore, microfinance benefits from the availability of donor (and development agency) support to help it develop and enhance capacity at no direct cost to the private investor. But there are other major challenges to developing the full potential of this $1000 billion market. There is insufficient start-up capital (both debt and equity) available. This in turn further limits the emergence of professionally managed start-ups, contributing to the existing shortage of absorptive capacity. Finally, there are significant regulatory challenges.

Much remains to be done in the area of capacity building, where publicly funded donors can play an important role in: building capacity in MFIs, regulators and supervisors, disseminating information on best practices and innovation, supporting microfinance to the poorest in rural and remote areas, innovation in product development, developing industry standards and financing infrastructure, economic development and operating in vulnerable (for example, war-torn) states. Both public and private donors can play a role in helping expand private sector involvement as debt and equity providers of funding to microfinance. This must be matched by a greater appetite for risk-taking among private commercial investors.[15]

Microfinance thrives in a supportive enabling regulatory environment. In general, there has been a shift from state-control towards more liberalized financial markets, which has been good for microfinance. But a recent paper by ACCION warns that this trend is under threat in some places. Weaknesses in the microfinance sector can invite political interference, such as happened in Rwanda and India in 2006. In Rwanda, the central bank closed down several weak MFIs, while in India a local government in the state of Andhra Pradesh closed two MFIs citing exorbitant interest rates and improper collection practices. The Indian action was later (and quickly) overturned by the central bank.[16] The industry must ensure that institutions maintain high standards of consumer protection, and educate the public about the principles of fair microfinance. Failure to do so, and anticipating similar issues that might arise, may result in heavier regulation.

Notes

1 In its first decade, ACCION's volunteers worked closely with local residents to identify the most pressing community needs such as electricity and water. The "ACCIONistas" then worked with residents to install electricity and sewer lines, start training and nutrition programs and build schools and community centers. Source: ACCION website: http://www.accion.org/ (accessed 24 November 2006).
2 See Chapter 3 by Benoît Leleux and Dinos Constantinou.
3 See the Preface 1 by Ivan Pictet.

4 Portfolio-at-risk (PAR) is the outstanding principle amount of all loans that have one or more installments of principal past due by a certain number of days, in this case by 30 days.

5 Using PAR > 90 as a benchmark.

6 For period FY2000–04: range of ROEs 51.2 percent $\leq \times \leq 8.1$ percent, a group of 10 MFIs. These were ASA, Bancosol, Banco Solidario, BRAC, CERUDEB, CMAC Arequipa, Compartamos, Los Andes, Mi Banco and PRODEM.

7 See Chapter 8 by Michael Hölz.

8 See Chapter 3 by Benoît Leleux and Dinos Constantinou.

9 See Chapter 8 by Michael Hölz.

10 See Chapter 3 by Benoît Leleux and Dinos Constantinou.

11 See Chapter 2 by Vijay Mahajan.

12 P. Goodman, "Raising MFI Equity through Microfinance Investment Funds", paper presented at the KfW Symposium in Frankfurt am Main (2005).

13 See Chapter 7 by Marc de Sousa Shields.

14 M. Otero and E. Rhyne. "Microfinance through the Next Decade: Visioning the Who, What, Where, When and How", paper commissioned by the Global Microcredit Summit 2006 (Boston: ACCION, 2006).

15 Op. cit.

16 Op. cit.

Transcript of former UN Secretary-General Kofi Annan's remarks at the Geneva Private Capital Symposium: Investing Private Capital in Micro & Small Business Finance, 10 October 2005

Microfinance is gaining general acceptance. A small loan, a savings account, an affordable way to send a paycheck home, can make all the difference to a low-income family, or to a small-scale enterprise. With access to microfinance, people can earn more and better protect themselves against unexpected losses and setbacks. And with the ability to collateralize their assets, they can move beyond day-to-day survival, towards planning their future. That means they can invest in better nutrition, housing, health, and education for their children. They can create productive businesses, and recover quickly in the aftermath of natural disasters. In short, they can take real strides towards breaking the vicious cycle of poverty and vulnerability.

Of course, much more than microfinance is needed to eradicate poverty and hunger. Sound macroeconomic policy. Good governance. Strategies to develop rural areas and the industrial sector. And of course, good regulatory systems that create the proper incentives for businesses. Investments in classrooms, clinics and human capital. These are among the essential elements in any national strategy for defeating poverty.

International support is crucial: more and better aid; more debt relief; and a trade regime that is open, fair, and truly gives the poor a chance. Only with such a sustained global partnership will poor people have a proper chance to lift themselves out of poverty.

Microfinance has much to contribute to that effort. And let us also be clear: microfinance is not charity. In some cases, it might have started out as philanthropy. But today it is real business.

Microfinance is a way to extend the same rights and similar services to low-income households that are available to everyone else. It protects people against shocks, and allows the majority of the population to become part of a country's economic activity. It can help to build markets, and show that profits and principles can reinforce each other.

However, microfinance is not as widespread as it could or should be. The vast majority of people in the world do not have access to financial services. In many countries, the financial sector reaches only a small fraction of the population, with very few people having even something as basic as a bank account. There are great disparities in the availability of banks, ATMs and other services. Some countries have less than one bank branch per 100 000 people, while others enjoy as many as 50 or more.

Thankfully, this situation is changing. A new mindset is taking hold. Where once the poor were commonly seen as passive victims, microfinance recognizes that the poor people are remarkable reservoirs of energy and knowledge. And while the lack of financial services is a sign of poverty, today it is also understood as an untapped opportunity to create markets, bring people in from the margins and give them the tools with which to help themselves.

Governments, public and private financial institutions, private businesses and others are recognizing the value of microfinance for poor individuals and for small- and medium-sized enterprises. The World Bank and the International Monetary Fund have embraced it as part of their strategy for alleviating poverty.

The United Nations, for its part, is making this a key issue in implementing the Monterrey Consensus on Financing for Development. Last month's The 2005 World Summit at the United Nations headquarters re-affirmed the need for access to financial services for the poor. And, as you all know, the General Assembly has proclaimed 2005 to be the International Year of Microcredit.

Our collective challenge is to sustain this momentum, and to meet the growing global demand for increased access to financial services. The International Year has served as an effective stimulus for action. More than 90 governments have undertaken initiatives to observe the Year. A number of microfinance leaders, development banks, credit unions, postal and savings banks and commercial banks are lending their support, for which we are most grateful. More than 300 events have been held around the world at which financial experts have been raising awareness and sharing their knowledge.

I believe microfinance offers another platform for private–public collaboration and for interventions by private solidarity institutions such as non-profit organizations and cooperatives. Through such arrangements, poor people can gain new choices, and a chance to increase their wealth. Small- and medium-sized enterprises can build up their infrastructure and capacities. Societies benefit in their efforts to defeat hunger and achieve other development goals such as better nutrition, gender equity and education for children. And private businesses profit from access to new markets and, not least, the boon to their reputations that comes with offering services that have a positive social impact.

I hope such engagement will intensify. The potential is significant. It is estimated that many millions of people around the world have unmet needs for financial services. The challenge is to scale up without losing sight of the poorest and the most vulnerable members of our society. Microfinance has been a small and, at times, partially subsidized venture. Now, the possibilities for commercial involvement have increased. We need to transform it into a viable and truly developmental effort on a mass scale that reaches the people, businesses and microfinance institutions that need to be supported. I hope financial institutions will continue to show that they are true entrepreneurs, and invest robustly in this line of business.

Last month's The 2005 World Summit in New York served as a real catalyst for development advances that we have been seeking for many years in key areas such as aid, debt relief and quick-impact projects. As we continue our efforts to achieve the Millennium Development Goals, microfinance can and must be part of that picture. Where people have a stake, a start, a piece of ownership, they are more likely to prosper. And where businesses are given a chance to develop, countries are more likely to flourish. I look forward to working with you to expand the reach of microfinance, and most importantly, to intensify our global struggle against poverty.

KOFI ANNAN
Former UN Secretary-General

Part I
Market Demand

Depending on the definition used for a microenterprise and the scope of microfinance, estimates of aggregate demand for capital range from $45 to $500 billion. While these estimates are notoriously unreliable, what is unquestionable is the enormous size of the market and its accelerated growth. Already a $30 billion industry today, microfinance is estimated to be growing at 15–30 percent per annum. In the next chapter, Vijay Mahajan looks at the breakdown, and drivers, of demand as well as some options for meeting that need.

2

The Demand for Micro and Small Business Finance: The $500 Billion Question

Vijay Mahajan[1]

Introduction: Defining micro and small business

After several decades of neglect, the private financial sector has finally started taking notice of the "fortune at the bottom of the pyramid", a phrase made famous by Professor C.K. Prahalad in a book by the same name.[2] In this chapter, we will try to take a view from below, that is, from the demand side. We will first clarify some definitions, then give rough quantitative estimates, then delve into the attributes of the demand, and finally make some comments on how private investors can meet this demand with a reasonable level of risk adjusted return.

The topic aggregates microenterprise and small business, as if they were one and the same. But the ownership, employment generation potential, geographical distribution and financial requirements of microenterprises and small businesses are very different. It is, therefore, more useful to consider them separately.

What is a microenterprise?

There is no single internationally accepted definition of the term microenterprise. The term was coined in 1973 by ACCION,[3] to distinguish the vast number of enterprises in the informal sector, which existed below the radar screen of the earlier categories, used – "small business" or "small enterprise" or "small-scale industry". The term was perhaps first officially used when the Act for Micro-Enterprise[4] was introduced in the United States House of Representatives in 1990. The bill's aim was to assist in the development of microenterprises and microenterprise lending. It defined a microenterprise to be "any unincorporated trade or business with five or fewer employees, one or more of whom own the enterprise", and limited a microenterprise loan to between $50 and $5000. The bill was referred to a House sub-committee, where it languished. Later, the United States enacted the Microenterprise Act, 1996.[5] The Act did not directly define microenterprises and indeed used the term "micro- and small enterprise" throughout the text. It also specified that credit to these enterprises would include at least 50 percent for "poverty lending"; a term defined as loans below $300 to very poor members of society, particularly women. The Act envisaged the provision of credit along with training and technical assistance:

> The support of private enterprise can be served by programs providing credit, training, and technical assistance for the benefit of micro- and small enterprises; and...
> - (3) Approximately one-half of the credit assistance authorized under paragraph (1) shall be used for poverty lending programs, including the poverty lending portion of mixed programs. Such programs:
>   a) Shall meet the needs of the very poor members of society, particularly poor women; and
>   b) Should provide loans of $300 or less in 1995 United States dollars to such poor members of society.

In India, the term is not used officially. Instead, the Central Statistical Organization (CSO) of India uses the phrase "Own Account Enterprise" for those enterprises in which the owner is self-employed, other workers are from his or her family and there is no hired worker. In contrast, an "establishment" is a business that employs at least one hired worker.

By contrast, China distinguishes enterprises by legal status: from "individually owned enterprises" to "legal entity enterprises", which can be non-state owned or state-owned.

Another categorization of business size comes from Peru. It compares micro businesses with the small and the medium sector, and gives an idea of the extent of capital employed at various levels. IDESI/Pro Empresa, Peru, divided the market into three areas:

- Micro business: Comprises 1–10 workers and has annual sales of up to US$40 000 by company. Loans granted to micro-business companies usually vary from US$50 to US$900 for an average term of 6 months.
- Small business: Comprises 10–20 workers and has annual sales of over US$40 000 by company. Loans granted vary from US$1000 to US$5000 for an average term of 2 years.
- Medium-sized business: Comprises 20–100 workers, and has annual sales of over US$750 000 by company. Loans granted vary from US$3000

to US$10 000 or more by company for an average term of 8 to 24 months.

IDESI/ Pro Empresa distinguishes its loans as follows: A micro-loan is granted for the growth of its recipients, a small loan is granted for market purposes (to a small business) and other loans are granted for development (to medium-sized and large companies).[6]

The institutions that aim to satisfy the financial needs of microenterprises are called microfinance institutions (MFIs). Many of them have their roots in non-governmental organizations (NGOs), often voluntary agencies, engaged in poverty alleviation and delivery of a range of service to the poor including education, health and housing. MFIs range across a wide spectrum in terms of their business model, from those that depend upon charity for their operations, to those that aim to be commercially viable outfits.

What is a small business?

The Small Business Administration of the US defines a small business as having less than $18 million in net assets and/or less than $6 million in net income. There are also alternate industry-based tests based on the number of employees.

It is obvious that these limits are far too high for any developing country. In India, for example, tiny industries are defined as below Rupees (INR) 2.5 million (about $55 000) investment, whereas small-scale industry is below INR 10 million (about $220 000) in plant and equipment.[7] However, even these numbers are too high. A better definition for a small business might be what the Central Statistical Organization of India terms a "Directory Enterprise" – an enterprise that has at least one hired worker on a "fairly regular basis" and more than five workers in total.

While the precise definitions may vary from one county to another depending on the local conditions, the general characteristics are clear: Compared with microenterprises, small businesses have more capital invested, employ somewhat better technology and enjoy slightly better access to formal financial institutions. They are served by small business finance institutions, SBFIs, which are often state owned or state sponsored. For example, the United States has the Small Business Administration, while India has the Small Industries Development Bank of India, SIDBI.

Why rule out agriculture?

The definition of a micro or small business generally makes no mention of agriculture. Generally, in developing countries, small and marginal farmers have been among the poorest, except for the rural landless house-holds and, as a result, governments have focused on them, providing them with support in the form of soft loans, subsidies and extension services. Seeing the sector well attended to, most microfinance institutions have traditionally stayed away from agriculture. But over the years, it has become evident that government alone will not be able to provide all the support needed by this sector. Factors such as bad policy design, poorly conceived and implemented schemes, corruption, and a lack of suffi-cient resources, have resulted in the small farmers staying poor.

In most developing countries, agriculture employs many more people than do enterprises. The majority of rural small and microenterprises use agricultural produce as their input, or have farmers as their customers. Hence, lack of growth in agriculture constrains the growth of the micro and small business sector as well. As the two sectors are so intimately connected and share similar problems, agricultural enterprises and their financial needs also deserve to be discussed here.

Demand for finance from microenterprises and small businesses

Estimating the number of microenterprises and small businesses

According to one recent paper, it is estimated that there are about 500 million microenterprises worldwide, most of them in the informal sec-tor in developing countries.[8] This number seems to be an over-estimate, if we go back to country statistics, starting with the two most populous countries, China and India.

In India, in 1998, there were a total of 30.33 million enterprises, 17.71 million in rural areas and 12.63 million in urban areas, employing a total of 83.4 million persons, or an average of less than three workers per enterprise (see Table 2.1 and Figure 2.1).[9]

According to another estimate, in the year 2000, there were about 39 million microenterprises in India, and about 5.6 million small busi-nesses.[10] In China, in 2001, there were an estimated 20 million "indi-vidually owned enterprises" in addition to 30.26 million "legal entity" enterprises.[11]

Putting together estimates from various sources, we find that in 2001 China had about 50 million microenterprises and small businesses, and India 45 million. The US had 22.9 million small businesses according to the Small Business Administration (SBA),[12] while Latin America had 18 million[13] and Indonesia, another large economy, 3 million.[14] These numbers add up to about 139 million, and perhaps the rest of the world,

Table 2.1   Enterprises in India by size (1998)

	Enterprises (millions)		
Size	Rural	Urban	Total
1–5 workers	16.95	11.56	28.51
6–9 workers	0.42	0.57	0.99
More than 10 workers	0.33	0.5	0.83
Total	17.7	12.63	30.33

Source: Economic Census, Government of India, Central Statistical Organization, 1998.

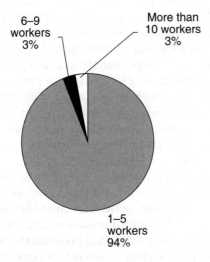

Figure 2.1   Percent of enterprises, by size, in India (1998)
Source: Economic Census, Government of India, Central Statistical Organization, 1998.

including Europe, has several tens of millions more, to take the number to 200 million. But it is unlikely that the world as a whole had 500 million microenterprises, as estimated by the paper cited above.

However, if we treat agricultural farms as enterprises, we may yet reach 500 million microenterprises worldwide, since China had nearly 210 million agricultural households[15] and India had 116 million farms in 2001. This adds up to 326 million, and thus the number of farming enterprises in the world is likely to be in the range of 400 million. If we add to this to the number of non-farm microenterprises and small businesses estimated above, the total does add up to 600 million.

Demand for credit from microenterprises

Formal credit institutions generally shy away from lending to microenterprises. A recent study[16] indicated that in most countries, micro and small business finance accounted for less than 1 percent of the broad money supply, with the major exceptions being Indonesia and Thailand (about 6 percent each) and Bangladesh (3 percent). It is difficult for microenterprises to obtain credit because of their lack of fixed assets, their low volumes of business and their existence on the margins of, or outside, the law.

Two studies of relevance to the topic were conducted by the National Sample Survey Organization, a part of the Ministry of Statistics and Programme Implementation of the Government of India. The first, in 1999–2000, was on the Informal Sector in India. In the next year, another study was done on the Unorganized Manufacturing Sector in India. In the unorganized manufacturing sector in India, which we can equate to the microenterprise sector, the total loan outstanding at 2000–1 was about $800 million. Of all the microenterprises involved in manufacturing, only about 4.4 percent had access to credit in 2001, and of these, about one-third obtained their credit from informal sources (moneylenders, family, friends, business partners, etc).

In a study carried out for the World Bank in India between 1994 and 1995, Mahajan and Ramola estimated the average annual credit usage by rural households in the survey area based on their credit usage for the previous three years.[17] The annual average credit usage per household from all sources worked out to INR 14 549 (about $300). Of this, 65 percent was for productive purposes and 35 percent for consumption purposes. Long-term productive purposes, including purchase of livestock, farm machinery, and so on, accounted for 16 percent of the total credit usage while short-term productive purposes like agricultural crop loan accounted for 49 percent. Loans for consumption purposes included long term purposes like house building and marriage (accounting for 15 percent of the total) and short-term purposes like household expenses, clothes, consumer durables, and so on (accounting for 20 percent).

We can try to estimate the annualized credit usage in rural India from the above data. The World Bank study was carried out in Raichur district of Karnataka, which, though a dryland region, has a higher credit usage compared with the poverty belt in Bihar, Madhya Pradesh, Rajasthan, Uttar Pradesh, Orissa and the North East. In view of the above, if we assume the average annual credit usage in 2004 to be INR 9000 ($200) per household per annum, the total usage comes to about $30 billion by rural households. Of this, roughly half of the demand is from poor households, or about $15 billion. In addition, the 25 million urban poor households in India also use microcredit to the extent of $200 per annum and this adds up to $10 billion. In short, the demand for micro-credit in India is in the range of $25 billion.

In China, the average loan size for micro-borrowers varied from $50 to $100 in the initial experiments on microcredit conducted in the late 1990s by projects sponsored by IFAD and the UN. The profile of usage is described below:

> The demand for productive loans generally depends on the economic activities of the households concerned. Nearly all households in the sample group pursued cropping and livestock activities, while less than half were engaged in wage earning (48 percent) and self-employment (29 percent). More households in the richest group were engaged in non-farm activities (56 percent in wage earning and 37 percent in self-employment), compared with those belonging to the poorer strata of the sample.
>
> Economic activities have different financing needs. More was needed for livestock (75 percent), followed by self-employment activities (64 percent), cropping (27 percent) and wage income (5 percent). The borrowing propensity was highest for cropping (29 percent), self-employment (22 percent) and livestock (10 percent). Borrowing for cropping was much lower in the richest asset quartile (17 percent), and for livestock, it was much higher in the poorest quartile (17 percent).[18]

Applying the average loan size of $100 from the microcredit project in China to its 210 million peasant households, we get straightaway a demand for $21 billion of microcredit. In addition, more than 50 million small and microenterprises all need at least $500 each, which adds up to another $25 billion. In short, China has a demand for at least $46 billion. Thus, even based on these very rough estimates, India and China alone constitute a $100 billion market for microcredit.

Demand for credit from small businesses

For all the benefit it brings in terms of stabilizing the incomes of millions of subsistence farmers and self-employed micro entrepreneurs, microcredit has not been shown to generate growth and additional employment.

In an article entitled "Is Microcredit a Development Tool?", Fernand Vincent of IRED, Geneva, wrote:

> Does micro-credit produce economic growth by enabling the creation of businesses and therefore partially solving employment problems? The answer is not that simple. Two studies carried out in Asia have delivered an initial interesting answer:
> Loans under US$100, usually made to women, rarely (less than 3 percent) permit the creation of small trader or new jobs. These loans help improve the social situation of the recipients who are able to satisfy vital needs such as healthcare, food, housing, schooling, etc., but few of them are able to cross over the poverty threshold. These loans must continue to be developed, however, as they have an essential role in social improvement:
>
> - Loans between US$100 and US$1000 result in the same but they also contribute to the creation of jobs and small trade (7 to 12 percent depending on the country and the case).
> - Loans above US$5000 are the ones that trigger a growth process by enabling investments in new production units, increases in productivity and an opening towards new markets.[19]

This phenomenon is visible in almost all countries – that microenterprises serve a purpose in supporting household subsistence, but real growth and employment comes from small enterprises. Yet, small businesses' access to credit is still incredibly difficult in most countries. We have another interesting description of the situation of small business credit in China, the fastest growing large economy in the world:

> China has always had a very high savings rate, and the total savings deposits are increasing quickly with the growing economic scale. In 2002, the balance for deposits and loans of all kinds, in domestic and foreign currency in all financial institutions reached 18.34 trillion Yuan and 13.98 trillion Yuan respectively (NBS, 2003). Since the 1990s, four state-owned commercial banks have occupied 60–63 percent of the business of deposits and loans. SMEs lack specialized financial-service institutions and suitable credit system. Most loans were extended to state-owned enterprises, especially large enterprises.[20]

The situation is further amplified in the citation below:

> SMEs still lack access to the resources lavished on larger state-owned firms, according to investment statistics. Widespread wariness by both

borrowers and lenders of the higher risks accompanying private projects is a key cause of the slower growth in private sector investment. Chinese officials have said that banks are "too conservative" to lend money to SMEs. Loan officers in state-owned commercial banks are not rewarded for making good loans but are penalized when they approve loans that are not repaid. Other officials are more blunt: The state-owned commercial banks will continue giving priority to large state-owned enterprises because of their implicit government guarantees. Some SMEs, usually former collectives, do in fact turn to the banking system for at least a small portion of their lending needs. In these cases, SME managers typically use their housing as collateral. As a result of the banking system's continuing preference for lending to large state-owned firms, SMEs usually raise money through indirect financing, primarily from family members or from their local communities. Retained earnings are another key source of financing.[21]

In India, too, the availability of credit to micro and small businesses is very much below the level of demand. The Indian Economic Census in 1998, for the first time, had a question about the source of finance for enterprises. It was found that 80.4 percent of the 30.4 million enterprises in the country were totally self-financed. Of the 19.6 percent who did use others' funds, only 4.7 percent of all enterprises, rural and urban, received any form of formal finance. Banks and financial institutions directly financed only 2.8 percent of enterprises, while 1.9 percent had received finance linked to poverty alleviation programs. The remaining microenterprises received credit from informal sources.

The acute shortage of credit for the microenterprise sector in India is not surprising, because microenterprises fell between the two priority sectors – agriculture and industry. Since the 1970s, in the wake of Green Revolution, the banking system has been expanded in rural areas, but primarily to cater to the needs of agriculture through the National Bank for Agricultural and Rural Development (NABARD). On the other side of the gap, the banking system and specialized institutions such as the Small Industries Development Bank of India (SIDBI) have mainly extended credit to the larger of the small-scale industries. SIDBI and its retail intermediaries, the State Finance Corporations, have focused on the larger end of the small-scale sector, largely neglecting microenterprises and smaller "small businesses". Both NABARD and SIDBI became conscious of the microenterprise gap in the mid 1990s and set up specialized windows for microcredit. NABARD used the self-help group bank linkage program and SIDBI established the SIDBI Foundation for Micro Credit.

In Indonesia, more than 40 million people out of the population of 210 million depend on micro and small businesses to earn a living. Yet the demand for credit from microenterprises and small businesses is hardly met:

> Out of 200 million Indonesian people, more than 40 million depend on micro and small-scale businesses to earn a living. Therefore, small and micro businesses form the backbone of the Indonesian economy. Micro-financial services like saving and credit are essential to keep these industries going. Today, there are approximately 10,000 MFIs in Indonesia. However, most of these institutions are concentrated in Java and Bali, while banking services in the outer provinces are far less developed. Recent studies by the Asian Development Bank show that in the rural areas only 50 percent of the people have access to banking services.[22]

> In 2003, banks (including rural banks) recorded a total of Rupiah (IDR) 26.9 trillion ($2.6 billion) in new SME loans and microcredit, representing 63.8 percent of the targeted IDR 42.4 trillion ($4.1 billion) in lending to this sector. This target was divided into IDR 7.5 trillion in microcredit (18 percent), IDR 15.2 trillion in new loans to small enterprises (36 percent) and IDR 19.7 trillion for medium enterprises (46 percent).[23]

In Latin America, ACCION estimated there were 17.9 million microenterprises and small businesses across the region in 2001, and that less than 15 percent of those had been reached by formal institutions and MFI/SBFIs.[24] ACCION estimated that 8 to 10 million urban micro enterprises in Brazil lack access to credit.

In summary, access to credit is well below the demand in almost all countries, even in the large and fast-growing economies of India and China. One can only imagine what adequate availability of credit for micro and small businesses could do in terms of supporting economic growth.

Demand for equity from microenterprises and small businesses

While microenterprises and small businesses overwhelmingly seek credit as a form of external finance, they also need equity, both at start-up stage and to enable later growth. Yet equity financing for microenterprises and small businesses is even more difficult to access than credit.

Several efforts have been made in this direction, such as the Small Business Investment Corporations (SBICs), a model created in the US in 1958, when the Small Business Investment Act was passed. The first

SBIC was licensed in March 1959. The SBIC program is generally credited with the development of the venture capital industry in the US, which has provided over $330 billion of equity in the last 15 years[25] and supported millions of small businesses including such celebrated successes as Intel, Apple, Sun and Google. (It should be noted that not more than 35 percent of SBIC funds can be from state and federal governments and the management is required to be private.) Using this experience, the US-based Small Enterprise Assistance Fund (SEAF), established in 1990, has set up over a dozen equity funds and financed 213 enterprises with $84 million of equity and quasi-equity investments in several countries.[26]

In India, the Small Industries Development Bank of India (SIDBI) has run a National Equity Fund (NEF) for two decades, which tops up the margin money to be put up by small entrepreneurs while borrowing from a bank. Though the term equity is used, in practice, banks use the NEF merely as a second source of credit willing to assume a higher risk, without the NEF benefiting from any of the upside. Several studies show that micro- and small entrepreneurs are starved for start-up and expansion stage equity funds in all other developing countries.[27]

The intermediation chain

As can be seen from the survey above, the demand for finance from microenterprises and small businesses is enormous. China, India, Indonesia and Latin America together have over 115 million microenterprises and small businesses and even if we assume a low average finance requirement of $1000 to cover both working capital and fixed assets, the total requirement is over $115 billion. It would not be an exaggeration to say that, for the world as whole, this number will be in the range of $150 billion. If we assume debt–equity ratio of 2:1, which is not uncommon, the debt requirements are at least $100 billion. If we add loans to agricultural enterprises and farms to this number, and assume that those would also need at least $1000 per farm to address badly needed long-term investments in land and water resources, we add another $400 billion to demand. Thus, the total amount of debt required to promote micro- and small businesses is in the range of $500 billion.

The aggregate number is very appealing, but the sobering fact is that the debt has to be distributed to more than 500 million microenterprises. These microenterprises make up a very amorphous and diffuse set of customers. They are often not legally registered, and may not have a fixed address. If they are farming enterprises, often the title may not be official. They are geographically very distant from each other and from the investor. There are social and cultural barriers to communication. It requires a high level of local knowledge to understand each enterprise. And, given that the value of each loan is very small, the transaction costs and verification costs are very high.

Thus, there is an obvious need for intermediation – perhaps a whole chain of it. This is true for both domestic and foreign investors. While domestic institutions may be in a position to build a retail network, it is generally more difficult for foreign investors to deal directly with the ultimate borrowers. A wiser approach is to channel investments through an intermediary, who is better placed to identify potential customers, disburse the loan amount and later collect the repayments, and verify from time to time that the loan is being utilized in the intended manner. Investors can invest in a fund, which then provides financial support to a local MFI or an SBFI. This local institution, owing to its closeness to the market, is able to channel the investment to borrowers in such a way as to obtain a social benefit as well as financial returns (see Figure 2.2).

In some cases, it is possible for foreign Micro and Small Business Finance funds to lend directly to domestic MFI/SBFIs, thus eliminating one rung in the chain. Indeed, BlueOrchard Finance, based in Geneva, has been doing this quite successfully. However, this is possible only when dealing with the larger MFIs and SBFIs. As these successful institutions are increasingly targeted by international and domestic banks, such as Citibank, Deutsche Bank, ABN Amro and in India, ICICI Bank and HDFC Bank, there is a need to reach out to the smaller MFI/SBFIs, which is possible only through a domestic fund.

We end this section by acknowledging that the unmet demand for finance for microenterprises and small businesses in enormous, perhaps

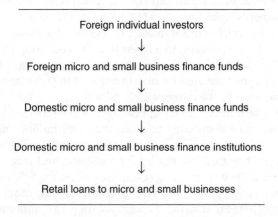

Foreign individual investors

↓

Foreign micro and small business finance funds

↓

Domestic micro and small business finance funds

↓

Domestic micro and small business finance institutions

↓

Retail loans to micro and small businesses

Figure 2.2   The intermediation chain for micro and small business finance

as much as $500 billion. However, as the market is highly dispersed, it can be addressed only by systematically building an intermediation chain between interested investors in the North and the user enterprises in the South. Thus, we now turn our attention to demand for finance from the intermediaries in the South.

Demand for finance from MFIs and SBFIs

CGAP estimates that the global total of microfinance loans outstanding, delivered through all institutions – including NGOs, commercial banks, state-owned and postal banks, credit unions and other institutions – is more than $15 billion.[28] Of this, foreign sources of funding, whether investment, or grants, or subsidized loans, comprise only a small percentage at about $1.9 billion.[29] (This amount includes the funding for all microfinance loans, including those to small businesses and agriculture enterprises.) Of this amount, about 73 percent is commercial and quasi-commercial debt. Equity comprises only 20 percent and guarantees just 6 percent. It is clear that of the three instruments – debt, guarantees and equity – debt is by far the most prevalent.

A recent study conducted by the Consultative Group to Assist the Poor (CGAP) and the Microfinance Information eXchange (MIX) provides very interesting data about the types of funding that MFI/SBFIs demand, and the barriers that prevent them from accessing funds.[30] In nearly every region, MFI/SBFIs ranked lack of funds as their greatest constraint on growth. However, the majority of respondents, even the financially sustainable ones, ranked grants and donor loans as the most appropriate sources of financing. Exceptionally, MFI/SBFIs in South and East Asia ranked commercial funding sources such as equity, debt and bank loans as more appropriate than did MFI/SBFIs elsewhere.

Profile of MFI/SBFIs eligible for private finance

The factor that has the most impact on the type of funds an MFI can access is its legal structure. For-profit Non-Banking Financial Institutions (NBFIs) can obtain funding through loans and equity. Institutions legally recognized as banks can mobilize deposits, which provide cheaper capital than borrowings. However, an NGO MFI has to support itself through grants and loans alone. Ivatury and Abrams have categorized institutions that receive foreign investment into two segments:

- Segment I institutions are regulated MFI/SBFIs (microfinance banks and non-bank microfinance institutions or NBFIs) which can receive both debt and equity investments.

- Segment II institutions are un-regulated MFI/SBFIs (such as NGOs and trusts), credit unions and cooperatives. These are legally structured to receive only debt, and not equity, investment.[31]

These Segment I and Segment II institutions represent only a small part of the wide variety of institutions that provide financial services to the poor. Other institutions – including state-sponsored agricultural and development banks, co-operative banks, commercial banks that are now expanding into microfinance, and small business funds – are not candidates for debt or equity funding from private foreign sources.

Risk levels

MFI/SBFIs generally consider lack of funds to be the biggest constraint to their expansion. This is particularly true in the early stages of growth for an institution. At an early stage, when equity investments are particularly important, the level of risk is also higher. Several barriers to equity investment exist, most notably the fact that the industry is not mature enough for the investor to rely on history as a reliable indicator. There are, in addition, regulatory pressures that inhibit investors. But the largest issue facing potential investors is risk.

The major risk involved in extending financial support to an MFI/SBFI is its likelihood of failure. Though there have been relatively few failures of MFIs so far, this has partly been due to the fact they are still relatively small and have access to several sources of operating support. SBFIs, which have a longer history, have failed in several countries, even where they were state owned. In India, for example, a large proportion of the state government-owned state finance corporations designed to finance small enterprises are virtually defunct, with a high ratio of non-performing assets on their books.

Another risk is that the institution may have low profitability. Low profitability can be caused by a combination of higher operating costs due to small loan sizes, dispersed operations, particularly when those are in rural and remote areas, and in many cases, official or normative ceilings on interest rates. As long as MFIs are small, as are the loan sizes of their clients, they are able to charge higher interest rates. But as the loan sizes go up and the MFI's size and visibility also increase, its interest rates begin to be compared with those available from banks.

Yet another risk is improper corporate governance. Many MFIs are established by or continue to be NGOs, whose Boards are not always active or effective. Many have been formed by charismatic individuals, who gathered together a group of supporters as Board members. As the MFI becomes larger, these Boards lack the capacity and skills to perform the functions necessary for a financial institution. Donors are often reluctant to seek changes in governance. Thus, it is only when private equity investors come on board that weaknesses in governance become obvious. There have been a few cases of MFI failure due to weak governance.

Another source of risk is exchange rate fluctuations. Currently, about 85 percent of all foreign debt investment to microfinance providers is loaned in hard currency. Some MFI/SBFIs, such as BASIX, have always borrowed from abroad in local currency (Rupee) denomination. In the case of BASIX, this arrangement was favorable because the Rupee depreciated with respect to the US dollar, from INR 36 to INR 44 in the nine years since BASIX has been borrowing. This example shows that unanticipated fluctuations in exchange rates can potentially be very costly, and so borrowers and lenders alike need to be aware of foreign exchange risk. Yet only about one quarter of MFI/SBFIs with hard currency borrowings fully hedge the foreign exchange risk.[32] Also, MFI/SBFIs often overlook the cost of hedging the foreign exchange risk, thus making the loan seem more attractive than it actually is.

Expected returns through the intermediation chain

Microfinance is an emerging asset class, with its own distinct rewards and risks. It has been shown to be an effective means of providing financial services for the poor. There are now numerous examples of successful microfinance programs that have scaled up, transformed into non-bank financial institutions or commercial banks and become commercially viable. There are several examples, notably in Latin America and South Africa, where MFI/SBFIs show a high return on equity. Yet, there is a widespread misperception in the capital markets about the potential rates of return in microfinance.

To help rectify this situation, let us compare MFI/SBFIs against mainstream commercial financial institutions engaged in lending. In one recent study it was found that 13 MFI/SBFIs exceeded the weighted average profitability of the world's five strongest banks over a three-year period from 2001 to 2003.[33] Likewise, 51 MFI/SBFIs were more profitable than the weighted average of the top 10 banks in the world in 2002. In 2003, 21 MFI/SBFIs were more profitable than the top five banks.

While the profitability of several MFI/SBFIs may compare favorably with that of commercial lending institutions, it should be noted that even the largest MFI/SBFIs today are small compared with other targets of international capital. The loans they can absorb are correspondingly small.

Therefore, the transaction cost per dollar lent is high, relative to other corporate loans.[34] Further, hard currency loans attract the added cost of hedging foreign exchange risk. These factors drive up the cost of foreign debt for MFI/SBFIs. However, MFI/SBFIs can insulate themselves from this risk by utilizing hedging solutions such as the International Finance Corporation's (IFC) Global Microfinance Facility.[35] The Facility provides credit enhancement products at commercial terms to MFI/SBFIs through local commercial banks who would not otherwise lend to them. These products include standby facilities (letters of credit, letters of guarantee, and direct funded loans or deposit products) to local commercial banks, to support local currency lending to MFI/SBFIs.

Thus, while MFI/SBFIs may be very attractive targets for foreign debt, established institutions on the ground may not find these loans as attractive. Most established MFI/SBFIs already have access to funds at or below market rates of interest, from sources such as international financial institutions and social investment funds. Besides, these institutions may also be able to mobilize funds from domestic financial institutions or deposits. Therefore, they have low incentives to obtain commercial international funding.

However, smaller and newer institutions may consider foreign debt more attractive, because of the perceived lower cost, as well as the easier conditions on collateral.[36] But a vast majority of these smaller MFI/SBFIs are not yet viable businesses or investments. They represent a potential market, but it is difficult for a foreign fund to invest in a large number of such small MFI/SBFIs, though these would offer a higher rate of return than established MFI/SBFIs in more mature markets, like Latin America, where the returns offered by MFI/SBFIs have declined as a result of increasing competition. A further complicating factor is that many MFI/SBFIs are run on a social – or double bottom line – basis that does not emphasize the maximization of profit or return on equity (see Table 2.2).

This quick calculation shows that investors can expect about 2 percent per annum on their investment in debt funds, and 5 percent per annum on their investment in equity funds. These estimates take into account indicative costs at each stage of the necessary intermediation chain.

Exit options

There are, as yet, few exit options for equity investors in MFI/SBFIs. There is a low probability of IPOs in this sector, and as a result, the main exit option is a buy-out by second stage investors. Encouragingly, this is starting to happen. Institutions such as the Soros Foundation, the Michael and Susan Dell Foundation, and the Omidyar Network (set up by the

Table 2.2   Returns and costs at each stage of the intermediation chain

Intermediation chain level	Returns and costs		Debt funds (%)	Equity funds (%)
Retail Loans	Interest and fees	+	24–36	24–36
Domestic MFI/SBFIs	Operations costs and credit risk	–	15–21	6–24
	Average net returns	=	12	15
Domestic	Fees	–	2–4	2–4
MF/SB Funds	Average net returns	=	9	12
Foreign	Currency risk	–	2–6	2–6
MF/SB Funds	Fees	–	2–4	2–4
	Average net return to investors	=	2	5

founder of e-Bay) have plans to invest in MFI/SBFIs. Mr Vinod Khosla, a well-known venture capitalist, has plans to invest personally in several Indian microfinance companies. In addition, the first generation of equity funds and investment companies also provide exits to primary investors. This includes the Ford Foundation from the USA, Oikocredit from the Netherlands, and the Triodos Bank managed funds – Hivos-Triodos, Triodos-Doen and Triodos Fairshare. Another possible buy-out opportunity is provided by large financial institutions, like insurance companies, looking to diversify into a new asset class. This has been tried successfully by the Deutsche Bank Microfinance Foundation, which has attracted mainstream investors into a $75 million fund.

Another possible way to liquidate the investment is by selling the equity to the community that is served by the microfinance company. In India, BASIX has done this with its subsidiary Sarvodaya Nano Finance Ltd, and SHARE Microfin has raised part of its equity in this manner. However, there are issues about what kind of valuation can be charged to the community, beyond book value.

Ways for potential investors to meet the demand

The funding environment

Currently, the foreign funding environment consists of private-sector funding arms of bilateral and multilateral donor agencies such as the KfW in Germany, AFD in France, BIO in Belgium, FMO in the Netherlands and the World Bank affiliate IFC. In addition, there are socially motivated, privately-managed investment funds financed by private investors, such as Calvert from the USA, Oikocredit and the Triodos Hivos and Doen Funds from the Netherlands. Although social investment funds are smaller than development investor funds, they are growing dramatically.

Both types of investors generally take a commercial approach in the rigor of their investment analysis and monitoring, but are not fully commercial in the sense of trying to maximize profit. They take greater risks and accept lower returns than purely profit-maximizing investors. In addition to these investors, there are a large number of donors, both private and public.

A recent paper by Tom Coleman comments on the contradictions in direct foreign investment in MFI/SBFIs globally:

> Direct foreign investment in MFI/SBFIs comes primarily from the US and Europe. The aggregate flow of direct foreign investment to MFI/SBFIs displays some interesting anomalies.
>
> Although the roots of microfinance, and microfinance equity in particular, came from donor and grant financing of NGOs, increasingly the financing of the microfinance industry comes from commercial capital. Microfinance is also increasingly being financed by local borrowing from commercial banks and other commercial investors.
>
> A smaller but significant portion of the financing of microfinance comes from direct foreign investment. This financing comes primarily from the United States and Europe. CGAP estimates that US$655 million of direct foreign investment is available to MFI/SBFIs in 2005. This is in addition to an estimated US$1 billion each year of grants and donations to microfinance. Of this US$655 million of direct foreign investment, less than 10 percent is private commercial capital.
>
> The vast majority of this direct foreign investment in microfinance, 90 percent, is development institution capital and private social capital invested at below commercial market rates. Looking at direct foreign investment in aggregate, $100 of social capital is only leveraging $10 of commercial capital investment in microfinance. If the $1 billion of grants and donations to microfinance is included, then each $100 of social capital is leveraging less than $4 of commercial capital.
>
> It should be possible to reverse this relationship. $100 of social capital should be able to leverage 5–10 times as much commercial capital or even more. Leverage of social capital has already been achieved by some MFI/SBFIs that have used social capital for equity to develop profitable institutions that now fund themselves primarily with commercial capital. Developing profitable MFI/SBFIs is one important way that social capital is beginning to leverage larger amounts of commercial capital, one MFI at a time.[37]

This inverse leveraging could be turned around in several ways. One way is to establish specialized funds for MFI/SBFIs. Funds may use any of the three methods – equity, debt or guarantee – or a mix of them.

MFI/SBFI funds – Debt

Debt funds are far more common than either guarantee or equity funds. One particularly interesting example is BlueOrchard Finance, based in Geneva. BlueOrchard began as the manager of the Dexia Micro-Credit Fund, which was the first private worldwide and fully commercial microfinance investment fund. It currently services about 50 microfinance institutions in 22 different emerging economies, with a current value of $58 million. BlueOrchard has also acted as adviser to the ResponsAbility Global Microfinance Fund since December 2003.

One of the innovations of BlueOrchard was establishing a long-term lending facility guaranteed by the Overseas Private Investment Corporation of the USA. The structured financial instrument BlueOrchard Microfinance Securities I & II provides loans of five to seven years. The total value of these loans is $92 million. The structuring on the liabilities side comprises three tiers – senior debt, junior debt and equity. The senior debt is fully guaranteed, while equity assumes all the risk. This kind of innovative structuring has enabled BlueOrchard to attract diverse investors with different risk-return appetites into the same fund.

Another example of a debt fund is the PlaNet MicroFund, which encourages and supports the development of the most promising young microfinance institutions. These young MFI/SBFIs seldom have access to commercial financing. PlaNet MicroFund helps them build their own credit history and develop relationships with financial backers, banks and other investment funds to obtain commercial financial resources and thus to diversify their financing sources.

Though there are many agencies that are willing to provide debt funding, the proportion of MFI/SBFIs satisfying their eligibility conditions is extremely low. CGAP estimates that there are only about 100–150 such microfinance institutions. These relatively mature institutions are easily able to obtain foreign and domestic funding. It is essential that more MFI/SBFIs develop to the point where it is feasible to lend to them. In this, the role of equity is critical.

MFI/SBFI funds – Guarantee

The first-ever loan guarantee fund for microfinance institutions was the ACCION Latin America Bridge Fund, established in 1984. By providing Standby Letters of Credit, the Fund enables ACCION's partner and affiliate programs in Latin American and the Caribbean to access short-term lines of credit from local banks. As of February 2005, the LABF was capitalized at over US$6.1 million with loans from socially responsible investors. Since 1987, the Fund has provided guarantees for close to $70 million, enabling over 23 institutions in 12 countries to access local commercial funding. This has the benefit that the MFI/SBFIs are able to avoid foreign exchange risk.

FUNDES in Latin America, established by Mssrs Ernst Brugger and Schmidheiny, was one of the pioneers in offering guarantees to banks to lend to small businesses. The principle was simple: Establish a fund in Europe or the USA, using philanthropic investors, then park the funds in an international bank and ask it to grant a guarantee to a local bank that, in turn, gives loans to local microenterprises or small businesses, with its risk partially or fully covered.

One of the pioneers in establishing guarantee funds for local currency loans in several countries is Fernand Vincent, who set out his experience as follows:

> Based on a comparative study of the impact of such funds, the following lessons have been learned: These guarantees have enabled tens of thousands of small producers, men and women, peasants, merchants, craftsmen and entrepreneurs from the informal sector to obtain a long awaited bank loan. Certainly, a guarantee is not the only risk coverage solution, but it is one of the most efficient. Over a period of 12 years, the experience of the RAFAD Foundation has resulted in the following conclusions:
>
> - The average annual loss of such a Fund is in the order of 5 percent.
> - The multiplying factor is 3.5, which means that local banks have granted loans of $350 000 based on a guarantee of $100 000.
> - The interest charged by banks was at market rate less 1 to 3 percent depending on the case, since risks were partially covered by the guarantee.
> - The borrowers reimbursed their loans in local rather than foreign currency.
> - After 6 years of positive experiences, local banks consider these partners as clients and no longer require a guarantee.[38]

For small business, the US SBA runs the world's largest loan guarantee program, having given out guarantees worth $40.5 billion to 486 000 small businesses. The SBA also provides guarantees for microenterprise loans of up to $35 000 with an average loan of $10 500.[39] Although guarantees in general have not been as successful in developing countries, the US SBA experience is worth studying to see what can be done to use guarantees more creatively, at both the enterprise and the MFI/SBFI levels.

MFI/SBFI funds – Equity

One of the most prominent examples of equity funds is ProFund. Incorporated as a for-profit investment fund in 1995, ProFund Internacional (ProFund) seeks a high return on investment for its shareholders while promoting the growth of regulated and efficient financial intermediaries whose main target market is the small and microenterprise sector of Latin America and the Caribbean. ProFund provides equity and quasi-equity resources to eligible financial institutions so that they can expand and improve their operations on a sustainable and large-scale basis. It invests only in financial institutions, which are financially stable, with a demonstrated ability to earn profits while serving the target market. ProFund earned a profit of $1.6 million in the year 2004.

The concept of equity funding for MFI/SBFIs is becoming more common. In India, for example, BASIX championed this idea for several years with proposals for what it initially called the SAMTEX Fund and later the Millennium Fund. Eventually, Gray Ghost and Triodos jointly established the $10 million Bellwether Fund in India with the former CEO of a BASIX finance company acting as the Fund Manager. At the same time, the government of India has established a $50 million Microfinance Equity and Development Fund, housed in NABARD, while SIDBI has begun to offer equity to MFIs. Private investors like Vinod Khosla have also made equity investments in several Indian MFIs.

Concluding comments

Mission versus returns – are both possible?

So let us return to the $500 billion dollar question: is it possible to be a socially responsible investor, and get respectable financial returns at the same time? The answer depends on your definition of "respectable".[40] In the current state of the industry, investors should not expect to earn any more perhaps than 2 percent on their investments in debt funds, and 5 percent on their investments in equity funds.

These returns may sound disappointing, but they are a beginning to establish a new asset class in the investment portfolios of private investors, many of whom are interested in a "bonus" non-financial return from the satisfaction of helping poor people achieve self-sufficiency. We expect financial returns will improve as better architecture reduces risk and an increase in the overall volume of funds reduces intermediation costs.

Building the sector from the bottom up

Today, the bottleneck in the intermediation chain is that there are not enough MFI/SBFIs that qualify to receive financial support. When this is the case, no amount of funds from the top can help. Thus, it is essential to build the sector from the bottom up rather than top down. Capacity building of new and young institutions is required. This involves both financial and non-financial capacity building. Financial capacity building is aimed at improving the ability of the MFI/SBFIs to absorb larger funds, and consequently to serve larger numbers of loans and customers. MFI/SBFIs may also be trained in developing new products. Non-financial capacity building includes developing the human resources of the company, improving institutional governance practices, and building up the management information systems.

While capacity building is essential to the growth of MFI/SBFIs, so that they can reach even larger numbers of the poor, there is no immediate or assured financial return from this exercise. So, capacity building is ideally funded through donor grants, rather than loans or equity. However, this is not to say that foreign debt or equity investments have no role to play in building the capacity of the recipient MFI/SBFIs. Private investments will stimulate MFI/SBFIs to adopt greater transparency and standardization, and to obtain the managerial and technical ability required to scale up. Also, the demands of private investors can encourage MFI/SBFIs to adopt higher standards of corporate governance and accounting.

The problem of capacity building becomes more acute when one looks at the different regions of the world. Coleman draws attention to a significant disparity in foreign investment reaching MFIs in different regions:

> The microfinance market coverage of the poorest is 23 percent in Asia, compared to 7 percent in Africa and the Middle East, 8 percent in Latin America and the Caribbean and 2 percent in North America Europe and the CIS. Asia, where the largest number of the poorest live, has already developed by far the largest microfinance coverage of the poorest at 23 percent.
>
> Direct foreign investment in microfinance is predominantly composed of social investment. Where does this direct foreign investment go? CGAP data estimates that 87 percent of direct foreign investment in microfinance is flowing to Latin America and Eastern Europe. Over

90 percent of the poorest people in the world live in Africa and Asia. Social capital would seem to have the greatest incentive to flow to the poor. Why is only 10 percent of this direct foreign investment in microfinance flowing to the regions of the world where 90 percent of the poor live?

Why then is such a small percentage of direct foreign investment in microfinance flowing to Africa and Asia? CGAP data also indicates that direct foreign investment in microfinance is highly concentrated in a relatively small number of MFI/SBFIs in Latin America and Eastern Europe. Two reasons may help explain why direct foreign investment in MFI/SBFIs is not more widely diversified or more aligned with the regions where most poor people live.

First, in the absence of well defined, transparent standards for MFI financial quality, it may be easier for investors, including social investors, to stick with a small number of familiar, well-known and successful MFI/SBFIs and to focus on low perceived financial risk. Second, in the absence of well defined, transparent measures of poverty effectiveness or social return, it may be hard for social investors to incorporate the social return of MFI/SBFIs reaching poor people and producing value for poor people into an investment decision.[41]

The role of the private investor

We have shown that there are very large numbers of farmers, micro-enterprises and small businesses that are unable to access credit to carry out their work. Financing such enterprises is one of the best ways to provide regular employment to billions of poor people. It has been shown by several MFIs/SBFIs over the years that this can be done in a financially sustainable manner. While there are a few high quality MFI/SBFIs with the capacity to utilize significant private investment, many more need to be incubated and their capacity needs to be built. This is where donor money should flow, largely as grants. Once the capacity is built, debt financing should be assured to the MFI/SBFIs from specialized funds, eventually to be replaced by commercial funding from local banks, perhaps with guarantees in the initial years.

As the MFI/SBFIs mature, they need equity financing, which is where the real role of the private equity investor begins. Socially conscious investors have to take some risks and initially be prepared for lower returns. Eventually there will be reasonable level of profits from such investments, and they will also measurably alleviate poverty in developing countries, thus offering double bottom line benefits. Private investors can help by making investments in guarantee, debt and equity funds and by prevailing on donors to use their resources to build institutional capacity, rather than engage in commercial functions that are better left to banks and investors.

Notes

1   The author thanks V.R. Prasanth, Senior Executive, Analytics, BASIX for assistance in writing this paper.
2   C.K. Prahalad, *The Fortune at the Bottom of the Pyramid: Eradicating Poverty Through Profits*, (Upper Saddle Hill, NJ: Wharton School Publishing, 2005).
3   ACCION International 2001 Annual Report.
4   101st Congress of the United States of America, H.R. 5918.
5   104th Congress of the United States of America, 2nd Session, H.R. 3846.
6   F. Vincent, "Is Micro-credit a Development Tool?", *IRED*, Geneva, http://www.ired.org/modules/
7   http://www.laghu-udyog.com/ssiindia/definition.htm, the official website of the Ministry of Small Scale Industries, Government of India.
8   "Engaging the Financial Sector", Discussion Paper by responsAbility – Social Investment Services AG.
9   Economic Census, Government of India, Central Statistical Organization (1998).
10 Unorganized Manufacturing Sector in India, NSS 56th round, National Sample Survey Organization, Ministry of Statistics and Programme Implementation, Government of India (September 2002).
11 Yanzhong Wang, "Financing Difficulties and Structural Characteristics of SMEs in China", *China & World Economy*, 12(2) (2004), 34–49.
12 United States Small Business Administration (SBA), Small Business Statistics http://www.sba.gov/aboutsba/sbastats.html
13 M. Beatriz and M. Otero, *Profile of Microfinance in Latin America in Ten Years: Vision and Characteristics*, (Boston, MA: ACCION, 2004).
14 Bank of Indonesia http://www.profi.or.id/engl/index.htm
15 Rural Development Institute www.rdiland.org
16 P. Honohan, "Financial Sector Policy and the Poor: Selected Findings and Issues", World Bank Working Paper No. 43 (2004), World Bank, Washington, DC.
17 Vijay Mahajan and Ramola Bharti Gupta, "Financial Services for the Rural Poor and Women in India: Access and Sustainability", *Journal of International Development* 8(2) (1996), 211–24.
18 Thematic Study on Rural Financial Services in China http://www.ifad.org/evaluation/public_html/eksyst/doc/thematic/pi/cn/cn_1.htm
19 F. Vincent, "Is Micro-credit a Development Tool?", *IRED*, Geneva, http://www.ired.org/modules/
20 Wang, "Financing Difficulties and Structural Characteristics of SMEs in China", *China & World Economy*, 12,(2) (2004), 34–49.
21 "China's Small and Medium Enterprises: Room to Grow With WTO", http://www.usembassy-china.org.cn/econ/smes2002.html
22 Bank of Indonesia http://www.profi.or.id/engl/index.html
23 Bank of Indonesia, Bureau of Communications Jakarta, 23 June, 2004.

24   M. Beatriz and Otero Maria, *Profile of Microfinance in Latin America in Ten Years: Vision and Characteristics*, (Boston, MA: ACCION, 2004).

25   National Venture Capital Association http://www.nvca.org/ffax.html

26   Small Enterprise Assistance Fund www.SEAF.com.

27   T. Fisher and V. Mahajan, *The Forgotten Sector: Non-Farm Employment and Enterprises in Rural India*, (New Delhi: Oxford and IBH Publishing Company Private Limited, 2004).

28   "Foreign Investment in Microfinance: Debt and Equity Form Quasi-Commercial Investors", Focus Note No.25, CGAP (January 2004).

29   G. Ivatury and J. Abrams, "The Market for Microfinance Foreign Investment: Opportunities and Challenges", KfW Financial Sector Development Symposium (November 2004).

30   G. Ivatury and I. Barres, "CGAP / MIX Study on MFI Demand for Funding".

31   G. Ivatury and J. Abrams, "The Market for Microfinance Foreign Investment: Opportunities and Challenges", KfW Financial Sector Development Symposium (November 2004).

32   "Foreign Investment in Microfinance: Debt and Equity form Quasi-Commercial Investors", Focus Note No.25, CGAP (January 2004).

33   J. Abrams, "The Microfinance Profitability Index", *The Microbanking Bulletin*, Issue No.11., May 2005.

34   "Engaging the Financial Sector", Discussion Paper by responsAbility Social Investment Services AG.

35   "IFC Creates Global Facility to Support Microfinance", References, http://www.microfinancegateway.org/content/article/detail/19079.

36   I. Gautam, and J. Abrams. "The Market for Microfinance Foreign Investment: Opportunities and Challenges", KfW Financial Sector Development Symposium (November 2004).

37   T. Coleman, "A Standardized Commercial Investment Vehicle (SIV) for MFI/SBFIs in India: Concept piece", August 2005.

38   F. Vincent, "Is Micro-credit a Development Tool?," *IRED*, Geneva, http://www.ired.org/modules/

39   United States Small Business Administration, Fixed-Asset Loans for Small Businesses   http://www.sba.gov/opc/pubs/fs70.html;   SBA   Micro-Loans http://www.sba.gov/financing/sbaloan/microloans.html

40   *Businessweek* Magazine; 'Micro Loans, Solid Returns' http://www.business-week.com/magazine/contest/05_19/b3932134_mz070.htm.

41   T. Coleman, "A Standardized Commercial Investment Vehicle (SIV) for MFI/SBFIs in India: Concept Piece", August 2005.

Part II
Institution Building

In Part I we provided support for the view that there exists a deep, grass-roots demand for microcredit in the world, with a credible market size of $500 billion or more. We also showed that such lending can be done in a professional, sustainable way. Even if funding were not a constraint, the sector would still face the challenge of getting the money to the farmers, microenterprises and small businesses that need it. There are simply not enough high-quality microfinance institutions to channel and manage the money. As Mahajan points out in Chapter 1, when such is the case, no amount of funds from the top can help; the sector must be built from the bottom up. Capacity building – financial and non-financial – of new and young institutions is required. Who builds microfinance capacity, and how, is the subject of Part III. We first take a global perspective – Constantinou and Leleux consider the microfinance institution builders, "developing" a tentative typology for generic business models. From general models we move to specific examples; Freytag and Chakraborty then illustrate some individual cases of capacity building: the "downscaling" model, the self-help group and the MFI–Bank linkage model.

3

An Analysis of Microfinance Business Models

Benoît Leleux and Dinos Constantinou

Introduction

Micro and small business finance ("microfinance" for the purposes of this chapter) has grown from humble origins into a vibrant industry over the last 30 years. ACCION issued its first microloans in Brazil in 1973. Professor Yunus, recipient of the Nobel Prize for Peace in 2006, followed with the launch of the Grameen[1] Bank Project in 1976 in Bangladesh; and, in the 1980s, Internationale Projekt Consult (IPC) set up a system of 13 municipal savings banks in Peru to provide credit to microentrepreneurs. From an estimated base of $200 million in 1984,[2] the industry has grown almost 15 000 percent over the last two decades to reach an estimated $30 billion[3] in outstanding microfinance loans (see Figure 3.1). The microfinance industry is now estimated to be growing at between 15 and 30 percent per annum to fill a potential demand estimated at between $300 and $1000 billion.[4/5]

Darwin and the microfinance industry

The industry's first steps were slow and marked by often-painful experimentation. A rich variety of business models emerged over time as microfinance institutions (and their promoters) developed new solutions to the financing problems affecting micro and small enterprises. Gil Crawford, CEO of MicroVest Capital Management, draws a parallel to biological evolution.[6] He suggests that the microfinance industry has gone down some dead ends over the last decades – with progress taking the form of an evolutionary development process.[7] Over the last few years, in particular, natural selection has led to a convergence of the different business models as microfinance organizations implemented proven "best practices".

Raging debates between the different schools of thought in the early days of microfinance (individual versus group lending, non-profit versus

49

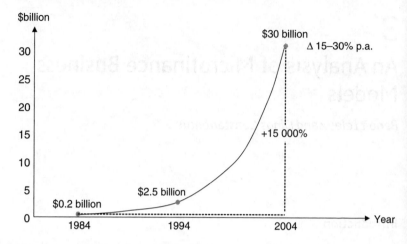

Figure 3.1   Microfinance[a] growth and size
Notes: a) The term microfinance here deployed broadly to denote finance for the poor and for micro and small enterprise.
Not drawn to scale.
Sources: CGAP; authors' own estimates.

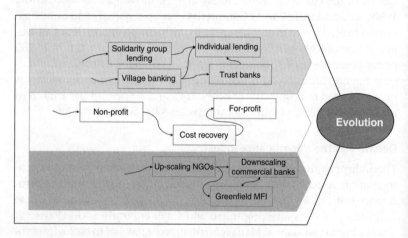

Figure 3.2   Evolution of microfinance business models

for-profit, downscaling versus up-scaling) are rapidly giving way to more pragmatic approaches, as operational microfinance entities face growing competition for clients and funding becomes increasingly commercial-based. Figure 3.2 illustrates the non-linear evolution of the sector.

Table 3.1   Selected microfinance players/business models

	Loan portfolio (US$)	Number of active clients	Number of countries
IPC–ProCredit (IPC–PC)	$1.294 billion	420 000	19
ACCION Network (ACCION)	$931 million	1 460 000	22
Opportunity International (OI)	$130 million	676 000	27
FINCA International (FINCA)	$100 million	370 000	23
UNITUS	$29 million	450 000	3

Note: Figures for IPC-PC, ACCION and OI from end-of-year 2004; FINCA from 30.09.2005 and UNITUS from 31.08.2005.
Sources: Websites of respective organizations; interviews with the representatives of respective organizations.

Driving this evolutionary process was the dynamic growth of a number of successful business models, which have achieved sustainable scale and broad international coverage. Foremost among these were ProCredit Group, the group of banks led by ProCredit Holding, and ACCION International, a network of affiliated microfinance institutions. By the end of 2004 (see Table 3.1), both ProCredit and ACCION had broken – or were within breathing distance of breaking – the $1 billion barrier in terms of the combined loan portfolios of their underlying subsidiaries, affiliates or partners. Expanding faster than the broader industry, ProCredit was nearing $2.5 billion (by September 2006) and ACCION had exceeded $1.3 billion (by end 2005) – with the former covering 19 countries and the latter 22. Between them, ProCredit and ACCION were offering financial services to micro and small businesses in 36 different countries – almost one-fifth of the member countries of the United Nations.

Methodology and scope of the paper

The sheer number and variety of entities active in microfinance render it impossible to cover more than a select number of microfinance business models in the context of a short study. This chapter offers a clinical investigation of some of the most interesting "networks" or "corporate groups"[8] in the industry, with a view to developing a tentative typology for generic business models in microfinance today.

Within a similarly defined category, the MIX listed over 140 national and international MFI networks worldwide. The selected players share four common characteristics of most interest for the purposes of this study, including (1) a focus on institution building, (2) an international scope, (3) scalability and replicability and, last but not least, (4) an identifiable business strategy to develop and expand the business model (see box below).

Key features of selected business models

A focus on institution building

The parent organization should play an active part in the development of underlying microfinance institutions (MFI) as institution builders. The aim is to analyse organizations that, as a matter of course, are interested in having such a role with respect to the MFI. In other words, the paper steers away from pure investment funds[9] providing capital but not necessarily involved in institution building.

International scope

International expansion should be an important aspect of the market strategy of the parent organization. The chapter thus focuses on business models with a clear objective to expand beyond national borders, independently of whether this has already occurred or not.

Scalability and replicability

The business model should be scalable (that is, should have the potential to reach significant scale in terms of client numbers and loan portfolio size) and replicable across different markets (that is, implementation should be feasible in different market and national contexts).

An identifiable business strategy

A commercially viable business strategy should underlie the development and expansion of the business model. While it may change over time, a business strategy should exist and be clearly identifiable. The existence of such a strategy distinguishes business organizations – whether for-profit or non-profit – from mere, associative networks.

While these criteria narrow the field significantly, they still provide a potent sample to draw from in terms of their potential impact on the industry. Within this field, we develop a simple typology of parent organizations and underlying MFI along four dimensions (see Figure 3.3):

1) Operating model – the credit methodology and other operational characteristics of microfinance institutions on the ground.
2) Revenue model – the means by which both the overarching entity and the underlying microfinance institutions sustain their operations.

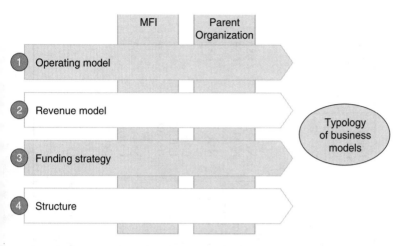

Figure 3.3 Dimensions of analysis of business models
Note: MFI = Microfinance institution

3) Funding strategy – the strategy followed by "parent" and operating entities with respect to funding for the loan portfolio and organic growth.
4) Structure – the way in which the "parent" and operating entities are organized and linked in terms of ownership and/or affiliation.

Operating and revenue models, together with funding strategy and structure, provide the pillars of a framework for describing the different models. The resulting typology, while neither perfect nor complete, aims to enhance our understanding of prevailing microfinance business models and provide a basis for mapping their evolution in the years ahead.

Background of selected players

The sample (see Table 3.2) consists of eight players currently active in the microfinance arena: five institutions with a long-standing history in the sector and three younger entities. As mentioned in the introduction, no attempt is made to make this sample representative in a statistical sense, nor is coverage comprehensive. The objective is to analyse a group of select entities with unique attributes and with the potential

Table 3.2 Selected microfinance players

Selected players (organizations or groups)/businessmodels		Launch of MF activities	Description	Legal status	Head-quarters
Estab-lished players	IPC-ProCredit (IPC–PC)	IPC: 1981 PC: 1998	MSME-focused banking group (PC) supported & parts controlled by consulting firm (IPC)	IPC: GmbH PC: AG	Germany
	ACCION Network (ACCION)	1973	Nonprofit that fights poverty through microfinance	NGO	USA
	FINCA International (FINCA)	1985	Global network providing financial services to world's poorest families	NGO	USA
	Opportunity International (OI)	1974	Global organization serving world's poorest through ME development	NGO	USA
	La Fayette-HORUS (LF-H)	H: 1994 LFP: 2001 LFI: 2004	Investment vehicle (LF) and consulting company (H) focusing on microfinance	LFP: SAS LFI:SICAR H:SARL	France
New entrants	UNITUS	2001	Microfinance accelerator, social venture capitalist	NGO	USA
	Investisseur et Partenaire pour le Développement(I&P)	2002	Private finance company investing in microfinance	C1/GBL (Mauritius)	France
	Global Microfinance Group (GMG)	2004	Private investment holding company focusing on micro & small business finance	SA	Switzerland

Sources: Websites of respective organizations; the MIX; authors' own research.

to help draw generic implications for the industry in general, as opposed to providing a statistical description of the industry or some of its sub-segments.

Of the established players, ACCION dates from the 1970s, IPC and FINCA from the 1980s and Opportunity International and Horus from the early 1990s. UNITUS, I&P and GMG are creatures of the twenty-first century, coinciding with what is widely seen as the "coming of age" of microfinance.

The ProCredit Group

The ProCredit Group (IPC-ProCredit, IPC-PC) is led by two Frankfurt-based entities: a management company, Internationale Projekt Consult GmbH (IPC), and a holding company, ProCredit Holding AG. While IPC is the exclusive supplier of management and advisory services to the 19 ProCredit banks, ProCredit Holding acts as the main provider of capital and corporate governance. IPC seconds qualified personnel to ProCredit Holding.

The ProCredit Group pursues a development agenda through the creation of commercially viable financial institutions for micro and small businesses in developing countries. ProCredit thus seeks to leverage commercial means to achieve development goals:

> Our core business is the provision of formal credit to micro and small enterprises. Our business model combines a development policy orientation with a commercial approach.[10]

The cornerstone of ProCredit's approach was the establishment of new, regulated institutions as the fastest and most effective way to develop institutional capacity to provide credit and other financial services to micro and small businesses.

By 2005 ProCredit banks operated in 19 transition and developing economies in Eastern Europe, Latin America and Africa – with only one ProCredit financial institution active in each country. ProCredit Holding, a non-regulated holding company founded by IPC in 1998, was typically the leading shareholder in the ProCredit banks, while other shareholders often included public institutions such as the IFC and the EBRD – and, in Eastern Europe, Germany's Commerzbank. Notwithstanding its young history, the ProCredit Group employed some 12 000 people and expected its staff to grow to 17 000 by 2010.

Ownership structure

IPC is the founder and largest shareholder of ProCredit Holding (see Table 3.3). IPC also has direct, minority shareholdings in some of the underlying institutions (for example, in the ProCredit banks in Ecuador, El Salvador, Bolivia and Romania) – although these emerged in the course of the development of the group rather than being based on (currently relevant) strategic motives.

In recent years, IPC has steadily increased its share of voting equity in ProCredit Holding (to currently over 20 percent), at the same time as shareholders from the public domain (such as IFC and FMO) have reduced their share. IPC, together with Doen Foundation and IPC Invest GmbH & Co. KG, form a stable nucleus of strategic private shareholders representing just over 43 percent of the holding company's voting shares. Overall, around 49 percent of the voting shares are in the hands of private shareholders, with the balance still held by public sector organizations.

Table 3.3   Shareholder structure of ProCredit as of September 2006

Name		Paid-in capital (€)	(%)
Voting shares			
IPC GmbH		31 695 040	*20.8*
KFW		27 697 800	*18.2*
DOEN		27 093 040	*17.8*
IFC		25 493 000	*16.7*
FMO		13 014 560	*8.5*
BIO		11 516 440	*7.6*
IPC Invest GmbH & Co KG		7 264 400	*4.8*
Fundasal		4 452 240	*2.9*
responsAbility		2 080 000	*1.4*
Andromeda		2 080 000	*1.4*
	Sub-total voting capital	*152 386 520*	*100.0*
Non-voting preferential shares			
TIAA-CREF		14 683 240	*53.0*
Omidyar-Tufts Microfinance Fund		8 637 200	*31.2*
Andromeda		2 800 200	*10.1*
responsAbility		1 560 000	*5.6*
	Sub-total non-voting capital	*27 680 640*	*100.0*
Total paid-in capitalt		**180 067 160**	

Source: Procredit.

These include one multilateral organization, the International Finance Corporation (IFC) and the German (KfW), Dutch (FMO) and Belgian (BIO) bilateral institutions. At this stage, the ProCredit Group personifies a public–private partnership. KfW and BIO have indicated that they intend to maintain their shares in ProCredit Holding for the foreseeable future; however, disinvestment by public shareholders and the transfer of ownership control to strategic parties led by IPC is a likely long-term scenario.

The introduction of preferred, non-voting shares in 2006 effectively allows ProCredit Holding to raise private capital without diluting ownership control. Table 3.3 shows the current ownership structure of both IPC and ProCredit Holding. The investment in ProCredit Holding of TIAA-CREF, one of the largest pension funds in the US, was particularly noteworthy – as it heralded an important step for microfinance in tapping mainstream private investment.

In tandem with the growing control of IPC and similarly minded private investors at the holding level, ProCredit Holding has pursued a parallel strategy at the level of the individual ProCredit banks, with the long-term aim of acquiring well over 75 percent of the equity in each institution. Increased control of the underlying operating entities has also been accompanied by the adoption of the ProCredit brand throughout the ProCredit Group.[11]

The funding strategy pursued by ProCredit represents an innovative approach to private–public and social–private partnerships in mobilizing private capital to pursue development-oriented goals.

The IPC micro and small business credit "technology"

Interdisciplinäre Projekt Consult GmbH (the original name of the company) was founded by Claus-Peter Zeitinger in 1981 and became widely known as IPC.[12] In the early years, IPC was indeed inter-disciplinary, executing projects for the German development agency Gesellschaft für Technische Zusammenarbeit (GTZ) in Peru in the area of both finance and energy. Its work in Peru in the 1980s, setting-up a system of municipal banks on the German Sparkassen (savings banks) model, marked the development of the now famous IPC microlending "technology" – and propelled IPC towards specialization in microfinance. The word "technology" was used by IPC to denote the broader approach and methodology – including credit policies, processes, information technology and incentive systems – developed to bring credit to the microentrepreneur.

A central element of the IPC "technology" was a focus on lending to individual entrepreneurs, as opposed to lending to groups. In the world of microfinance, the emphasis on individual as opposed to group lending was something of a revolution, sparking a long-standing debate between IPC and the more established camp of ACCION (see below) and Grameen Bank.[13] Despite early opposition, ACCION affiliates such as BancoSol of Bolivia moved to introduce individual lending alongside their existing group lending methodology in the course of the 1990s, so that most of the ACCION network's loan portfolio today (with the notable exception of highly successful Compartamos of Mexico) is on an individual basis.

The IPC "technology" derived partly from the principles of credit evaluation prevalent in the German financial system (especially in the Sparkassen) at the time, but also from an application of rigorous microeconomic analysis to loan underwriting. Thus, IPC contributed to the more general move in microfinance from collateral-based to cash flow-based lending and the deployment of a personal relationship between loan officer and borrower to better understand the latter's economic situation.

Over the last decade, the incursion of the IPC "technology" into formal microenterprise and SME lending – most notably in the context of the "downscaling" program of the Russia Small Business Fund (RSBF) – has further encouraged the move away from group and towards individual-based lending in microfinance. Established by Elizabeth Wallace at the European Bank for Reconstruction and Development (EBRD) in the early 1990s, the RSBF aimed to facilitate transformation from a command to a market economy by providing capital to Russian entrepreneurs. In the event, the RSBF was only the first of several EBRD initiatives that culminated in the establishment of a series of banks specializing in micro and SME finance in the former Eastern bloc.

The recent introduction of the Grameen II package of innovations, including individual lending, at Grameen Bank in Bangladesh is possibly the ultimate recognition of the shifting ground in microfinance.

ACCION Network and ACCION International (ACCION)

Joseph Blatchford founded ACCION International in 1961 "to address the desperate poverty in Latin America's cities".[14] Blatchford was studying law at the time and ACCION started as a student volunteer initiative in the slums of Caracas. The roots of ACCION in combating poverty permeate the mission of the organization to this day, although the means used to achieve this goal have changed markedly over the years.

> The mission of ACCION International is to give people the tools they need to work their way out of poverty. By providing "micro" loans and business training to poor women and men to start their own businesses,

ACCION's partner lending organizations help people work their own way up the economic ladder.[15]

In 1973 staff at the ACCION program in Recife (Brazil) began experimenting with loans to small-scale entrepreneurs, in the process inventing both the term "microenterprise" and, possibly, the microfinance industry, as we now know it.[16] ACCION developed a microlending methodology centered on "créditos solidarios" (solidarity loans), whereby small groups of three or more microentrepreneurs came together to guarantee each other's loans.

By the early 1990s, ACCION led the way again with the establishment of Banco Solidario S.A. (BancoSol) in Bolivia through the transformation of a former NGO, PRODEM. BancoSol was the first specialized, commercial microfinance bank in the history of the industry. The "financial systems approach", as it was named by ACCION, aimed to allow microfinance institutions to reach scale financial sustainability through a for-profit business model. More recently ACCION has advised and/or cooperated with commercial banks in Ecuador, Brazil and Argentina as an alternative channel to specialized microfinance institutions through the so-called downscaling approach (see also below).

Organizational structure

While ACCION International is a non-profit, recognized charity organization operating out of the United States, many – but not all – of the "affiliated" or "partner" microfinance institutions in the various developing countries are organized as for-profit companies, in many cases as fully regulated financial institutions.

ACCION International provides technical assistance and – through a number of fund vehicles – equity, debt and loan guarantees to partner institutions. The main equity vehicles – ACCION Gateway Fund and ACCION Investments in Microfinance (AIM) – are each capitalized at $5 million and $19.5 million respectively. The ACCION Latin America Bridge Fund (LABF), the first microfinance loan guarantee fund, is capitalized at $4.85 million and provides guarantees that facilitate partner institution access to short-term lines of credit from local commercial banks, while the ACCION Global Bridge Fund (GBF), with a capital of $2.52 million, is a similarly structured vehicle with a more global radius of action.[17] ACCION Network was conceived in 1984 to bring together the various microfinance programs established and/or supported by ACCION International – under a common umbrella – with the declared mission to "collaboratively create, grow and lead the microfinance industry".[18]

The link between the "parent" and partner or affiliate MFI in the network is usually enhanced equity and board participation of ACCION International (directly or through its financing vehicles) in the MFI.

ACCION Network members can choose from an extensive offering consisting of capital combined with corporate governance, technical assistance and advisory and management services. Unlike ProCredit, the approach of ACCION varies markedly between countries and partner organizations, ranging from partial ownership and management to arms-length advisory.

By 2005 ACCION was active in 21 countries through partnerships with and/or investments in 18 regulated financial institutions, 5 NGOs in the process of transformation into regulated financial institutions and a further 2-3 NGOs with no immediate transformation plans.[19] The ACCION portfolio was composed mainly of "upgraded" (that is, transformed) former NGOs or similar organizations (for example, Financiera Compartamos of Mexico) but also joint ventures with "downscaling" banks (namely Banco del Pichincha in Ecuador[20] and, more recently, Banco Columbia in Argentina).[21] Moreover, ACCION was taking a leaf from the book of ProCredit with the proposed establishment of a greenfield microfinance bank in Nigeria.[22]

Opportunity International (OI)

Opportunity International has its origins in the "merger" of two distinct microlending programs set up in Latin America and Indonesia respectively in the early 1970s by Al Whittaker, a former president of the pharmaceuticals giant Bristol Myers, and the Australian entrepreneur, David Bussau. Whittaker was a deeply religious man who imbued the nascent nonprofit organization with his moral values and social vision:

> The bottom line...is to always remember this is not our business, this is the Lord's business. We are the ones He has chosen to carry it out. That is all we need to know. That is how it started. That is how it blossomed. Let's keep it that way.[23]

OI was marked by the intent of Whittaker and Bussau to give poor people a "working chance" by providing access to working capital loans and business training. OI describes itself as "a Christian ecumenical organization serving women and men of all beliefs":

> Our mission is to provide opportunities for people in chronic poverty to transform their lives. Our strategy is to create jobs, stimulate small

businesses and strengthen communities among the poor. Our method is to work through indigenous partner organizations that provide small business loans, training and counsel. Our commitment is motivated by Jesus Christ's call to serve the poor. Our core values are respect, commitment to the poor, integrity and stewardship.[24]

At the same time, OI has been highly successful over the years in mobilizing grants and donations (and, more recently, debt through the issue of international obligations) to finance expansion internationally.

At the grassroots level, OI has applied a pragmatic approach to achieve its goals. In 1992 it introduced the "trust bank" model as a way to reach poorer women entrepreneurs. OI loan officers encouraged the creation of Opportunity Trust Banks, borrowing groups consisting of 15 to 40 women and allowing members to receive loans of $80 or more. The members guaranteed each other's loan obligations and elected a treasurer to collect and manage repayments and savings. In the 1990s, OI started working with independent self-governing organizations in different countries to extend its global outreach – a development that led to the creation of the Opportunity International Network in 1998. By 2000, following in the footsteps of ACCION, Opportunity began to convert a number of OI members into formal financial institutions through the establishment of commercial banks, development banks or credit unions, which in turn absorbed the loan portfolios of the existing NGOs. Transformation into regulated entities allowed the mobilization of savings, equity and debt finance – and thus a more aggressive expansion in the provision of loans and other financial services to the target clientele.

OI Network members employed some 6000 staff worldwide in 2006. The network had two categories of members in 28 countries: 42 "Implementing Partners" (microfinance organizations) and five "Support Partners" (resource providers). While all but one of the network members had been initiated by Opportunity International, the pattern of ownership of the different MFI was heterogeneous. Information from the MIX was available only with respect to 24 of the 42 OI microfinance operations. Of these, only one was fully owned by OI, four were majority-owned by OI and five were minority-owned by OI. Almost 60 percent of the MIX sample had no OI equity stake whatsoever.[25]

FINCA International (FINCA)

FINCA was founded in 1984 by social visionary John Hatch, a Fulbright-trained economist and international development expert. FINCA International describes itself as a provider of financial services to the poorest families (and in particular women) through a global network of locally managed, self-supporting institutions:

> FINCA International is a network of community-focused credit and savings associations employing the Village Banking™ methodology. Our programs are established in areas largely underserved by the formal financial sector. Village Banking is a means of delivering financial services – small loans and savings products – to those who could not otherwise obtain them. The village banking method is unique in the responsibility and autonomy given borrowers to organize and run their banks, resulting in individual development, higher self-esteem, improved quality of life for families and the overall empowerment in their communities. FINCA works through local affiliates that have nonprofit status. FINCA plans to transform a number of affiliate programs to deposit-taking institutions.[26]

FINCA is a far more centralized and homogeneous network of microfinance organizations than either ACCION or Opportunity International. According to the MIX, all of the partner organizations in the FINCA network had been created by FINCA International; moreover, all were linked exclusively to FINCA through dedicated service agreements.[27] By 2006 two FINCA programs, in Ecuador and Uganda, had been transformed into regulated microfinance institutions with a view to financing growth and lowering funding costs by taking deposits from the public.[28]

At this time, FINCA was active in 21 countries in the Americas, sub-Saharan Africa, Eurasia and the Caucasus through 23 partner organizations. In recent years FINCA had grown especially fast in countries of the former Soviet Union and other ex-communist countries in Eastern Europe and Central Asia – where it had to adapt its approach by adding individual loan offerings to its traditional village-banking model.

FINCA envisioned the next phase in its development as one of "forging partnerships with some of these organizations who can deliver our clients other services – whether health care, education, nutrition, potable water or many others – that they value."[29]

La Fayette-Horus Group (LF-H)[30]

La Fayette Participations (LFP) is an investment company controlled by the Horus Group. Horus Group was founded in 1994 and LFP in 2001 in France. Horus Development Finance is the consulting division specializing in microfinance. In 2004 the funding "firepower" of the LF-H group was enhanced by the establishment of a Luxembourg-based investment vehicle, La Fayette Investissements (LFI). Horus manages both financial vehicles and holds just over 80 percent of the equity capital of LFP but only an 8 percent minority stake in LFI.

The main objective of LFP is to have an active role in the creation of new MFI by providing investment and technical assistance (through Horus).[31] Although a technical assistance agreement with Horus is not a pre-condition for accessing LFP funding, in practice public institutions co-investing with LFP habitually stipulate this as a necessary condition for their investment. LFP has minority investments in three microfinance institutions: AMRET, Cambodia (20 percent), FINADEV Chad (7 percent) and FINADEV Benin (10 percent). Moreover, LFP has a 2 percent share-holding in Financial BC Togo – which in turn holds 40 percent of FINADEV Benin, 73 percent of FINADEV Chad and stakes in two further microfinance institutions in Gabon and Guinea.

LFI, on the other hand, aims to invest mainly in equity capital with a controlling stake and the investment strictly conditional upon the provision of technical assistance by Horus. The capital of LFI is held (in addition to Horus) by a number of multilateral and bilateral institutions: International Finance Corporation (IFC), European Investment Bank (EIB), FMO of Holland, AFD of France and KfW of Germany. LFI aims to promote the creation and development of microfinance institutions by providing (alongside equity and technical assistance) quasi-equity, debt instruments and guarantees.

The main focus of LFP and LFI is on the less developed economies of Africa and Asia. Both entities are long-term investors and do not require an exit window in undertaking their investments.

UNITUS

UNITUS was founded by ex-Apple and Microsoft top executive Mike Murray and a group of businesspeople including Bob Gay of Bain Capital[32] and Joseph Grenny of VitalSmarts in January 2001, building on the experience of the Unitus Action Groups.

Reflecting the origins of its founders in the United States high tech and venture capital scene, UNITUS describes itself as a "microfinance accelerator" – seeking to "combine ... best practices from the venture capital, investment banking and strategy consulting industries to help create large-scale, poverty-focused and commercially sustainable microfinance institutions."[33]

Funding is provided in the form of grants, equity and/or debt – and originates from the "parent" NGO (UNITUS), an equity vehicle launched and managed by UNITUS and (in the case of debt) from its partnership with Dignity Fund (which is led by the current vice-chairman of UNITUS, Elizabeth Funk).

The UNITUS–ACCION "Alliance for India," consummated in 2005, aims to enrich the UNITUS approach with specialist technical assistance from a pioneer in the area of microfinance technology and institution building. UNITUS and ACCION thus work together through the India Microfinance Centre, which provides expertise in microfinance products and services through a locally-based team.

By 2006 UNITUS was supporting eight MFI in India and one MFI each in Argentina, Kenya, Mexico and the Philippines.

Investisseur et Partenaire pour le Développement (I&P)[34]

Investisseur et Partenaire pour le Développement (I&P) is a private finance company, established in 2002 by a group of European entrepreneurs with backgrounds in private equity, industry and consulting. Although registered in Mauritius, it is effectively managed out of Paris and relies on its French consulting arm I&P Études et Conseils (I&P EC) for research, marketing and investment follow-up.

The core business of I&P is the provision of equity capital to emerging MFI coupled with active board membership.[35] I&P also provides short and medium-term hard currency loans to affiliated and non-affiliated institutions – on a presumably opportunistic basis. I&P describes investments in affiliates as "strategic," while (non-equity) investments in other MFI are viewed as "non-strategic".

By September 2006 I&P had four equity investments in Cambodia (AMRET, see also LF-H above), Cameroon (ACEP), Mexico (Semilla Solidaria) and Uganda (U-Trust); moreover, it had provided loans to a further four MFI (in Kenya, Madagascar, Nicaragua and Peru) and the LACIF fund.[36] The total paid-in equity of the holding company at this time was EUR 10 million, counting among its shareholders 17 private individuals and one public limited company.

Global Microfinance Group (GMG)[37]

Global Microfinance Group SA (GMG) is a privately funded, investment holding company founded in 2004 in Lausanne by a group of former IPC consultants and IMD MBA graduates. The objective of GMG is to seek profitable opportunities through greenfield investments and acquisitions – acting as a single platform for funding, building and managing nascent microfinance institutions.

The GMG business model encompasses two main areas: (1) establishment of greenfield MFI and (2) investment in brownfield MFI with a view to acting as a consolidator in fragmented markets. The first aspect entails the creation of new institutional capacity in relatively virgin microfinance markets. The second thrust of the model is to strengthen and preserve the installed capacity of promising small and medium MFI lacking the critical scale to survive in competitive markets by providing the key ingredients required for growth (capital, management, know-how) and pursuing a consolidation strategy with other MFI.

GMG provides mainly equity capital and subordinated or convertible debt to affiliated companies, combined with the installation or reinforcement of experienced management teams and the enhancement of institutional capacity through consulting on an occasional basis. GMG started its first MFI in Argentina in 2004 as a pilot project and aims to expand its activities to other countries over the coming years.[38]

While the holding company is funded by private individuals and institutional investors, at the MFI level GMG seeks investment from multilateral and bilateral organizations to help deal with complex emerging market environments.

The list of selected models is by no means exhaustive. At the time of writing, several new creations were in the making or had just been launched. Examples include Access Microfinance Holding AG (set up by LFS Financial Systems GmbH in 2006)[39] and Microcred Holding (established by the PlaNet Finance network in 2005).[40]

Analysis of the business models along four dimensions

The selected business models are described below along four key dimensions, in each case looking at both the parent organization and the MFI. As described in the introductory section, the structural dimensions are: (a) Operating model, (b) Revenue model, (c) Funding strategy and (d) Structure. Taken together, these dimensions provide the four pillars of a business model typology.

Operating model

The operating model of the parent is described here through its offering to the MFI (see Figure 3.4), which can include: capital (that is, funding in terms of equity, debt or grants), corporate governance (that is, supervision and strategy formulation through participation on the board of directors), know-how (in particular, credit methodology and processes), information

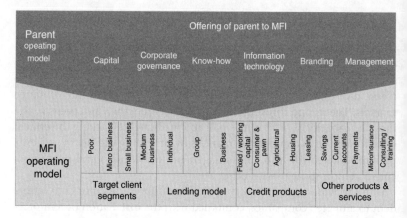

Figure 3.4 Dimension 1: Operating model (a) (parent organization and MFI)

technology (information systems are crucial in allowing MFI to manage relationships with a large number of clients), branding (which defines the identity of the MFI and the degree to which this is aligned with that of the parent) and management (the selection or secondment of the management team). These elements also define the degree of control exercised by the parent vis-à-vis the MFI.

Figure 3.4 also shows how we define the operating model of the MFI in terms of: target client segments (low income and micro, small or medium enterprise), lending model (that is, methodology), credit products, and other products and services.

The analysis suggests that the business models have been shaped by a dynamic interplay between the respective operating models of parent and MFI. On the one hand, the offering of the parent in the way of capital, know-how and information technology plays a significant role in determining the palette of products and services the MFI can provide and the market segments it can serve. On the other hand, the parent's branding strategy and the way the parent interacts with the MFI through the board and management team influences the commercial and operational strategy of the MFI.

ProCredit banks, for example, steer clear of the group lending model in line with ProCredit-IPC business philosophy; whereas ACCION affiliates or partners use either individual or group lending (or indeed both) methodologies. Similarly, whereas FINCA, OI and others may encourage (or even expect) the MFI to include training in the package offered to microentrepreneurs, this would go against the grain of ProCredit policies and procedures.

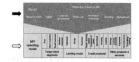

Organization (parent)	Offering of parent to MFI						Objective of parent	
	Capital (equity, debt or grants)	Corporate governance	Technical capacity	Proprietary MIS	Branding	Management	Exclusive relationship to MFI	Influence vs. control
IPC-PC	A	A	A	A	A	A	Yes	Control
ACCION	P	P	P	P	P	P	No	Influence
FINCA	P	A	A	A	A	A	Yes	Control
OI	P	A	A	A	P	A	Yes	Control
LF-H	A	A	P	P	P	P	No →Yes	Control
UNITUS	A	A	P	N	N	N	No	Influence
I&P	A	A	P	N	N	N	No	Influence
GMG	A	A	P	P	P	A	No	Control

Figure 3.5 Dimension 1: Operating model (b) (parent organization)
Note: A = always; P = possibly; or N = never offered.

Three aspects are highly indicative of the business model type of the parent: the comprehensiveness of the offering to the MFI, the degree of integration of the offering, ranging from a menu approach to a "take-it-or-leave-it" package, and the degree of exclusivity in the relationship between parent and MFI.

The analysis (see Figure 3.5 above) shows that ProCredit (IPC-PC), FINCA and OI share certain key characteristics – with ProCredit at the extreme end of the spectrum in terms of comprehensiveness, integration and exclusivity. As such, ProCredit is beginning to resemble an international banking group, albeit one focusing on a particular segment of the market (micro and small business loans). The analysis also suggests that OI and FINCA are uniquely positioned to follow along the path marked by ProCredit given their comprehensive, integrated offering and their aspiration to exclusivity in the relationship parent–MFI. ProCredit, OI and FINCA aim for majority ownership and/or control of affiliated or partner MFI.[41]

The ACCION offering may be comprehensive – but it is neither fully integrated nor exclusive. Moreover, ACCION has been quite flexible in structuring partnerships and taking investment positions. Although acting as strategic investor in several ACCION Network members, and being close to establishing a greenfield microfinance bank in West Africa, ACCION is rarely a controlling investor. And while investments by ACCION (through ACCION International and internally managed AIM)[42] are of unlimited duration, its long-term role as minority shareholder is difficult to pin down. In many ways, ACCION International is more of a technical adviser to MFI affiliates and partners, a vision that sits well with its role in the UNITUS–ACCION Alliance for India. How far this vision is compatible with long-term minority positions in the equity of disperse MFI or (the subsidiaries of) downscaling banks remains an open question.

A similar question can be asked about the La Fayette-Horus group, which aims to be a long-term investor but has accumulated only a series of minority equity stakes to this date through the LFP equity vehicle. The larger LFI could conceivably aim at majority stakes, which in turn could form the basis for the development of a banking holding in the ProCredit mold – but how its investment strategy actually plays out remains to be seen. The experience of Horus Development Finance allows the group to offer a comprehensive package of services to MFI (which at this stage is neither exclusive nor integrated) so that a twist in the stra-tegy of LFI could move the La Fayette-Horus model closer to that of ProCredit.

The broader question is whether the two La Fayette equity vehicles, in spite of not requiring an exit window, intend to monetize their invest-ment in the longer run. The public sector investors holding much of the equity in LFI must face at least some pressure to exit from the parent at some point in time – which in turn would apply pressure either to exit the underlying MFIs or find alternative avenues to provide its investors with liquidity options.

Microfinance venture capitalists UNITUS and I&P, on the other hand, stipulate a 5–7-year investment horizon for MFI investments – that is not very different from that pursued by the mainstream venture capital indus-try.[43] Geoff Davis, CEO of UNITUS, explicitly suggests several exit possi-bilities such as public listing, M&A[44] and share buyback[45] (although neither UNITUS nor I&P provide guidance with respect to expected return on investment). As might be expected, UNITUS and I&P are less comprehensive and less integrated than the other models in the sample – and not only do not seek exclusivity but also may prefer to operate with complementary partners. In particular, as the UNITUS–ACCION alliance shows, players such as UNITUS and I&P are often happy to leave the oner-ous task of providing technical capacity (consulting) to external parties.[46]

Despite important differences in culture and philosophy, the operating models of the MFIs are undergoing what seems to be an inexorable convergence process (see Figure 3.6 below). Driven partly by market considerations (such as investor and client preferences) and partly by efficiency considerations (such as the need for higher productivity), the MFIs are increasingly offering a similar range of financial products and services – often to the same client segments. Ancillary (that is, non-financial) services, such as business training and consulting, are fading in significance or are being moved outside the MFIs in mature microfinance markets such as South America – largely as a result of the decreasing importance of group lending methodologies such as solidarity credit, village banking and trust banks.

The development of small business lending in Eastern Europe as the natural complement to traditional microlending has since been transported to Latin America – through the ProCredit group and the move of several former IPC experts to established players such as ACCION and FINCA or new ventures such as GMG.

The convergence of the underlying operating models leads to an astonishing similarity in terms of the long-term vision for these MFIs. Cultural differences may persist, yet the dynamic development of the respective operating models seems to be driving the various players to the same conclusion – namely, to seek regulatory status to access savings and offer a variety of financial services (such as current accounts and payments) to the target market segments.

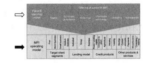

Organization (underlying MFI)	Target client segments				Lending methodology				Credit products offered to clients					Other prod./services offered to clients					Long-term vision for MFI
	Poor	Micro business	Small business	Medium business	Individual	Group (solidarity, village or trust banks)	Business	Fixed / working capital	Consumer & pawn	Agricultural	Housing	Leasing	Savings	Current accounts	Payments	Microinsurance	Consulting / training	
IPC-PC	A	A	A	S	A	N	A	A	A	S	S	S	A	A	A	N	N	RB
ACCION	A	A	S	N	S	S	S	A	A	S	S	S	S	S	S	S	S	RB
FINCA	A	A	N	N	A	A	N	A	S	S	S	N	S	N	N	S	N	RFI
OI	A	A	N	N	S	A	N	A	S	S	S	S	S	S	S	S	S	RFI
LF-H	A	A	S	N	S	S	N	A	S	S	N	N	S	N	N	N	S	RFI
UNITUS	A	N	N	N	N	A	N	A	S	S	N	N	S	N	N	S	A	RFI
I&P	A	A	S	N	S	S	S	A	S	S	S	S	S	S	S	N	S	RFI
GMG	A	A	A	S	A	N	A	A	S	N	S	N	S	S	S	N	N	RB

Figure 3.6 Dimension 1: Operating model (c) (MFI)
Keys: A = always; S = sometimes; or N = never served/deployed/offered. RB = regulated bank; RFI = regulated financial institution.

Revenue model

Figure 3.7 below shows the extent to which the parent organizations are sustainable through earned revenue: interest and other investment income, management fees, membership fees and consulting income.

While the bulk of revenue usually stems from affiliated or partner MFIs, organizations such as Horus and IPC have significant consulting income from external clients. In the case of IPC, however, the tendency is to focus increasingly on the needs of the ProCredit banks and less on outside contracting.

Non-profit parent organizations such as ACCION, FINCA, OI and UNITUS rely significantly on direct grants and donations to support their activities (refer also to Funding Strategy of parent organizations below) – although UNITUS has stated its intent to move towards sustainability through earned revenue. IPC-ProCredit, La Fayette-Horus, I&P and GMG have only occasional or no access to grants and depend on the different types of earned income to ensure their long-term sustainability.

All players, however, attract more or less significant grants and donations at the level of the MFIs (see Funding Strategy below) – a significant share of which is channeled to the operating or consulting arm of parent organizations to finance consulting (for example, for technical capacity) and management services provided to the MFIs. Indirectly, therefore, both non-profit and for-profit parent organizations usually draw on a similar pool of technical assistance grants and donations – whereby the former typically access such subsidies directly and the latter indirectly.[47]

Organization (parent)	Types of earned revenue					Long-run sustainability on basis of earned revenue?
	Interest income	Investment incomde (incl.dividends)	Management fees	Membership or affiliation fees	Consulting income	
IPC-PC	L	H	H	N	H	Yes
ACCION	L	L	N	N	H	No
FINCA	L	N	N	H	N	No
OI	L	L	N	L	N	No
LF-H	N	H	L	N	H	Yes
UNITUS	H	H	N	N	N	No →Yes
I&P	H	H	N	N	N	Yes
GMG	L	H	L	N	L	Yes

Figure 3.7 Dimension 2: Revenue model (a) (parent organization)
Note: Importance in terms of share of long-run revenues: H = high importance; L = low importance; N = no importance.

The revenue models are more straightforward and uniform at the level of the MFIs (see Figure 3.8 below), where all players seek sustainability through profitability in the long term. Practically all MFIs rely on loan income and increasingly on revenues from other financial products and services – a trend that is reinforced by the ongoing transformation of formerly non-regulated (and usually non-profit) MFI organizations into regulated banks, finance companies and other regulated structures.

Funding strategy

An interesting dichotomy is also evident in our comparison of the funding strategies of the different parent organizations vis-à-vis that of underlying MFIs.

Significant variations are to be found in the mix of funding – between equity, debt and grants/donations – available to (or pursued by) the parent organizations (see Figure 3.9 on p. 72). And while the five established parent organizations tap significant funding from public sector sources (such as IFC, EIB, FMO and KfW), new players UNITUS, I&P and GMG rely mainly or exclusively on private funding. Parent organizations also diverge widely with respect to envisaging and pursuing exit scenarios – where applicable – for their equity investors.

There are few differences, on the other hand, in the funding strategies of the underlying MFIs, where the tendency moreover is towards ever-greater uniformity. Figure 3.10 distinguishes between equity, deposits (savings, current accounts), debt and grants/donations. In particular, the role of deposits as a source of funding is poised to rise over time, although surrogate

Organization (underlying MFI)	Types of revenue			Long-run sustainability on basis of earned revenue?
	Loan income	Other financial services income	Training & consulting income from clients	
IPC-PC	H	H	N	Yes
ACCION	H	H	N	Yes
FINCA	H	N	N	Yes
OI	H	L	N	Yes
LF-H	H	L	N	Yes
UNITUS	H	N	N	Yes
I&P	H	L	N	Yes
GMG	H	N	N	Yes

Figure 3.8 Dimension 2: Revenue model (b) (MFI)
Note: Importance in terms of share of long-run revenues: H = high importance; L = low importance; N = no importance.

forms of refinancing such as portfolio securitization may be deployed in markets where regulatory obstacles stand in the way of the emergence of regulated, specialized microfinance banks.

Divergent approaches, however, emerge with respect to parent exit intentions, where the players are divided in three camps: parents that have no exit intentions whatsoever (ProCredit, OI and FINCA), strategic

Organization (parent)	Types of funding			Sources of funding	Investor exit possibilities envisaged for equity investors?
	Equity	Debt	Grants and donations		
IPC-PC	H	H	N	Private & public	Possibly
ACCIÓN	L	L	H	Private & public	Not applicable for NGO but yes forAIM fund vehicle
FINCA	N	L →H	H	Private & public	Not applicable
OI	N	L	H	Private & public	Not applicable
LF-H	H	N	N	Private & public	Not known
UNITUS	N→H	N	H	Private	Not applicable
I&P	H	N	N	Majority private	Not currently
GMG	H	H	N	Private	Yes

Figure 3.9 Dimension 3: Funding strategy (a) (parent organization)
Note: Importance in terms of share of funding in the longer run: H = high importance; L = low importance; N = no importance.

Organization (underlying MFI)	Types of funding				Parent exit intentions?
	Equity	Deposits	Debt	Grants and donations	
IPC-PC	H	H	H	H	No
ACCION	H	H	H	H	No exit horizon, but exit not excluded
FINCA	H	L →H	H	H	No
OI	H	L →H	H	H	No
LF-H	H	L →H	H	H	No exit horizon, but exit not excluded
UNITUS	H	L →H	H	H	Yes (exit horizon 5–7 years)
I&P	H	L →H	H	L	Yes (exit horizon 5–7 years)
GMG	H	N →H	H	L	No exit horizon, but exit not excluded

Figure 3.10 Dimension 3: Funding strategy (b) (MFI)
Note: Importance in terms of share of funding: H = high importance; L = low importance; N = no importance.

investors without a defined exit horizon but who do not preclude an exit scenario (ACCION, the La Fayette investment vehicles, GMG) and financial investors with a defined exit horizon of five to seven years (UNITUS, I&P).

Structure

The legal structures adopted by organizations, as illustrated in Table 3.2, range from a series of finance vehicles (holding companies, stock corporations, limited offshore companies, SICAR funds) to non-profit NGOs. Finance vehicles, moreover, are often managed by and/or use the services of separate operating companies (such as IPC, Horus, I&P Etudes & Conseil).

Closer analysis shows that structure (including legal and regulatory status) is driven by funding strategy, at the level of both the parent organization and the MFI affiliate/partner (see Figure 3.11). The attractiveness of deposits as the cheapest and most sustainable way to fund loan portfolios, in particular, is impelling MFIs of all colors to seek regulatory status. On the other hand, the desire to tap both grants/donations and commercial money is driving NGOs like ACCION and OI to embrace new instruments such as for-profit equity vehicles and collateralized debt obligations[48] while maintaining non-profit status for the main parent organization. It can be expected that the push to diversify and expand sources of finance from private/commercial sources will continue to shape the structure of the industry in the years to come.

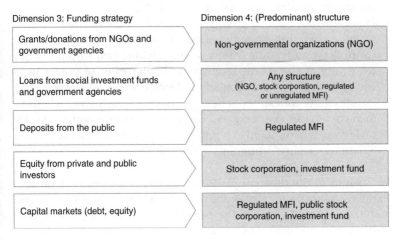

Figure 3.11 Funding strategies and (predominant) structure

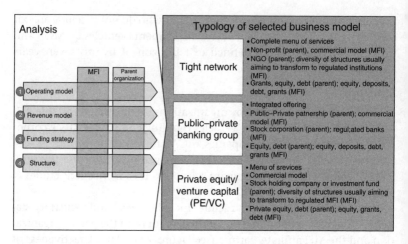

Figure 3.12 Typology of business models

A tentative typology of business models

The detailed examination of the four dimensions (operating model, revenue model, funding strategy and structure) provides a basis for dividing the various business models into three main categories (see Figure 3.12):

- Tight networks – characterized by a comprehensive (but not necessarily integrated or exclusive) menu of services from parent to MFIs, led by a non-profit NGO, and relying on a broad array of funding types including grants/donations at both parent and MFI levels.
- Public–private banking groups – defined by a comprehensive, integrated and exclusive offering of parent to MFIs, with regulated MFIs controlled by a holding company, and relying heavily on public sector equity at the parent level and a combination of public sector equity/debt/grants and commercial deposits at the MFI level.
- Private equity companies – offering a (not necessarily comprehensive) menu of services, operating on a commercial model at both parent and MFI levels, relying mainly on private equity at parent level and a combination of equity/debt/grants at the MFI level.

An analysis of the different players along the two important variables "funding strategy" and "relationship parent–MFI" (see Figure 3.13) suggests that: the ProCredit Group is the clearest example of the private–public banking group model, FINCA and OI the archetypal tight network model and I&P the most representative private equity model. ACCION

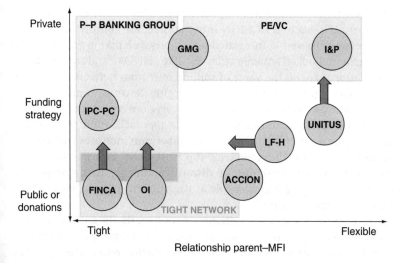

Figure 3.13 Funding strategies and interrelationships

is closest – but does not quite fit – the tight network model, while La Fayette Horus is tending towards the ProCredit banking group archetype and UNITUS is moving to the private equity model as it approaches more commercial sources of funding to fund its investments. GMG is nearest to the private equity model, although the tight relationship between parent and MFI also brings it close to the banking group model.

Conclusions

Over the past two decades, the microfinance industry has grown from a little-known area of development finance into a $30 billion industry. A rich variety of business models proliferated as different players sought solutions to the financing gap affecting micro and small businesses. Over time, an evolutionary development process is leading to the propagation of the more successful business models as microfinance institutions on the ground converge to similar operating, revenue, funding and organizational strategies. The business models of parent "networks" and "groups", on the other hand, are still marked by differentiating features resulting from their past history and current objectives.

Our integrative analysis of both parent organizations and underlying microfinance operators suggests that three main types of business models are emerging in the industry, differing mainly in terms of funding strategy and the relationship between the parent organization and the

MFIs. Tight networks offering choice among a broad menu of services to member MFIs, such as ACCION International, are competing against a rising class of powerful, integrated public-private banking groups on the ProCredit model. Dynamic players like FINCA and Opportunity International are on the verge of spilling over from network to banking group types. In the meantime, fledgling private equity/venture capital players such as I&P and UNITUS seek to carve out a permanent space in the market on the basis of a more flexible approach, while the impending consolidation of the industry (as competition increases and markets mature) is spurning the emergence of private equity type models such as that of GMG. In the midst of disruptive change, partnerships and alliances are playing a greater role as the different players prepare for a more challenging future.

The chapter is but a first attempt to systematically analyse microfinance business models that focus on institution building on an international scale. Further research can undoubtedly refine the typology proposed by the authors and expand the analysis to existing participants and the ever-growing wave of new entrants in the microfinance industry.

Notes

1 Grameen means "rural" or "village" in the Bangla language.
2 Source: authors' own estimates.
3 Source: Consultative Group to Assist the Poorest (CGAP).
4 Sources: CGAP; authors' own estimates.
5 Different sources (for example, CGAP, Microfinance Information Exchange (MIX) and Microcredit Summit) provide a wide range of estimates for both microfinance industry size (between $10 billion and $30 billion) and growth rates.
6 Source: Conversation with Gil Crawford in Santa Cruz, Bolivia, on 4 October 2005.
7 The evolutionary story in microfinance has been constrained to a significant extent by the prevalence of non-market forces, mainly in the form of social and public support for microfinance programs (especially from multilateral and bilateral agencies) and regulatory factors. At the same time, with subsidies for a number of more mature institutions drying-up and the growing commercialization of the sector, market forces are likely to take on an increasing role in weaning out the weakest and ensuring the survival of the fittest organization through an impending cycle of industry consolidation.
8 The term microfinance "network" is used by the Microfinance Information eXchange (the MIX) to denote adherence, affiliation or outright ownership of a number of microfinance institutions to overarching organizations. A number of these networks, in particular the set of microfinance institutions grouped under the ProCredit Holding, are becoming increasingly similar to multinational banking groups with a focus on microfinance. Others were established

– or have evolved into – organizations more akin to the venture capital and private equity entities that provide much of the early stage and growth capital to companies in mainstream western economies.

9   Patrick Goodman provides an excellent overview of "Microfinance Investment Funds: Key Features" in a recent paper (ADA, February 2005).

10   Source: ProCredit Holding.

11   The holding company of the ProCredit Group was founded in 1998 as Internationale Micro-Investitionen AG (IMI), while the operational entities of the Group each featured different brands that could be traced back to the origins of each institution.

12   It would not be an exaggeration to claim that the acronym IPC became legend in Latin American microfinance in the course of the 1980s and 1990s.

13   Grameen Bank does not figure in the selected sample, since it does not share the Key Features set out in this chapter.

14   Source: ACCION International.

15   Ibid.

16   Ibid.

17   Ibid.

18   Source: ACCION Network.

19   Sources: Maria Otero; ACCION International.

20   ACCION was initially a minority shareholder of Credifé, which is the service company Banco del Pichincha, one of the leading commercial banks in Ecuador.

21   ACCION (or one of its finance vehicles) will own 20 percent of Columbia Microcrédito once the deal is completed. Columbia Microcrédito does not provide credit in its own name but acts as a service provider to Banco Columbia in the nascent Argentine microfinance market.

22   The IFC, six local financial institutions, ACCION International and AIM agreed in November 2003 to establish an MFI lending to micro, small and medium enterprise (MSME). The proposed venture was later given the name ACCION Nigeria; and in 2005 ACCION was seeking to recruit management staff for the planned entity. In August 2006, the Central Bank of Nigeria authorized ACCION and seven other companies to operate as microfinance banks (sources: IFC; MicroCapital; ACCION).

23   Source: Opportunity International.

24   Ibid.

25   Source: The MIX.

26   Ibid.

27   Ibid.

28   Source: FINCA.

29   Ibid.

30   Sources: The MIX; Horus.

31   Technical assistance usually refers to consulting services funded by public investors such as the IADB.

32   Bob Gay was at the time managing director of Bain Capital, a private equity firm.

33   Source: UNITUS.

34   Sources: The MIX; I&P.

35   A further field of activity of I&P involves investments in medium enterprises (only in Africa).

36   Latin American Challenge Investment Fund, managed by Cyrano.
37   Source: GMG (note that the authors are involved in GMG as investors and directors).
38   Source: GMG.
39   EIB, KfW, IFC and the Omidyar Tufts Microfinance Fund each purchased a 19.2 percent shareholding in AccessHolding – with the balance of 23.2 percent held by LFS and its employee investment company MicroAssets in what is practically a replication of the ProCredit ownership model. LFS is the technical partner in a similar way to the role of IPC in ProCredit.
40   The shareholders of Microcred are PlaNet Finance, IFC, AXA Belgium and Société Générale. PlaNet Finance is the technical partner.
41   In the case of FINCA and OI, where many MFI are still non-profit organizations and therefore have no "owners," the parents strive for control. The trend, however, is for new FINCA and OI MFI to be established as commercial organizations which, as ProCredit has shown, provides an attractive model of corporate governance.
42   AIM is managed by AIMCO, a wholly owned subsidiary of ACCION International.
43   Sources: Presentation by I&P at Geneva Microfinance Symposium, October 2005; Geoff Davies, CEO of UNITUS (see note 44).
44   M&A = merger with, or acquisition by, another MFI.
45   Source: http://unitus-microcredit.blogspot.com/2005/09/unitus-fund-profile-by-microcapital.html.
46   A parallel can be found in the private equity industry, where prominent investment houses often outsource the operational restructuring to external specialized consultants. Interestingly, however, the legendary buyout firm Kohlberg Kravis Roberts & Co. (KKR) has, in recent years, chosen to reinstate an in-house consultancy (Capstone) to provide consulting services to its investments and to KKR itself.
47   These differences are not absolute, as non-profits also access subsidies indirectly by providing services to affiliated or partner MFIs; and for-profits on occasion receive direct grants to finance specific activities or projects.
48   OI recently placed a collateralized debt obligation (CDO), Microfinance Loan Obligations (Switzerland), among a combination of public and private investors to raise debt funding for a number of OI affiliates/partners.

Appendix: Interviews

Organization	Interviewee	Date	Form of interview
IPC-ProCredit	Christoph Freytag	October 2005	Personal conversation (Geneva)
ACCION International	Maria Otero	04.10.2005	Personal conversation (Santa Cruz)
FINCA International	Geremy Birchard	05.10.2005	Telephone conversation
Ibid.	Volker Renner	09.10.2005 25.10.05	Telephone conversation
	E-mail		
Opportunity International	Diane Ferguson	06.10.2005	Telephone conversation
UNITUS	Geoff Davies	October 2005	Personal conversation (Geneva)
Investisseur et Partenaire pour le Développement	Jeremy Hajdenberg	06.06.06 27.06.06	Telephone conversation E-mail

4

Downscaling Projects in CIS Countries – Revisited

Christoph Freytag

Summary

There are numerous approaches and project designs that share the common goal of making credit available for microentrepreneurs and small businesses. Creation of credit-granting NGOs, their formalization and – increasingly – their commercialization and upgrading into microfinance banks are most prominently discussed. IPC- has been involved in a variety of different kinds of projects including the following:

- Greenfield creation of microfinance banks in Macedonia, Kosovo, Bosnia, Serbia, Bulgaria, Ukraine, Georgia, Angola, Congo, Ghana, Mozambique, Ecuador.
- Creation of microfinance companies in Moldova, Haiti.
- Transformation of credit-granting NGOs, credit-granting foundations and microfinance companies into fully-fledged microfinance banks: El Salvador, Bolivia, Nicaragua, Albania, Romania.

One of the most widely discussed questions over the course of 2005, the international year of microfinance, has been why private capital and/or commercial banks do not engage in microfinance although there is sufficient evidence in all continents that microfinance is profitable. It is therefore worthwhile revisiting a project design that was developed some 20 years ago by the IDB, later modified and replicated by EBRD and KF,[1] and entered the literature under the term "downscaling."

One could ask why a choice in favor of private commercial banks is made at the outset of a project that is aiming to create capacity for a sustainable and massive supply of credit to micro and small enterprises (MSEs). The answer is simple: Because they have a number of attractive characteristics, NGOs usually cannot offer. First of all, a bank allows (better) utilization of existing institutional infrastructure in terms of their branch network, support facilities, management capacity, and – last but not least – their ability to mobilize deposits and other funds which play a crucial role in growing the loan portfolio. Secondly, when a bank is entering the business for the sake of profit, that is, the "commercial approach", which is a precondition for sustainability of the project, it does not require painful restructuring or a "cultural revolution" as would be the case for other donor supported microfinance providers. Finally, banking is a highly regulated activity; although bank regulators can cause inefficiency in microlending operations, regulation is a precondition for accessing long-term funding from private sources.

All in all, we believe that the type of institution providing the best long-term perspective for significant outreach and sustainability in MSE lending is a private commercial bank.

Introduction

For more than 15 years IPC has been advising commercial banks in developing countries and transition economies in their efforts to build capacity to lend to micro and small enterprises (MSEs). We find it particularly advisable to work with existing banks in countries, which cover a very large area, where the creation of a target group-oriented financial institution might prove too costly and time-consuming. This assumes of course that there are banks that are willing to aggressively enter the market for micro and small firms and that they can satisfy financial stability and integrity requirements.

The goal of these complex consulting projects is to build capacity in the financial sector for lending to MSEs. Therefore, they involve setting up microlending departments in a number of different banks. Projects are long term in nature because they require in-depth training of large numbers of loan officers, implementing appropriate procedures, and ensuring that all functions necessary for smooth lending operations are in place. These activities include entry-level and advanced training, back-office functions, IT support, auditing and marketing. IPC assumes responsibility for project management; in addition to providing advisory services, we (IPC) have an obligation as a company to ensure that significant results are achieved in lending to the target group.

In implementing this "downscaling" approach, simply transferring knowledge or monitoring the credit lines provided by public-sector donors is not sufficient to create a sustainable supply of credit for the target group or to build lasting capacity. Banks must make fundamental institutional commitments and achieve a volume of lending to MSEs, which makes a substantial contribution to their overall revenue. When banks fail to engage at this level, making only cosmetic or half-hearted changes, the funding International Financial Institution (IFI) and IPC respond through incentives, persuasion or pressure (as appropriate) focused on the banks being advised. Success requires that the owners of the banks be genuinely committed to developing MSE lending. If they are not then all parties are wasting their time and it is better to reallocate resources to other banks where they can be put to more productive use.

MSE credit operations are usually only one of the activities, and seldom the main activity, of the commercial banks advised. That is one reason why usually better lending results are achieved in institutions that focus only on the MSE target group. However, downscaling universal commercial partner banks does offer the advantage of creating competition in the financial sector right from the start of a project. This leads to an expansion in the supply of credit – particularly in remote regions – and an overall increase in efficiency in the sector. In markets in which successful microfinance institutions were created this impact is only indirectly achieved through a demonstration effect that, by definition, stimulates competition.

IPC's best-known downscaling consulting projects currently under way are the "Russia Small Business Fund", the "German–Ukrainian Fund/ Ukraine Micro Lending Programme", the "Kazakhstan Small Business Programme", the "German–Armenian Fund/Armenian Micro Lending Programme" and the "Micro and Small Enterprise Finance Facility" in Kyrgyzstan. As of the end of 2005, these projects represented about 200 000 loans outstanding at 33 partner banks, amounting to more than $1.3 billion. Currently,[2] about 26 000 loans are issued per month by the banks participating in these projects. The average loan amount is about $6700 (lowest in Kyrgyzstan: $1700; highest in Russia: $8500). 85 percent of all loans had an initial loan amount of less than $10 000 (70 percent less than $5000). Portfolio-at-risk across the region is stable around or less than 1 percent. Without doubt the MSE loans issued under these programs account for a substantial share of the small business credit market in each of the countries listed above.

Project design

Typically, a downscaling project combines three different actors: An international financial institution (IFI; the examples discussed in this chapter

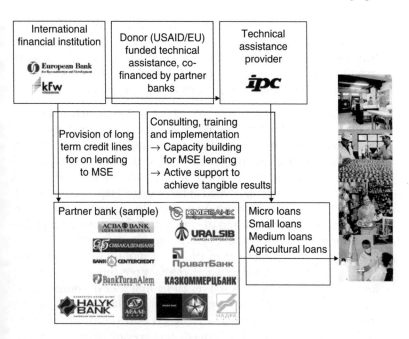

Figure 4.1 "Downscaling" project-design

are EBRD and KfW), providing long-term funding and technical assistance funds, the implementing consultant and local private commercial partner banks (PB) (see Figure 4.1).

Choosing the right partner for a downscaling project has a decisive bearing on the results that can be achieved, and on the inputs necessary for achieving these results. The importance of the selection process and the ongoing management of the relationship with the partner bank cannot be overestimated. The partner bank is probably the biggest risk factor in the project. The criteria for choosing the right partner can broadly be summarized under three headings:

Financial standing and reputation: Clearly a partner bank needs to pass a standard credit review, not only to safeguard the IFI's loan to that PB, but also because MSE lending (no matter how successfully implemented) will be unsustainable if the PB itself is unstable. The investment of public resources makes it imperative that the PB gives no cause for doubt about its future prospects in the market. The PB should also be in good standing with regulatory authorities and enjoy a good reputation with the public. On the other hand, banks that are too profitable often lack the motivation needed to embark on MSE lending. Hence, the bank should be sound and stable, but should also need MSE finance in order to improve its profitability. For example, young banks striving for a share in underserved market niches can be good candidates.

Partner banks' motives for joining the project: It is extremely important to analyse, understand and test the true motives of a potential PB. The desire to obtain long-term funding, receive training support and participate in a prestigious international project is an insufficient motive in itself. The bank must also demonstrate a willingness to change and to adopt a serious strategy aimed at becoming a major player in MSE finance in the market in which it operates. Understanding the ownership structure of the bank and the interests of major owners is probably among the most important tasks in this context. Furthermore, the bank's level of commitment to the target group can be tested. For example, the type of manager whom the bank presents as a counterpart for the team of consultants is a revealing indicator of commitment. The counterpart should be a promising, bright, ambitious manager who combines his/her personal career prospects with a vision of successful MSE lending development. A formerly unsuccessful or essentially passive manager is an unacceptable counterpart and raises doubts about the PB's motives. Another good test is money: The structure and size of the budget (in terms of both operating costs and loan funding) that a bank is willing to allocate for MSE lending provides ample evidence of its level of motivation.

Other characteristics of the partner bank: Partner banks should have a certain "proximity to the target group". An analysis of the current trends in the customer portfolio and its segmentation provides good indicators. Also the manner in which the bank presents itself to the public, and the appearance and location of its branches should be compatible to MSE lending. Other important characteristics are the quality of staff and their degree of motivation (test: appropriate salary levels and moderate staff turnover), the systems in place, and the presence of other successful retail products.

For a consultant, a downscaling project is attractive since it is long term in nature and requires a lot of input, but it is also demanding, as such a project binds substantial resources long term, which are thereby unavailable for other projects. Terms of reference (TOR) for a well-designed, institution-building project go far beyond those of pure implementation of credit lines. They aim at creating capacity on various levels. The main goals of a typical "Downscaling Project" are as follows:

- Fostering commercial micro and small business finance.
- Reaching large numbers of micro and small enterprises (MSEs) on a sustainable basis.
- Training local banks as well as providing these banks with on-lending funds.

These goals are closely interlinked. Reaching large numbers of MSEs on a sustainable basis means that the provision of financial services needs to be profitable for the partner bank so that it has an incentive to continue and expand operations. For the target group it provides a clear signal that the service offered is not a one-off opportunity, but a serious endeavor to embark on a long-term commercial relationship. This sets strong incentives for MSE borrowers to disclose accurate financial information and to honor their repayment obligations. Without a commercial approach, the project would be limited in its outreach and sustainability from the outset. Fostering commercial MSE finance – reaching large numbers of MSEs through local banks – requires the creation of capacity in the broadest meaning of this term through training and consulting.

Building technical capacity: At the outset of any lender–borrower relationship there is an asymmetrical distribution of information about the probability of successful debt service. The methods that are traditionally employed by banks to overcome the resulting incentive problems, namely credit analysis based on reliable documented financial information and an insistence on liquid, "bankable" collateral, cannot work with MSEs because enterprises of this type are generally unable to provide either reliable financial data or the requisite kinds of collateral. The financial service provider will therefore have to deploy alternative methods to resolve the information and incentive problems. IPC's micro and small business credit technology has been developed and tested over 20 years in diverse environments, ranging from very poor and under-developed markets in Africa to highly competitive environments in Latin America. Over time micro and small loans totaling more than $10 billion have been disbursed through IPC's ongoing projects, with historic loss rates of less than 0.5 percent in every single country.

HR capacity: The provision of financial services is a "people business". One of the core elements of a successful downscaling project is the creation of a large body of professionally competent loan officers who become particularly expert at evaluating informal and poorly documented businesses and assessing their capacity and willingness to repay loans. The ability to recruit, train, develop, motivate, manage and retain MSE credit staff is probably the decisive success factor for any financial service provider. IPC is probably the world's largest and most experienced trainer of MSE credit staff. In the above-mentioned CIS countries downscaling projects alone more than 9000 loan officers have been recruited and trained, a contribution to financial sector development, which cannot be overestimated.

Management capacity: The largest bottleneck for scaling up microfinance operations is the absence of trained, experienced, motivated and ethically proven managers. We conceive of our core function – in the early phase of a project – as being a "manager" rather than merely an "adviser". Partners will be convinced that MSE lending is a viable business proposition only if the results are convincing. We believe that in order to achieve convincing results it is necessary to apply a consultancy approach that centers around the assumption of management responsibility and a commitment to produce results. From time to time project partners have found this approach disquieting given the commonly accepted notion that the role of a consultant is usually limited to the provision of know-how, advice and training. But as project managers we have learned that introducing micro credit to an institution frequently gives rise to conflicts or even open resistance, and almost always engenders fear or irritation at least to some degree. A consultant who shies away from such situations will not achieve results and therefore cannot contribute to the accomplishment of the project goals. We believe it is too easy to blame the project partner for such outcomes: Financial institution building requires a more active, interventionist approach on the part of the consultant. Of course, as we build institutions we create local managers, and train those managers to create more managers. During this process, IPC gradually retreats from the role of manager, progressively limiting itself to that of a coach, until the institutions have finally graduated and we can withdraw completely.

Advisory capacity: The role of advisory capacity in a large-scale downscaling project is self-evident. Clearly, substantial input will be required in order to achieve the project goal of "reaching large numbers of MSEs". For a team of expatriate bank advisers – even if they have the necessary methodological know-how, credit expertise and interpersonal skills – operating in a foreign language environment represents a challenging task as does reaching more and more bank branches and towns and cities over time. Therefore, if the expatriates were to act alone they would pose a potential bottleneck for the achievement of the project's objectives. Consequently, further local advisory capacity needs to be created. IPC has always regarded this as one of its main tasks, and in fact we have trained and coached a large number of local consultants throughout our downscaling projects in CIS countries. We systematically recruit ambitious, intelligent young individuals from the countries in which we operate, and train them in the skills and methods needed in MSE finance, a field that is generally new to them. Whenever we have identified local people with the potential to take on a managerial position, a talent for training, an ability to convince others, and a certain degree of flexibility and mobility, we have embarked on an intensive dialogue with these individuals and "molded" them into IPC consultants with the ability and the desire to take a pro-active approach to their work. Today, a large number of former local consultants have further grown into managers and senior managers at MSE lending banks.

IT capacity: In order for a microfinance project to achieve sustainability, maximizing the efficiency of loan processing is of utmost importance. Lending is also an information business, and this is especially true of MSE lending since capturing information about the borrowers' repayment capacity is at the core of our credit technology. The process of gathering, systemizing, storing, evaluating and processing information therefore requires strong IT support. If IT support is insufficient, loan officers will be unable to serve large numbers of MSE clients, and costs in relation to interest income will become prohibitive as a result. Already during the early years of our work in Latin America, IPC realized the importance of IT support. Over the years the business logics, support functions, reporting capabilities and the platform of our credit management system have been improved on an ongoing basis and adapted to numerous different languages and financial systems.

Control capacity: Many traditional bankers are afraid of microfinance for the wrong reason: The perceived high default risk associated with lending to MSEs. International practice (ours and that of a number of other providers) has demonstrated that if incentive systems and a sound micro credit technology are in place credit risk is manageable. The loss potential in microfinance is represented by operational risks, arising for example as a consequence of inefficient procedures and processes or fraud. MSE lending relies on loan officers capturing and processing information that serves as the basis for credit decision making but which is difficult for managers to verify. One of the challenges in building successful MSE lending institutions therefore lies in designing procedures and processes that create an effective control environment (minimizing operational risk) but that simultaneously increase loan officer productivity.

The first line of defense against operational risk is a well-trained and functioning credit committee composed of two or three decision makers with the necessary level of experience to "sense" problems. The consultant's participation in credit committees during the early stage of cooperation with each new PB will ensure that in addition to performing efficient credit risk assessment credit committee members learn to ask the right questions and to make the right judgments. The credit committee institutionalizes discussion and is therefore undoubtedly one of the most important "learning workshops" in the course of financial institution building. Another important factor in the implementation of efficient MSE loan procedures is the creation of back offices that assume responsibility for documentation, loan disbursement and portfolio monitoring. Supported with a strong IT package, an MSE back office embodies the establishment of a powerful institutional "four-eyes principle". Another important issue is the creation of a management unit on the level of the PB's head office (or regional centre, if the bank is very large) which also assumes control functions. Lastly, capacity for internal auditing needs to be built. These internal audit units should not only focus on individual loan files but should consistently monitor the efficiency and functionality of internal control procedures.

Financial capacity: The presence of funding is a prerequisite for a financial service provider. Even if liquidity levels at the PB are high and the deposit base is strong, the willingness of an IFI to support the project by providing targeted credit to PBs is needed at least in early stages of a project before microfinance has proven its potential to compete in profitability with other business lines. It will create additional incentives for partner banks to develop MSE lending if they know that they can tap long-term financial resources to support this business. This will also leverage the IFI's influence over the PBs and – over time – create income for the IFI to cover the costs of coordinating the project. On the other hand, IFI should refrain from becoming too commercial and "deal orientated" – they would clearly risk their development goals and undermine the consultant's authority to implement target group orientated lending operations. In IPC's ongoing downscaling projects our clients (EBRD, KfW) currently have $200 million in credit lines outstanding with partner banks. IPC's presence in these institutions and markets reassures our clients that their investment is safe. Most prominently, we demonstrated our abilities following the Russian financial sector crisis of 1998, when IPC arranged portfolio transfers to recover the debt owed by failed Russian partner banks to EBRD. IPC also sought and realized other assets from the PBs, thus helping EBRD to recover as much of the debt as possible.

Building financial capacity also has another dimension, which is beyond typical TORs for this type of project, but should also be included. All too often in microfinance projects the financial needs of MSEs are narrowed to credit, and the institutions involved provide only this single product to the target group. Building links and relationships between local banks and MSEs can and should go further; that is, it should include deposit mobilization. If banks are enabled to capture deposits from the target group and the target group is given access to deposit services the self-sustainability of a microfinance project is greatly enhanced. Banks will have additional incentives to promote MSE finance, informal finance can be further reduced and relationships between banks and their MSE clients can become stronger, since they will then be based on mutual trust. To summarize our thinking about "financial capacity building", we promote the development of a project approach that places the MSE as a client at the center of our work, rather than the loan disbursed to an MSE. We believe that MSEs will be better served and more firmly integrated into the formal financial sector if this approach is adopted. Banks will have opportunities to earn additional income and will find it easier to incorporate MSE lending into their business, which consists of financial intermediation in the broad sense.

Typical TORs further specify that the consultant should advise on legal and regulatory impediments to banks and/or borrowers that affect the project on the local level. During our long-term work in developing and transition economies, we have developed a profound understanding of legal and regulatory constraints for efficient MSE lending. On the one hand, a sound regulatory environment is clearly necessary to protect the rights of both the creditor and the borrower. But regulation almost inevitably produces transaction costs. Reducing these costs is usually not high on the regulators' list of priorities, yet the reduction of transaction costs is crucial in MSE finance since their weight relative to the size of the loan is greater than in, say, corporate lending and therefore drives up the real cost of the loan (sometimes prohibitively). Transaction costs can take various forms: Among the most obvious are the registration fees or notary fees associated with collateral arrangements. But documentation requirements for loans or accounts can also translate into costs for the borrowers if obtaining the documents in question means that the borrower has to go through lengthy, bureaucratic procedures (which, in addition to the time and effort entailed, may also involve additional payments). Time is money, and microentrepreneurs cannot afford to waste any.

It is important to identify which regulatory issues represent genuine impediments, and which merely serve as an excuse for a "traditional" banker to obstruct efficient MSE lending. In many countries, we have found that there is a difference between the wording of a regulation and its interpretation and application. By and large, it can be said that the degree to which the deliverables in terms of lending performance will be achieved will also depend on the way in which counterparts at partner banks interpret the regulations. In summary, we consider it important to stipulate the following principles for a functioning legal and regulatory environment:

- Banks need to obtain full authority to design and launch MSE loan products, including the authority to determine their pricing.
- Documentation requirements for microloans need to be minimized, that is, reduced to the following: Client's identity documents; consistent documentation of credit analysis and credit decision making; concise, practical contracts.
- Providing collateral needs to be easy and inexpensive; otherwise, collateral requirements will hinder microentrepreneurs from gaining access to finance.
- Microbusiness is a cash business – loan disbursement and repayment procedures need to take this into account.
- Loan provisioning regulations should focus on portfolio at risk and demand high generic provisions for loans in arrears. Setting aside individual loan loss provisions for microloans is not advisable or indeed practicable.
- Supervisors should focus on monitoring whether the internal control procedures are functioning effectively, whether loan portfolio repayment performance is satisfactory, and whether adequate levels of provisioning are being maintained.
- Improved financial infrastructure, such as central credit registers that provide timely (on-line) information about the borrower's credit history, and central pledge registers can cut transaction costs significantly and greatly enhance credit culture.

Success drivers and challenges

Beyond project design related issues, the economic environment has a strong impact on inputs required vis-à-vis outputs to be expected. The importance of this simple wisdom must not be underestimated. It makes a huge difference, whether banks operate in an environment offering ample other opportunities for making (a perceived) "easy profit" (for example, Russia before 1998) or whether banks face increasing competition, declining margins, increasing fixed costs and therefore look for a stable mass-market high-margin credit product (for example, Russia, Ukraine since 2004). Continuous crisis, notorious instability of the banking sector and failing or absent financial sector reform represent substantial risks for any downscaling project. At the outset, we believe a positive medium to long-term assessment has to be made for the development of the banking sector. If this is not possible, the risk of failure, or – at best – inefficient investment of technical assistance funds, is very high. Looking back, it could be said that two of IPC's downscaling project started "too early". The Russia Small Business Fund (RSBF) was launched in 1994 and started full-scale operations in 1995, at a time when Russian banks simply speculated against their domestic currency and invested heavily in short-term high-yielding Russian government debt. Competition was hardly an issue. Not only was it extremely difficult to convince Russian bankers to change their relation-, document- and asset-based way of doing lending, in fact the project was completely dependent on EBRD's willingness to grant refinancing credit lines for MSE lending. Banks were simply not interested in investing other (scarce) funds. Finally, with the bank sector crisis in 1998, the project witnessed a financial sector meltdown, severely damaging or even destroying the results of four years of heavy institution-building work. Also in Ukraine, where the project started in 1997, partner banks initially were extremely reluctant to cooperate. Only in Kazakhstan (since 1998), Armenia (since 1999) and Kyrgyzstan (since 2002) have the projects developed successfully from the start. We believe it has a lot to do with financial sector reform being in place and a market structure, which provided few alternatives to MSE lending. However, one should not underestimate the importance of learning and the time it requires to understand markets, banks and the sector, or the importance of breaking new ground and – even in immature markets – showing what the future could look like. The early years of downscaling in CIS countries might have been expensive and inefficient, but the lessons learned yielded great benefits when the project design was later replicated. Donors planning to initiate a downscaling project need to keep this in mind and should not expect that just by putting the right banks with the right consultant together a project will function like a "plug and play" application. Again, learning requires time and is necessary.

Initially designed as a rescue vehicle for the RSBF, KMB Bank, a micro and small business bank with initial major shareholding of EBRD, managed by IPC, soon after the crisis became one of Russia's best performing MSE banks. Similarly, in the Ukraine the creation of a microfinance bank (today: ProCredit Bank) helped to achieve not only tangible results within the project, it also demonstrated to other banks that MSE lending is a serious proposition and profitable business. Ever since then, both projects, the RSBF and particularly the Ukraine Micro Loan Program (UMLP), have grown at exponential rates and become very successful. In the Ukraine (without the "specialized" ProCredit Bank) more than 10 000 micro and small business loans with an average amount around $5000 are being disbursed monthly. The loan portfolio of the downscaling partner banks has grown by 200 percent to $400 million over the last 12 months and continues to grow dynamically without loss of quality. At present, these PB have 70 000 MSE loans outstanding (including ProCredit Bank: 100 000). Interventions on the institutional level in the form of creating microfinance banks have therefore not challenged or harmed the downscaling projects, but through successful demonstration of sustainable MSE operations strongly leveraged further input, guaranteed stability and made sure that the lower end of the market is served.

Another clear driver for success is the role the IFI assumes vis-à-vis both partner banks and the consultant. EBRD's and KfW's strong commitment and involvement in the projects, in terms of willingness to enter into relationships with bank managers/owners and to push harder for results and institutional change, has been and continues to be of utmost importance. At all times, IPC was challenged to do its best and felt that its point of view was understood; both institutions engaged in a genuine dialogue with the consultant, which greatly facilitated the learning process. An IFI that limits its role to granting/monitoring credit lines and simply supervising the consultant's performance will achieve far less. Since downscaling projects are long-term, and they are intended to have a long-term impact, careful attention needs to be paid to what kind of incentive structures are created amongst the parties involved.

There are or have been, however, also a number of "home made" problems in downscaling projects, which should be avoided in the future:

Donor driven "microcredit only" culture: By and large, IFIs tend to measure the success of (not only) downscaling projects with parameters that need to be questioned. Focusing on "number of loans", that is, on transactions rather than on clients, can result in clients not being properly or comprehensively served. Almost inevitably, this "number of loans" focus will alienate the partner bank and lead to the unintended creation of "a MFI inside the bank" versus "the bank as MFI." This is the case because bank(er)s measure success usually in terms of income generating volume figures or number of clients. The microloan department within a PB is already distinct from other departments: It enjoys (?) a special status due to its support from an IFI and the presence of international advisers; it is new and serves "other" clients than were served traditionally and applies "other rules" for this activity. In most cases, its staff is young and has been trained under the program (not by the bank). If performance is determined with different yardsticks, the alienation is complete. This "MFI inside the bank" has a number of undesirable consequences:

- From the viewpoint of a banker, it means lots of lost opportunities in terms of client attraction, broadening the deposit base, fee income and reputation gains.
- From the viewpoint of the IFI/Consultant, it makes the exit from the partner bank very difficult and risky. By changing what is "alien" to the partner bank after the alienation has taken place, the target group orientation can get lost (at least out of focus) as PB are triggered to move gradually upmarket to SME.
- The "MFI inside the bank" is in itself sub-optimal in terms of efficiency and represents the main reason why specialized microfinance banks (for example, ProCredit Banks) achieve better results in terms of efficiency and – consequently – target group orientation.

It took a lot of time to overcome this approach. Today only during a pilot phase with a new PB, are "autonomous" microcredit departments permitted. As soon as the PB's management and owners buy into the concept, integration of MSE lending into an overall MSE client policy needs to be addressed. In this context, it has proved helpful to budget overall input of technical assistance per PB from the start and by doing so signaling clearly that TA support is limited in volume and time. If this is not clear to the partner bank (or consultant, or IFI) there are incentives to delay the exit from the PB, which again cements the "MFI inside the bank" and represents suboptimal use of donor funds.

One example for this is giving too much preference for "regional expansion" versus "institutional strengthening on head office levels".

Although microlending is an activity that requires a great degree of decentralized decision making, which in itself is often revolutionary to PBs, it needs to be carefully considered whether institution-building efforts should be continuously invested to create additional outreach or directed towards strengthening head office's supervision, support and planning capacities for microlending. While substantial input on a branch level is required to build an MSE portfolio representing "critical mass" for the PB to buy into the concept, the sustainability of these operations is at stake if the PB's head office is insufficiently built up to support MSE lending. The head office, not the branch, is the place where integration of MSE lending conceptually needs to be addressed and achieved. Beyond technical issues of integrating a new field of banking activity, this requires a major shift away from traditional banking culture. Traditionally, credit operations are document-based and centralized to a maximum degree. This does not work out in development-orientated microfinance.

Outlook

In all projects (with the exception of the RSBF), sufficient capacity for mass lending and training of local lending staff has been built up, and "microcredit" is not perceived as a "donor-driven" product but as a standard banking product. A logical next step is the expansion of MSE lending into rural areas with special focus on agricultural producers. The target is to disburse 20 percent of all loans in rural areas and 5–10 percent to farmers. This goal is in reach within the next 12 months. First lessons learned are that surprisingly little has to be changed in terms of credit technology. Two important issues were addressed, and they have helped to overcome typical prejudices and fears of traditional lenders:

- Substantial knowledge has been or is being accumulated about the different production cycles of farmers in the different regions with varying climate and soil conditions. Data about typical benchmarks on inputs and expected outputs has been gathered in the form of "technological maps" and is available for lending staff in the form of a database. Additionally, numerous loan officers were recruited from agro-economic faculties. Often, these recruits – apart from bringing their specific know-how to the projects – come from a rural environment and "speak the right language".

- The more difficult issue has been to find efficient delivery mechanisms. In essence, we believe that the increased transaction cost in rural lending (for attracting clients, conducting credit analysis and monitoring outstanding loans) impose the only real problem. Wherever a PB has built a branch network that reaches into rural areas, the problem was easily solved. In other cases, mobile branch offices were introduced which visit branches as soon as a number of loan applications from the community have been collected.
- Another quite often-debated alternative in recent conferences was to go via the food processors: They in general are interested in credit supply to farmers since this helps to increase their production capacity or quality of products. It was expected that food processors could be helpful in screening "good" farmers for the PB and decrease credit risk wherever timely cash payments can be expected from them. However, our observation has been that farmers with long-term supply contracts to food processors either do not necessarily honor these contracts (especially if better prices can be achieved on the markets) or (probably a counter-measure of the food processor) are already heavily indebted towards the food processor. In essence, we believe that – as in urban microfinance – credit supply should be arranged in a way as to provide the borrower with some degree of independence. After all, the borrower should know best how to make best use of the loan funds.

Beyond rural credit, this important "frontier of finance", we expect that the technical assistance support for the above-mentioned downscaling projects will be gradually reduced and phased out beginning 2007 and ending 2010. By that time, we are confident the objectives will have been fully reached and a substantial contribution made for better, deeper and inclusive financial sectors.

In Armenia and Kyrgyzstan, the impact of downscaling is highest relative to the size of the banking sector and market. More than 2/3 of all loan officers in Kyrgyz banks have been trained under the project, more than 50 percent of all loans outstanding in the banking sector are MSE loans of the project. The share in the bank sector's total credit to the economy is 13 percent in Armenia and 15 percent in Kyrgyzstan. But also in Kazakhstan, Russia and particularly the Ukraine commercial banks have firmly integrated microcredit into their business models.[3] PB's in Russia and Kazakhstan have provided funding for MSE loans at 325 percent and 350 percent respectively of funds provided by IFI. In the Ukraine, this ratio is above 500 percent. Until recently there was widespread doubt that this could happen.[4]

A major challenge ahead is still the RSBF, where as a result of the financial sector crisis of 1998 and widespread corporate governance problems the project was until very recently limited to working with regional banks only. Although on a regional level this has turned out to be successful (Urals, Central Siberia, Nizhny Novgorod), the limited absorptive capacity of these banks of course represented constraints to the goal of achieving countrywide outreach. At present, there is reason for optimism as larger, Moscow-based banks with nationwide branch networks have expressed interest in participation, offering even to co-finance the technical assistance component.

Results

Here, and in Figures 4.2, 4.3 and Table 4.1, some results of the five mentioned downscaling projects are presented. For the sake of making a clear distinction, the results of ProCredit Bank Ukraine have been excluded from the statistics, even though it is a partner bank of the UMLP. KMB Bank, an RSBF partner bank, was managed by IPC staff from 1999 to 2003. Since neither IPC nor ProCredit Holding were shareholders of the bank at any point in time, however, and since KMB Bank "inherited" substantial downscaling TA input that had been provided between 1994 and 1998, this bank's MSE lending data is included.

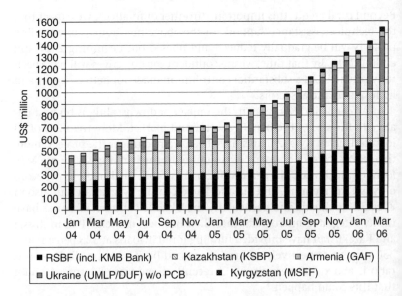

Figure 4.2   MSE loan portfolio

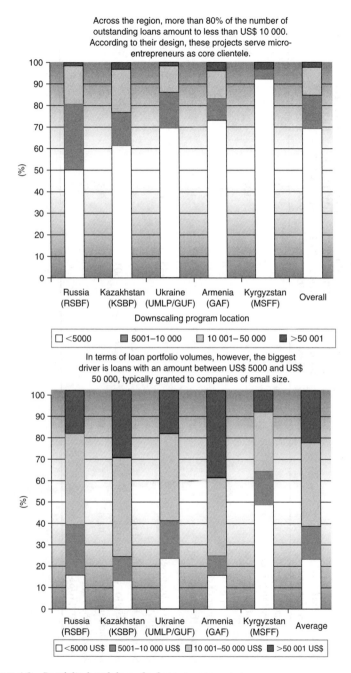

Figure 4.3 Portfolio breakdown by loan management

Table 4.1 IPC's downscaling projects – 2005 overview

Country Client PROGRAMME year of inception	Russia EBRD RSBF 1994	Kazakhstan EBRD KSBP 1998	Ukraine EBRD/KfW UMLP/GUF 1997	Armenia KfW/EBRD GAF/AMBFF 1998	Kyrgyzstan EBRD MSEFF 2002	Total
Advised banks (completed/ongoing)	4/5	5/1	1/4	3/4	1/5	14/19
Number of loan officers trained & retained	803	666	1242	107	247	3065
in number of branches	317	139	200	35	54	745
in number of cities	145	50	94	12	15	316
Cumulative number of loans disbursed 2005	65 666	49 529	74 013	11 571	21 662	221 441
Cumulative disbursements 2005 (US$ million)	671	453	445	66	44	1679
Number of loans outstanding	63 251	52 785	57 294	8245	16 207	197 782
Loan portfolio (US$ million)	530	429	301	46	28	1334
PAR (arrears over 30 days, in %)	1.0	0.9	0.4	0.5	0.8	<1
Average loan amount outstanding (US$)	8400	8100	5300	5600	1700	6700

Notes

1 DB: Inter-American Development Bank; EBRD: European Bank for Reconstruction and Development; KfW: Kreditanstalt für Wiederaufbau. Throughout the chapter these institutions are also referred to as International Financial Institutions (IFI).
2 March 2006 results.
3 A critical review of MSE lending at exited PBs (that is, PBs which have graduated from technical assistance) is beyond the scope of this chapter. Privat Bank, however, the biggest bank in the Ukraine, is definitely one example of a successfully exited PB; it is currently granting more than 5000 loans monthly without TA support. The loan portfolio comprises 40 000 loans outstanding with a combined volume of over $200 million. Without any external support, Privat Bank is rolling out MSE lending to additional regional branches and is fully capable of, and committed to, achieving dynamic growth in this line of business without any tendency to "drift" into other client segments – as is the case at some of the graduated PBs in Kazakhstan, where, it should be noted, there is no large MFI or specialized microfinance bank to set the pace and raise standards.
4 See S. Forster, S. Greene and J. Pytkowska: "The State of Microfinance" (Washington: CGAP/The World Bank Group, 2003.) The ratios provided in the paragraph are based on data as of 30 June 2005.

5
Case Study – ICICI Bank

Suvalaxmi Chakraborty
Former Head, Rural, Microbanking & Agribusiness Group
ICICI Bank ltd, India

An introduction to institutional credit in India

The administrative structure has, since Independence in 1947, tried to alleviate poverty and take financial services to under-served segments through a variety of programs. Early strategies included setting up Development Financial Institutions,[1] which were established with the objective of supporting industrialization and infrastructure development. Another strategy adopted was the nationalization of commercial banks,[2] in an effort to improve the delivery of financial services and take access nationwide. Furthermore, several directed target-approach poverty alleviation programs were initiated.[3] Most of these had a financial access component built in, either in the form of creation of income-generating assets, or for start-up capital to support entrepreneurial activities and indirectly generate employment.

Over the decades, a plethora of institutional credit providers came into existence in India, including the cooperative banks, the regional rural banks and branches of the commercial banks, which were given special area-specific responsibilities. Long-term credit requirements of the rural sector were to be met by a network of state and primary co-operative agriculture and rural development banks. Frequent loan waivers led to high default rates.[4] Priority sector lending was recommended as a means of ensuring that banks aligned with the development objectives of the country, and that some investment was made in agriculture, small-scale industry and micro enterprise, as well as other sectors that the administration felt were under-funded by the commercial banks. The priority sector commitments stand at 40 percent of the overall lending of commercial banks, and 18 percent of all advances must be made to the agriculture sector as direct lending.

For decades, financial service provision to the under-served was regarded as synonymous with credit delivery to rural areas, predominantly for the purpose of agriculture. Very few programs focused on micro enterprises, or encouraged diversification away from agriculture. This led to a focus on geographical expansion to rural areas, where bank branches offered credit in amounts to the very poor, rather than a suite of products designed to cater to the needs of this segment. These practices in turn led to high default rates.[5]

It was during the early 1990s that the National Bank for Agriculture and Rural Development (NABARD[6]) introduced the NABARD Self Help Group (SHG) bank linkage model[7] and it began to gain attention as a useful means of expanding rural reach, while achieving lower transaction costs through serving several persons at one point. Furthermore, the group would also act as an outsourced risk assessment and monitoring system, with local level presence and knowledge. The co-guarantee given by the members also served as a check on default, as the threat of denial of further credit to the entire group for the default of a single member incentivized the group to pay up themselves, or put pressure on the borrower to pay back the dues.

An introduction to ICICI Bank

ICICI Bank was originally promoted in 1994 by ICICI Limited (a development financial institution for providing medium-term and long-term project financing to Indian businesses), and was its wholly-owned subsidiary. After consideration of various corporate structuring alternatives, the managements of ICICI and ICICI Bank formed the view that the merger of ICICI with ICICI Bank would be the optimal strategic and legal structure for both entities. After the merger in January 2002, the ICICI group's financing and banking operations, both wholesale and retail, were integrated into a single entity.

ICICI Bank is India's second-largest bank with total assets of about $38.5 billion at 31 March 2005 and profit after tax of $461 million for the year ended 31 March 2005 ($376 million in fiscal 2004). ICICI Bank has a network of about 610 branches and extension counters and over 2000 ATMs. ICICI Bank offers a wide range of banking products and financial services to corporate and retail customers through a variety of delivery channels, specialized subsidiaries and affiliates. ICICI Bank set up its international banking group in 2002 to cater for the cross-border needs of clients and to offer products internationally. ICICI Bank has subsidiaries in the UK, Canada and Russia, branches in Singapore and

Bahrain and representative offices in the United States, China, United Arab Emirates, Bangladesh and South Africa. ICICI Bank's equity shares are listed in India and its American Depositary Receipts (ADRs) are listed on the New York Stock Exchange (NYSE).

ICICI Bank's foray into rural markets

Banking with the poor is a challenging task as the nature of demand requires doorstep services, flexibility in timing, timely availability of services, low value and high volume transactions and requires simple processes with minimum documentation. The nature of supply however involves a high cost of service delivery, rigid, inflexible timings and procedures, and high transaction costs for the customers. With these features on the supply side, traditional banking is not poised to meet the requirements of the demand side. The reach of the banking sector in the rural areas was as low as 15 percent in terms of credit potential, and 18 percent in terms of population with physical access to a bank branch.

ICICI Bank chose to pursue the unreached rural markets as part of its strategy of being a universal bank. However, instead of taking the conventional branch-banking model for increasing its outreach, the Bank decided to work with models that would combine the strengths of intermediary forms of organization with the financial bandwidth of a banking institution.

Initiation to microfinance – The SHG bank linkage model

To enable its foray into the rural markets, ICICI Bank merged with the Bank of Madura (est. 1943), which had a substantial network of 77 branches in the rural areas of a South Indian state – Tamil Nadu. The Bank of Madura had expertise in catering to the needs of the small and medium sector and a strong network of SHGs. At the time of the merger, the Bank of Madura had 1200 SHGs. However, the program was still not sustainable. To reach profitability ICICI Bank devised a three-tiered structure (see Figure 5.1). A project manager, who would be an employee of the bank, would oversee six coordinators who would in turn oversee the work of six promoters. The target for promotion of groups was 20 groups within 12 months, upon which the promoter would receive financial compensation from the Bank. The coordinator would usually be an SHG member who would coordinate the activities of the promoters.

Women who had finished a year of promoting the requisite 20 groups were given the designation of Social Service Consultant. They would

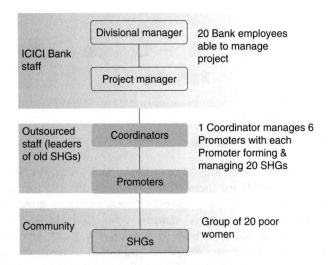

Figure 5.1　ICICI Bank's three-tier structure

travel within a radius of 15 kilometers, in order to promote as many groups within their area as possible. Strict guidelines were set for selection of SHG members and SHGs would focus on those who were illiterate and below the poverty line so that there would be homogeneity in the socioeconomic background as well. The SHGs followed the normal pattern of saving until they had internally collected a total of INR 6000 in a bank account held in the group's name, through small weekly payments by each member of the group. After this, the amount collected would be lent internally at 24 percent p.a. This rate of interest was much less than was available from the informal lenders, and all the groups stood to gain as the interest was churned back into the group.

ICICI Bank achieved a high rate of growth, reaching 8000 SHGs in March 2003, with its team of 20 project managers. Within three years of the merger with Bank of Madura, ICICI Bank had extended its reach to 12 000 SHGs. However, the pace of outreach was still slow, and the Bank began to experiment with other models of reaching the unreached (see Figure 5.2). This was because existing branches could be leveraged for outreach, but in areas where there were no ICICI Bank branches, it would not be viable to set up branches solely for the purpose of rural outreach, as such branches would have a very long gestation period and would be costly in terms of overheads. ATMs were also a costly proposition and the infrastructure required was not in place in most of the remote areas.

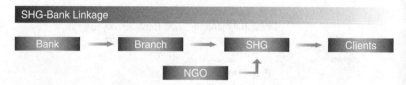

* Branches assess credibility and monitor repayment from SHGs
* Group formation by NGOs

Figure 5.2   SHG–Bank linkage model

Once the groups were formed and linked to bank credit, the NGO was no longer responsible for them. Thus it was felt that the social inter-mediary (the NGO) had no financial or performance stake in group forma-tion, nor did it participate in risk sharing. Although the SHGs had been repaying at very good rates, above 95 percent, it was still important to control the quality of group formation and link it to credit discipline. ICICI Bank worked with Self Help Promotion Institutions to outsource the work of group formation to institutions whose core competence was social intermediation. Yet even in this case also, the misalignment of incentives remained the same. The bank's staff was replaced by an exter-nal entity, which, even if competent and having the best of intentions, could not vouch for the quality of the groups it created. So, in spite of having a good increase in outreach, the model failed to scale up further.

It was felt that in the case of the SHG formation, there was no risk sharing or financial stake/performance stake of the social intermediary (NGO) in the process of group formation. Once the groups were formed and linked to Bank credit, there was no more responsibility on the part of the NGO. The SHGs had been repaying at very good rates, above 95 percent, yet there was a need to control the quality of group formation and link it to credit discipline. ICICI Bank also worked with Self Help Promotion Institutions to outsource the work of group formation insti-tutions whose core competence was in social intermediation. In this case, the alignment of incentives remained the same, as the bank staffs were replaced by an external entity, who albeit with the best of inten-tions and competencies, would not be able to vouch for the quality of groups created by it. Thus, despite having considerable increase in out-reach, the model failed to scale up further.

Microfinance institutions (MFI) intermediation model

ICICI Bank began to experiment with the microfinance institution (MFI) as a substitute for the more granular Self Help Group. The MFIs

Figure 5.3 Bank–MFI linkage model

were willing to take on the risk of the financial performance of individual and group borrowers. Therefore, the stake in good quality group formation was also built in. Also, this channel was better for leveraging large amounts of funds without necessarily having a grassroots level presence of the bank staff. The MFI would undertake the processes and operationalization in terms of group formation, cash management, disbursement and recovery, and also record keeping. The Bank would lend to the MFI on the basis of its balance sheet and portfolio performance and the MFI would repay the bank.

The MFI–Bank linkage model paved the way for taking a wider range of services to the financially under-served populace (see Figure 5.3). These financial services include provision of micro-insurance tailored to the cash flows and insurance needs of low-income clients. Micro-insurance ensured the end client support in case of accidents or disablement as well as loan insurance in case of death. This was a significant step towards reducing household vulnerabilities.

The intermediation model at first looked scalable, but there seemed to be constraints in this model as well. For instance, there was a double charge on capital created, once at the level of the Bank lending to the MFI and secondly at the level of the MFI on lending to the client. This seemed to be a sub-optimal lending structure due to the double counting that also, because of the small balance sheet size, unduly affected the risk perceived about the MFI, even if it had very robust systems and processes. Other key challenges to performance were that the MFIs could not grow and scale up as fast as their capabilities would permit, because of severe capital constraints. Most MFIs had potential access to large debt funds, but because of their small balance sheet (which would represent the limited initial capital of the promoters); they were constrained to operate with limited debt funding. In the complete absence of equity investors in the microfinance institutions, there was hardly any scope for the MFI to scale up rapidly.

On the other hand, MFIs were exposed to the entire risk of lending to the end clients, despite their constrained risk appetite. Most MFIs were operating in a single geography, and the systematic risk that they were exposed to was large. This put undue risk-bearing on these organizations, especially in the light of their limited geographical risk-diversification capabilities. Banks, which were lending ostensibly to the end-clients, could not get access to information regarding repayment capacity, or repayment behavior of the end-clients, as the MFI not only acted as an operating and servicing agent, but also assumed the entire risk. If the MFI collapsed because of any internal organizational issues as opposed to client default, the entire client segment, which had demonstrated credit-worthiness, would be deprived of a service provider. On the one hand were the competencies of the Bank (which had a large amount of finance waiting to be channeled into the sector) and on the other, the social intermediation expertise of the MFI (which had a grassroots presence, customer outreach and contact, and could also achieve better economies of scale if it scaled up and extended outreach faster). There was a need to combine the strengths of both players, while also building in the correct incentives and using capital parsimoniously to leverage the maximum value and client outreach from it. Furthermore, there was a need for close supervision and information tracking so that at no stage would rapid expansion lead to undetected default owing to slackness in monitoring. Costs would have to be recovered to ensure sustainability. The model would also have to incentivize growth and preserve the incentives of the originator (of the portfolio) to maintain portfolio performance.

Notes

1 The principal DFIs were the Industrial Credit and Investment Corporation of India, set up in (1955), the Industrial Finance Corporation of India (IFCI), established in 1948, and the Industrial Development Bank of India (IDBI), created in 1964.
2 In 1969, 14 banks were nationalized; six more were nationalized in 1982. The process of nationalization involved the government buying out majority stakes in an existing private bank.
3 Including the Integrated Rural Development Programme (IRDP) (restructured as Swarnajayanti Gram Swarojgar Yojana (SGSY) in 1997) and schemes for employment generation and training of rural youth.
4 In 1989, the Agriculture and Rural Debt Relief Scheme was introduced, which waived all loans below INR 10,000, thereby creating an even less conducive environment for rural and agricultural lending.

5 In the absence of insurance, many rural borrowers were unable to cover production and price risks and therefore defaulted on loans. For many, low
  productivity, variations in weather conditions, and lack of access to good
  quality inputs resulted in shortfalls in production, for others, the inability to
  access markets with favorable prices resulted in inability to repay.
6 NABARD is an apex institution, accredited with all matters concerning policy,
  planning and operations in the field of credit for agriculture and other economic activities in rural areas.
7 NABARD intended to overcome the problems associated with rural outreach
  through this model, which used participation, social intermediation and financial intermediation for advancement through access to financial services.

Part III
Private Capital in Microfinance

Part II highlighted the need for institution building, i.e. the development of appropriate business models for microfinance institutions and their dissemination. Part III moves from operations to funding. We have seen how commercial banks can "downscale" their operations to serve the microfinance market, and the variety of ways in which grassroots MFIs have grown into full service banks – offering savings as well as loans – to their customers. The ability to mobilize savings is critical as a means of accessing cheaper capital and reducing the borrowing costs of MFIs. In addition to savings and donor funding, in recent years, the microfinance industry has started to access private commercial capital. In this part, Michael Steidl traces the development of private commercial investment into microfinance through a series of structured investment vehicles. Marc de Sousa Shields focuses on some of the challenges faced by private investors entering the microfinance market. Finally, Hanns-Michael Hoelz presents the view of one of the largest commercial players, Deutsche Bank, giving some examples of the bank's involvement in microfinance.

Part II
Private Capital in Microfinance

6

Capital for Microfinance: From Public and Social Investment to Integration into Mainstream Financial Markets

Michael Steidl

The start-up of an industry: Public money

Not too long ago private investors and commercial financial institutions regarded microenterpreneurs as "unbankable", mainly because of the supposed elevated default risk involved in microlending and the high transaction costs for small loans. Thus, it was public funders, together with investors motivated by social intentions rather than commercially, who in the 1980s started the initiatives that led to the success story of microfinance. Most often, development agencies, non-profit organizations based in the developed world and some highly motivated local businessmen and women worked together to start the non-profit organizations that disbursed the first loans to the poor.[1]

In the process of growing from a "microfinance community" to a "microfinance industry", microfinance institutions and their stakeholders have struggled to find a balance between their social and development objectives and financial return. Although "return" was not a goal in itself for most of the institutions during their initial stages, many have begun to accept it as a requirement for sustainability, because they want to see their institution persist in the market beyond an initial period of public subsidy. Out of this perspective, many of these non-profit organizations began to behave as if they were for-profit firms providing financial services to a formerly under-served clientele.

The development of a quasi-commercial approach to microlending has been a crucial factor in the success of early microfinance institutions (MFIs), as these specialized organizations soon became known. Organizations such as Pro Crédito (now transformed into Banco Los Andes) and Prodem (the incubator of Banco Sol and Prodem FFP) in Bolivia or Servicio Crediticio AMPES (later converted to Financiera Calpiá and today Banco ProCredit) in El Salvador have proven that microlending activity can be managed on a sustainable and profitable basis. The most visionary MFIs knew back in the 1980s and 1990s that the flow of subsidies would stop one day, and that commercial sources of capital would have to step in. A special indicator was defined, called "financial self-sufficiency", to measure the degree to which an MFI would cover its costs if it did not receive any subsidies at all.[2]

Many of these more successful MFIs took the logical step of transforming themselves into formal financial institutions (banks or finance companies) that operate under the banking laws in their respective countries and mobilize resources from the general public to finance their operations. These leading MFIs have grown into serious actors in their local financial systems, and their continued success into a third decade proves that microfinance can indeed be a profitable business. Table 6.1 provides data for a five-year period on the return on equity (ROE) for ten of the largest MFIs reporting to the Microfinance Information Exchange (MIX), an important online resource for the industry. All of the MFIs listed in Table 6.1 had a total asset volume of more than $100 million as of 31 December 2004, and most of these institutions had originally been launched as non-profit organizations.

The data shows that microfinance has proven to be a profitable activity for these formerly non-profit ventures. The average ROE for the period

Table 6.1 Annual return on equity for ten of the largest MFIs (2000–4), in percent

MFI	Country	2000	2001	2002	2003	2004	Average
ASA	Bangladesh	26.2	28.8	36.2	37.9	32.0	32.2
Bancosol	Bolivia	3.8	0.4	1.7	13.0	21.6	8.1
Banco Solidario	Ecuador	−6.0	−9.3	19.7	23.2	22.9	10.1
BRAC	Bangladesh	12.2	N/A	N/A	14.5	10.4	12.4
CERUDEB	Uganda	40.9	32.7	18.8	21.0	35.5	29.8
CMAC Arequipa	Peru	33.2	43.9	50.7	42.9	33.7	40.9
Compartamos	Mexico	61.6	39.5	53.7	52.8	48.5	51.2
Los Andes	Bolivia	13.5	14.4	17.5	19.3	12.4	15.4
Mi Banco	Peru	9.4	21.0	26.4	26.6	20.1	20.7
PRODEM	Bolivia	0.7	1.5	8.9	12.0	17.9	8.2
Maximum		61.6	43.9	53.7	52.8	48.5	51.2
Average		19.6	19.2	26.0	26.3	25.5	19.6
Minimum		−6.0	−9.3	1.7	12.0	12.4	8.1

Source: MIX Market (www.themix.org).

has been 19.6 percent, and four MFIs have even generated an average annual ROE of 30 percent and more over the five-year period.

The only MFI that shows negative returns in two years during the period is Banco Solidario from Ecuador.[3] However, these results are mainly due to the aftermath of the deep financial crisis in Ecuador in the late 1990s, and even Banco Solidario shows an average annual ROE of 10.1 percent for the period under consideration. It is even more noteworthy that in the last two years even the MFIs with the "worst" performance of this group generated over 12 percent, and that the smallest average annual ROE over the whole period is still a respectable 8.1 percent.

While the large MFIs cited above have achieved a significant degree of commercial success, not many of the estimated 10 000 microfinance institutions in the world can be regarded as such a good investment. In 2001, only 64 MFIs out of 124 that reported to the Micro Banking Bulletin were fully sustainable financial institutions.[4] A more recent paper published by the German development bank KfW speaks of "approximately 100 to 200 MFIs considered economically viable".[5]

An analysis of the data of 620 MFIs listed on the MIX website confirms the result at least partially: Out of 283 institutions that reported data on their ROE for 2004, 152 MFIs showed ROE higher than 10 percent, some 68 reported ROE between 0 percent and 10 percent, and 63 a negative ROE. Taking into account that the sample is not representative, as most of the more developed and more commercial MFIs are listed on the MIX and provide data of good quality, this would confirm that there were not many more than 220 MFIs in the world that generated a positive ROE in 2004. This means, in other words, for one MFI that has reached a stage of institutional and commercial viability, 50 to 100 other MFIs have not. Therefore, outsiders to the microfinance market require cost-effective mechanisms for screening investments.

Nobody has measured the volume of subsidies that public and social organizations have dedicated towards the building of the microfinance sector.[6] Only the result is clear: A growing number of microfinance institutions offer ever more financial services to the poor, and some of them have now reached full financial self-sufficiency, which means that are ready to operate without subsidies.

Scattered private investment from insiders starting in the late 1990s

Given this evidence of the profitability of many microfinance institutions, it was only a matter of time before private investment came to the sector. In the first years of private investment during the 1990s, however, the private resources devoted to microfinance came from either microfinance or financial market insiders and were usually leveraged by public resources.

The German consulting firm Internationale Projekt Consult (IPC) has played an important role in the commercialization of microfinance. The activities of IPC involve a high degree of commitment and "intervention" in the client institutions, which created some controversy when the organization first became involved in microfinance in countries such as Peru, Bolivia and El Salvador. In the mid-1990s, IPC was commissioned by two of the most influential multilateral organizations – the International Finance Company, IFC, and the European Bank for Reconstruction and Development, EBRD – to participate as a shareholder in the set-up of a microfinance bank in Bosnia Herzegovina. Following the success of IPC's first investment, the company looked to replicate it in other Eastern European countries and founded the investment fund Internationale Micro Investitionen (IMI) in 1998. Initial investors included a public company, the Deutsche Entwicklungsgesellschaft (DEG), two private non-profit organizations (the Dutch Doen Foundation and Pro Crédito from Bolivia), and two commercial investors, IPC itself and IPC Invest GbR, an investment vehicle for IPC employees. Later, IMI was strengthened by the involvement of large investors from the public sector (mainly IFC and KfW) as well as private non-profit investors. Today, IMI has been converted into the Pro Credit Holding, which holds equity stakes in 19 MFIs worldwide.[7]

A second group of private investors includes local banks and finance companies that have been persuaded to "downscale" their activities to serve a microenterprise clientele. Among these are, for example, several Russian banks that participated in the Russian Small Business Fund, a program sponsored by EBRD, and Paraguayan finance companies that participated in the Micro Global scheme sponsored by the Inter-American Development Bank. In both cases, international development agencies offered rediscounting schemes for microloans at market prices and technical assistance in the introduction of product know-how that was free of cost for the participating financial institutions.

Finally, some private commercial institutions from the developed world collaborated with microfinance insiders in the establishment of MFIs in new markets. Particularly remarkable is the experience of Commerzbank, one of the largest commercial banks in Germany, and its joint ventures with IPC/IMI in Eastern and South-East Europe. It should be noted, however, that the main focus of Commerzbank has been the management of more traditional banking products, such as international bank transfers and other services, and not the small business lending, which was managed by IPC staff.

These examples tell the story of the first wave of involvement of private, commercial investors in the microfinance activity. One shared characteristic is that private investment has been limited to insiders from either the microfinance sector or the financial market. Involvement of public resources has almost always been necessary to pave the way for private investors by assuming the set-up cost and start-up risks of the new financial institutions in Eastern Europe or the downscaling efforts of financial institutions. While by the late 1990s, private capital involvement in microfinance had made great steps forward, it was still a long way from reaching mainstream investors from national and international capital markets.

Structured investment opportunities for individual investors

As Marc de Sousa Shields points out in his chapter, "On the big capital playing field, a good ROE is just a start. Domestic and international conventional investors have many other requirements before MFIs become attractive."[8] Conventional private investors, who are not insiders to the microfinance market, require – above all – structured investment vehicles that give them the opportunity to invest into relatively liquid instruments without excessive transaction costs.

Just as international development agencies and non-profit organizations played a major role in the establishment of the first generation of MFIs during the 1980s, they have also been crucial in the development of structured investment opportunities for international capital. In 1995, a group of purely non-commercial investors launched the first specialist microfinance investment fund, Profund. This Panama-based institution was incepted as a closed investment fund with a duration of 10 years. Among its initial investors were non-profit organizations (for example, ACCION International, Calmeadow, FUNDES and SIDI), multilateral organizations (IFC, the Multilateral Investment Fund, MIF, the Andean Development Corporation, CAF, and the Central American Bank for Economic Integration) as well as some bilateral development agencies.

Profund has proven that a specialist investment fund can work as a vehicle for funding MFIs on a profitable basis. According to data from Profund, the fund is expected to have an annualized internal rate of return of between 6 and 7 percent.[9] This has had a significant impact on the integration of microfinance into the worldwide capital markets.

In the wake of Profund, a series of specialty funds have been established, and some older social investment funds (such as Oikocredit and the Calvert Foundation) have dedicated more and more resources towards microfinance. Patrick Goodman recently counted 38 investment funds active in the funding of microfinance.[10] In another recent paper, he has developed a helpful typology of microfinance specialty funds.[11] He classifies them into three categories, according to several characteristics, such as the products proposed and the terms offered to MFIs, the shareholder structure and target investors, the returns offered to investors, and the Fund's involvement in the governance of the MFIs:

- Microfinance Development Funds, which typically put more emphasis on development aspects than on financial return, and offer favorable financing conditions and frequently also subsidized technical assistance.
- Quasi-commercial microfinance investment funds, that usually have clearly defined financial objectives, while maintaining a clear development mission. Goodman categorizes the Pro Credit Holding and Profund as quasi-commercial.
- Commercial microfinance investment funds that mainly target mainstream financial investors. The most important funds in this category include the Dexia Micro-Credit Fund, the responsAbility Global Microfinance Fund, Micro Vest I, the Triodos Fair Share Fund, and Impulse.

Dexia Micro-Credit Fund

The launch of the first commercial microfinance investment fund – the Dexia Micro-Credit Fund – in Luxembourg in 1998, was a qualitatively new step for the microfinance industry. For the first time, private investors had an investment vehicle in microfinance that combined a social return with a potential financial return. The Dexia fund started to grow more rapidly than the donor-sponsored specialty funds, especially after 2000, when BlueOrchard, a Swiss-based microfinance investment adviser company, began to manage it professionally.

In March 2005, the Dexia Micro-Credit Fund had grown to a total asset volume of more than $56.5 million. This corresponds to an average annual growth rate of more than 50 percent. Besides offering investments in US dollars, it started to offer shares in Swiss francs in 2002 and in Euro in 2003. The return on investment has been between 1.64 percent and 6.78 percent in all currencies (see Table 6.2).

Table 6.2 Development of the Dexia Micro-Credit Fund

	31 Dec 2001	31 Dec 2002	31 Dec 2003	31 Dec 2004	30 Mar 2005
Fund assets (US$)	14 000 000			51 669 512	56 538 562
Microfinance portfolio (US$)	11 200 000			46 334 570	46 800 071
Number of active investments	N/A			49	49
Instruments					
Loans and debt securities	94.40%			100.00%	N/D
Guarantees	5.60%			0.00%	N/D
Regions of investment					
Africa	0%			2%	N/D
East Asia and the Pacific	12%			5%	N/D
Eastern Europe/Central Asia	2%			16%	N/D
Latin America/Caribbean	80%			52%	N/D
Middle East/North Africa	0%			3%	N/D
South Asia	6%			4%	N/D
Other	0%			18%	N/D
Return on investment					
USD asset class	6.78%	4.10%	3.21%	3.95%	(YTD) 0.94%
CHF asset class	N/A	1.64%	2.18%	2.74%	(YTD) 0.47%
EUR asset class	N/A	N/A	1.65%	4.40%	(YTD) 0.85%

Source: MIX Market (www.themix.org), BlueOrchard Finance.

The responsAbility Global Microfinance Fund

The responsAbility Global Microfinance Fund was launched in November 2003 as an investment fund under Luxembourg law ("fonds communs de placement") at the initiative of responsAbility Social Investment Services Ltd, Zurich. This company was founded by four Swiss banks and a social venture capital fund. The fund manager is again BlueOrchard, and the promoter is Credit Suisse. The responsAbility Global Microfinance Fund offers investment opportunities for private individuals and places investments between $50 000 and $1.5 million in MFIs or other microfinance investment companies. responsAbility mainly invests in the form of debt with up to five years' maturity at market prices.

The responsAbility Global Microfinance Fund has recently experienced exponential growth. In six months in 2005, the fund grew in assets from $11.4 million to $37.9 million, which accounts for a remarkable annualized growth rate of 462 percent. The Fund plans to allocate an additional $30 million over 2006. The Fund increasingly focuses its investments in two regions: Latin America and Eastern Europe/Central Asia, which currently account for some 92 percent of the portfolio (see Table 6.3).

MicroVest One

MicroVest One is an investment fund that was founded in 2003 as a Delaware Limited Partnership on the initiative of three US-based non-profit organizations – CARE, the Mennonite Economic Development Associates (MEDA) and the Seed Capital Development Fund (SCDF). The fund was conceived with a 10-year life span, which may be extended up to four additional years. MicroVest is the first private microfinance investment firm in the US, and it channels investments from private investors to MFIs worldwide. However, as a limited partnership, the number of MicroVest's shareholders is limited by law, so that the Fund focuses mainly on high net worth individuals.

So far, MicroVest has placed $13.5 million in debt and equity investments with 16 MFIs in nine countries. Initially, the fund focused in Latin America, and more recently it expanded its scope of operations to Asia and Eastern Europe (see Table 6.4).

Triodos Fair Share Fund (TFSF)

The Triodos Fair Share Fund (TFSF) was set up at the initiative of the Dutch Triodos Bank in 2002. Triodos already managed successfully two other microfinance investment funds, Triodos-Doen and Hivos-Triodos, which belong to the category of quasi-commercial investment funds.

Table 6.3 Development of the responsAbility Global Microfinance Fund

	31 Mar 2003	31 Mar 2004	31 Mar 2005	30 Jun 2005	30 Sep 2005
Fund Assets (US$)	3 750 000	N/D	11 449 997	22 704 465	37 877 206
Microfinance portfolio (US$)	1 900 000	N/D	11 449 977	21 991 748	34 619 832
Number of active					
investments	6	N/D	40	59	73
Instruments					
Loans and debt securities	100%	74%	88%	94%	97%
Equity	0%	26%	12%	6%	3%
Regions of investment					
Africa	12%	5%	11%	5%	5%
East Asia and the Pacific	28%	11%	9%	4%	3%
Eastern Europe/Central Asia	11%	21%	39%	59%	52%
Latin America/Caribbean	48%	62%	41%	32%	40%

Source: MIX Market (www.themix.org).

Table 6.4   Development of MicroVest One

	31 Mar 2004	30 Jun 2005
Fund assets (US$)	15 000 000	14 400 000
Microfinance portfolio (US$)	7 700 000	13 500 000
Number of active investments	7	16
Instruments		
Loans and debt securities	100%	89.3%
Equity	0%	10.7%
Regions of investment		
East Asia and the Pacific	0%	15.7%
Eastern Europe/Central Asia	33.0%	36.2%
Latin America/Caribbean	67.0%	42.4%
Other	0%	5.7%

Source: MIX Market (www.themix.org).

Table 6.5   Development of Triodos Fair Share Fund

	31 Dec 2003	31 Dec 2004
Fund assets (US$)	3 708 345	11 073 367
Microfinance portfolio (US$)	1 702 449	6 983 086
Number of active investments	6	11
Instruments		
Loans and debt securities	94%	92%
Equity	6%	8%
Regions of investment		
Africa	0%	10%
East Asia and the Pacific	15%	15%
Eastern Europe/Central Asia	10%	10%
Latin America/Caribbean	75%	65%

Source: MIX Market (www.themix.org).

In contrast to the other two Triodos funds, which are established as foundations, TFSF has the form of a closed mutual fund under Dutch law. TFSF mobilizes funds from Dutch private investors and invests into MFIs in the form of debt and equity, as well as in selected companies that operate under fair trade and organic production schemes. Again, very strong growth rates confirm the viability of commercial investment in microfinance (see Table 6.5).

Other private investment vehicles

Impulse is an investment fund incorporated in 2004 as a private limited company in Belgium. It was established at the initiative of Incofin, a

Belgian cooperative company with a track record of investments in microfinance. At the end of 2004, Impulse had a total asset volume of $6.25 million.

In addition to the above mentioned structured investment opportunities in the form of investment funds, US-based investors also had the opportunity to participate in the funding of the worldwide microfinance industry in the context of the world's first international securitization of MFI portfolios in July 2004. BlueOrchard and Developing World Markets, a US-based investment management company, structured the transaction with a volume of $40 million distributed to nine MFIs in seven countries. The bonds were issued as fixed-rate notes with a seven-year term in three subordinated and one senior debt series. The senior debt is guaranteed by the Overseas Private Investment Corporation (OPIC), a US federal agency. In a second closing under similar terms, but with a lesser degree of OPIC involvement, some $47 million of investor funds was channeled to a total of 14 MFIs in Latin America, Eastern Europe and Southeast Asia. The $87 million of securitizations has been sold to a total of 60 investors, the bulk of which have been commercial institutional investors such as pension funds or mutual funds. However, foundations, individuals and even universities can also be found among the investors.

In parallel to the growth of international investment vehicles, the options for local commercial investors are also growing. While local commercial money in the form of savings has being mobilized in large quantities since the first transitions of MFIs into formal financial institutions, the use of more sophisticated financing mechanisms such as corporate bonds is relatively new.

In July 2002, Compartamos issued bonds in Mexican Pesos for a value of roughly $10 million. The deal was handled by Banamex, the local affiliate of Citigroup, and backed by a Standard & Poor's mxA+ rating. The issue was guaranteed merely by the MFI's financial strength rather than by its loan portfolio. The International Finance Company (IFC) played a crucial role in the issue by assuming the first-loss risk. In Peru, MiBanco issued a $6 million bond.[12] And in Colombia, Fundación WWB Cali was the first non-regulated MFI to issue corporate bonds in 2005. The issue was driven by competitive pressure in the Colombian microfinance market and the need to attract longer-term funding at lower interest rates. WWB Cali was awarded an AA+ credit rating by Duff & Phelps Colombia, reflecting a very high credit quality and a modest risk. Out of the $52 million total bond issue (denominated in Colombian Pesos), $25 million were offered, and $30 million were sold through an over allotment mechanism. Investors included brokers (36 percent), pension funds (32 percent), financial institutions (24 percent), other institutions (7 percent) and individuals (1 percent).[13]

In recent years, microfinance has clearly developed in a direction that increases the potential for involvement of mainstream financial investors, both local and international. Growth rates of commercial international microfinance investment funds are impressive. However, compared with the $15 billion portfolio of MFIs worldwide, the capital provided by the five commercial funds (approximately $108 million), the two successful cross-border securitizations ($87 million) and three local bond issues (for a total of $68 million) mentioned in this chapter still accounts for only a very small proportion of the funding sources of MFIs – less than 2 percent of the total microfinance portfolio.

How far will microfinance go in exploiting the investment potential of local and international high net worth investors, socially responsible investors and institutional investors?

The prospect of full integration of microfinance in the mainstream financial market

In November 2001, Tor Jansson, then a senior microfinance expert at the Inter-American Development Bank, closed a widely recognized paper on the commercialization of microfinance with the following remarks: "Admittedly, it would be an exaggeration to claim that the microfinance industry is knocking on the door of Wall Street at this point. However, it is clearly set on a path leading in that general direction. It may still take many years before the liability/equity side of microfinance institutions is fully integrated in local and international financial markets, but there is little doubt that it is just a question of when, not if."[14] Only four years later, as we have seen, the prospect of MFIs knocking on the doors of Wall Street, the Geneva private capital market or their local stock exchanges is a very realistic scenario.

However, obstacles remain for microfinance to become part of the financial mainstream. There are two important barriers on the side of the MFIs: attitude and size. First, most MFIs are still reluctant to behave as normal businesses that distribute dividends, trade their shares in an anonymous secondary market and are open for mergers and acquisitions under commercial terms. This reluctance, which originates in the high importance MFIs place on institutional mission, does not provide the most appropriate incentive structure for commercial investors, as pointed out by de Sousa in the following chapter.[15]

Secondly, only a few of the specialized microfinance investment funds have reached a size that would allow them to generate economies of scale and provide efficient services to investors. In 2003, Patrick Goodman analysed the size of the specialty investment funds and concluded that, mainly because of their short maturity at that point, very few had reached a volume of more than $20–30 million, which would be considered a minimum size for a viable investment fund.[16] Our more recent data, presented in this chapter, shows that at least the Dexia Micro-Credit Fund and the responsAbility Global Microfinance Fund have already reached larger volumes. However, these volumes may still not be sufficient to attract institutional investors, who need targets of a larger size in order to reach their minimum volumes of investment. Despite these obstacles, several trends are encouraging and suggest a positive outlook for the commercialization of funding sources for microfinance.

On the demand side for capital, the leading MFIs continue to progress towards integration into the financial markets of their respective countries. Upgrading of NGOs to banks, non-bank financial institutions or specialized formal financial institutions, on the one hand, and the downscaling of commercial banks to microfinance, on the other, both point towards a further commercialization of microfinance. It should, however, be clear that only the group of fully commercially viable MFIs will present opportunities for commercial investment, and that many of the 10 000 existing MFIs will remain outside the reach of the commercial investor in the foreseeable future.

As for the requirements of the intermediation chain (as outlined by Mahajan in Chapter 2 of this volume), increasingly structured investment opportunities are becoming available that will work ever more efficiently as they grow and reach economies of scale. Just as MFIs have become gradually more formal with the transformation of NGOs into finance companies and banks, investment funds have graduated from the initial fund structures, which were basically vehicles to pool donor resources, into transparent investment fund structures with clear development and financial objectives, managed by specialized professionals. And just as MFIs are on a path to becoming totally integrated into the financial market of their respective countries, specialty microfinance investment funds will one day be fully integrated into the "big capital" market.

Finally, capital is increasingly interested in microfinance. If more high net worth individuals and, above all, large institutional investors, gain enough confidence in microfinance as an investment opportunity, and public money concentrates on creating the necessary political frameworks and structured investment opportunities, microfinance finally will be fully integrated into the mainstream of financial market activity.

Notes

1 For an in-depth analysis of the early days of microfinance in Bolivia as an outstanding example for the development of a microfinance sector see: E. Rhyne, *Mainstreaming Microfinance: How Lending to the Poor Began, Grew, and Came of Age in Bolivia* (Washington, DC: World Bank, 2001).

2 According to the Micro Banking Bulletin, financial self-sufficiency "measures how well an MFI can cover its costs taking into account a number of adjustments to operating revenues and expenses. The purpose of most of these adjustments is to model how well the MFI could cover its costs if its operations were unsubsidized and it was funding its expansion with commercial-cost liabilities." See: *Micro Banking Bulletin* (November 2002): Issue 8, Focus on Standardization, Washington, DC, p. 10.

3 It is interesting to note that Banco Solidario is the only one of the Latin American MFIs in the sample that was originally designed as a private, for-profit venture.

4 See R.P. Christen and D. Drake, *Commercialization: The New Reality of Microfinance. In: The Commercialization of Microfinance*, eds, D. Drake and E. Rhyne (West Hartford, CT: Kumarian Press, 2002), p. 6.

5 See C. Schneider and H. Hüttenrauch, "Securitisation: A Funding Alternative for Microfinance Institutions?," draft presented at the Financial Sector Conference 2005, "New Partnerships for Innovation in Microfinance", p. 15.

6 To get an impression of the magnitude of the involvement of public money in microfinance, note the figure presented by de Sousa Shields and Frankiewicz that "development institutions (such as multilateral financial institutions, bilateral aid agencies and national development banks) over the past five to ten years have invested between $5 billion and $10 billion in microfinance". See: M. de Sousa Shields and C. Frankiewicz, "Financing Microfinance Institutions – The Context for Transitions to Private Capital", (Washington, DC: USAID – US Agency for International Development, 2004), p. 25.

7 For a history of the foundation of IMI and a discussion of the model of consultants as shareholders see R.H. Schmidt, "The Perspective of Participant Observers – A Brief Account of the History of IPC and IMI from an Institutional Econonomics Perspective", Frankfurt am Main (2004).

8 See Chapter 7 by Marc de Sousa Shields.

9 Data according to Alejandro Silva, Profund's manager, as quoted in P. Goodman, "Raising MFI Equity through Microfinance Investment Funds", paper presented at the KfW Symposium in Frankfurt am Main (2005) p. 9.

10 See P. Goodman, "Microfinance Investment Funds – Key Features", Luxemburg (2005) p. 9.

11 See P. Goodman, "Raising MFI Equity through Microfinance Investment Funds", paper presented at the KfW Symposium in Frankfurt am Main (2005).

12 See S. Fischer, speech held at the Asia Society and Women's World Banking Annual Microfinance Conference in New York (2003).

13 See C. Serra de Akerman, "WWB Colombia Foundation Bond Issue", presentation held at the Geneva Private Capital Symposium in October 2005.

14 T. Jansson, "Microfinance, From Village to Wall Street", Washington DC (2001) p. 18.

15 See Chapter 7 by Marc de Sousa Shields.

16 See P. Goodman, "International Investment Funds: Mobilising Investors towards Microfinance", Luxembourg (ADA, 2003) p. 15. See http://www.microfinance.in/comas/media/fondsiv_endef1%5D.pdf

7

Challenges in the Transition to Private Capital[1]

Marc de Sousa Shields

Introduction

Years ago, Hunter S. Lovins of the Rocky Mountain Institute eloquently persuaded a large gathering of social investors that owning as much capital as possible was key to sustainable development.[2] Socially responsible investment, she said, makes a lot of sense, for only through pooling and investing massive volumes of capital can major social and environmental problems be overcome: "What new drug has been developed without enormous investments; which transit systems have been built on civic good will; and what alternative energy system has not consumed great volumes of capital?" Lovin's axiom unquestionably applies to microfinance: Only big capital can meet a $300 billion dollar challenge (see Majahan's Chapter 2 in this volume for a detailed estimate of the size of the market).

As will be essential to respond to the scale of the challenge, microfinance is in the process of transforming from a sector dominated by a mission-driven ethos to one responding to the needs and interests of private capital. The sector must do this if it is to provide an ever-larger number of poor people with access to financial services. Given the $300 billion demand for microfinance credit products alone, there should be no mistaking the importance of transitioning from a dependence on public money to private capital. Early advances have already been described by Michael Steidl in the previous chapter. This chapter focuses on the challenges that are constraining the growth of private capital investment in microfinance.

Development agency capital, and increasingly MFI specialty fund capital, has in the past and will continue to play a key role in leveraging private capital for MFIs. Leverage comes with a price to sector development

126

as allocation patterns greatly favor larger MFIs (which arguably do not need subsidized capital). It also replaces direct subsidies to MFIs with indirect subsidies, as most specialty funds depend on a variety of subsidies to remain in business. This said, when used wisely, donor and MFI specialty funds remain a critical springboard to commercial capital and are vital to the transition to private capital. This chapter gives an overview of some advances and challenges in this transition to date.

Generating capital from deposits

Deposits are the most abundant and readily available form of private capital available within the financial system in most countries. Savings is the also the most stable and potentially least costly funding source for MFIs. Indeed, savings should – as they have in commercial banks the world over – fuel most long-term MFI portfolio growth.

Unfortunately, the ability to collect savings is one thing, collecting enough to fuel growth another. As Table 7.1 indicates, even many large and successful MFIs – many having long been able to mobilize savings – have yet to reach the ideal deposit to loan funding ratio for small financial institutions (around 90 to 95 percent). Savings mobilization is not easy for MFIs, and is fraught with many challenges, such as lack of appropriate regulations, lack of management capacity, cost of start up, and increasing competition from commercial banks.

A recent MicroBanking Bulletin article noted that few MFIs rely exclusively on savings for portfolio funding.[3] Moreover, those MFIs that do not fund themselves with savings are less likely to be profitable than those

Table 7.1   MFI deposit to loans rates

MFI	Year transformed	Deposits/Loans (%) 2003
BancoSol, Bolivia	1992	78
Caja los Andes, Bolivia	1995	60
Prodem, Bolivia	1992	64
Finamerica, Colombia	1996	26
Banco Ademi, Dom. Republic	1998	5
Banco ProCredito, El Salvador	1995	53
Fincomun, Mexico	1994	24
Nirdhan Utthan, Nepal	1997	26
First Microfinance Bank, Pakistan	2002	596

Source: Anne Miles, MicroBanking Bulleting, Issue 11, September 2005.

that do. This is because MFIs cannot efficiently leverage external borrowing the way they can deposits.

The market for debt

The debt appetite in microfinance is driven, most practically, by pricing. Very often, commercial bank debt is available to MFIs with decent performance, but for pricing reasons few MFIs actually borrow from this source. Instead, they prefer to use retained equity, funding from national development banks, or international specialty MFI funds. There are three primary reasons for this. First, few MFIs have serious liability management strategies to allow them to access the short and long-term advantage of sourcing local commercial bank debt. The calculus is complex because it is necessarily based on a strategy that assumes sourcing local, initially more expensive, funding will ultimately yield lower financing costs. Second, there is just enough development agency capital, particularly from national development banks, to keep MFIs from creating serious private capital networks. This situation continues despite the facts that long-term local capital is virtually unlimited (most national banking systems are seriously over-liquid) and that the "all in" price of development agency is usually about the same as private capital. Finally, because a good and long credit history begets better terms and price, the sooner MFIs establish a diversified range of private sector debt suppliers, the better.

Global demand for external debt will increase even as the number of MFIs allowed to take deposits increases and their capacity to mobilize savings improves. The estimated demand for external debt (that is, non-savings and equity portfolio funding) will top $3 billion by 2009, up from $700 million in 2005 (see Figure 7.1*).

Supply of debt – of any kind – is unevenly available by region. This is particularly true of the "risk tolerant" debt capital that comes from non-commercial sources, such donor agencies (bilateral aid agencies, international financial institutions, foundations, etc.), quasi-commercial MFI specialty investment funds and national development banks.

Access to commercial debt capital is highly limited in most countries. Commercial lenders typically have a poor understanding of microfinance and offer only expensive, short-term and relatively small loans, where larger, longer-term larger loans are required. Moreover, commercial bank lenders, the most common debt providers available in most developing countries, often face reserve requirements that make lending to an MFI prohibitively expensive. This is particularly true in countries where MFIs cannot use their loan portfolio as collateral.

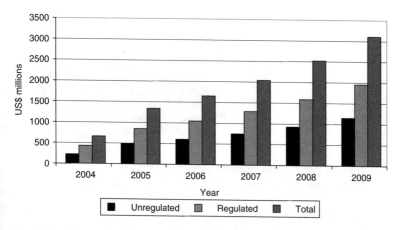

Figure 7.1   Estimated global MFI demand for debt
Note: *Based on assumptions: 30 percent annual growth of loan assets and 5 percent of debt being replaced by savings annually.

Commercial debt is available with strong guarantees – usually 100 percent coverage or more. This has led to interesting, but legally grey, collateral provision practices, as well as a number of interesting guarantee mechanisms. In one eastern African country, for example, MFIs used obligatory savings held in commercial banks to back loans. Others provide savers term deposit promissory notes and on-lend capital to their own portfolios. More promisingly (and legally), MFIs from Peru to Cambodia have used international loans to back local commercial bank loans. Other MFIs have received development agency (for example, USAID Development Credit Authority or International Finance Corporation) guarantees for commercial bank loans, which is initially more complex and costly to organize, but ultimately less expensive used repetitively. In some cases, such as Women's World Banking affiliates in Colombia, guarantees have not only improved access to private capital, but over the long term, decreased the average cost of borrowing, allowed affiliates to diversify sources of capital, and, importantly, increased loan tenor from fairly short terms to medium-length terms.

While several of the most sophisticated MFIs have gone to commercial capital markets for bonds or securitizations, the vast majority of MFIs does not have market credible ratings or are unable to bear the cost of accessing these more complex forms of debt. In almost all issues that have gone to market, a development agency guarantee was required to ensure investment grade ratings. Faulu's Kenya Limited $7 million five-year bond in Kenya had its guarantee from Agence Francaise de Developppment, MiBanco's

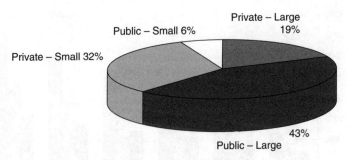

Public = donors, government, government agents etc.

Private = non-public sources which expect commercial rate of return

Figure 7.2   Foreign MFI debt funding
Note: Large MFIs as defined by the MicroBanking Bulletin.

$10 million bond in Peru had a guarantee from Corporacion Andeno de Fomento and IFC. Compartamos successfully went to market with its first $10 million Mexican denominated issue in 2004 without a guarantee, but returned to a broader market in 2005 with IFC guarantees. In many countries, however, regulations are far too restrictive or transaction costs too high relative to the volume of funding available to expect bond issues to fund MFIs.

Despite advances, very few MFIs have cracked commercial debt markets. Only 14 of 159 significant MFI debt deals between April 2005 and April 2006 reported on the MicroFinance Capital Markets Update (MFCM) were private sector deals.[4] Total private deal volume was $111 million with two deals of about $70 million dominating. The average private debt deal was $7.9 million ($4.5 million median), much larger than the average specialty fund and about the same size as development agency deals, which were $900 000 and $4.5 million respectively (see Figure 7.2). Clearly, one key to accessing private capital is the volume of funding required: The greater the volume, the more private sector interest and the lower the transaction costs.

This means that in the interim period, while there are many small MFIs growing to become larger MFIs, private capital markets will continue have selective interest in the sector. One conclusion is that specialty microfinance funds, like Triodos-Doen, BlueOrchard, responsAbility Global Microfinance Fund and others, are important to the transition to private capital. Their value, however, will be judged less for the volume of capital they supply (which is an estimated 10 percent of demand worldwide) than for their willingness and ability to lend where private capital is not yet interested.

These funds have relatively high-risk tolerances, can lend for longer terms and often require low or no collateral. The demonstration effect – that MFIs can pay near or at market rates for funding – to private capital may, ultimately, be the most important impact of the specialty funds.

There are about 20 or so highly active specialty funds in the market worldwide. Their number is growing, as is the amount of funding they can access. BlueOrchard Finance of Geneva, which lends exclusively to MFIs, is on target to manage over $300 million by the end of 2006. The Zurich-based responsAbility fund will likely top $75 million by the same period. Some funds such as Triodos Fair Share and NOVIB (both of the Netherlands) are also growing quickly, thanks in part to tax incentives provided by the Dutch government. As a result of this rapid growth, reported annual disbursements from specialty funds topped $165 million in the period April 2005 to 2006. An estimated $75 to $100 million in disbursements likely came from other funds for a total of at least $250 million of funding.[5]

Unfortunately, less than 20 percent of funding for specialty funds is from private sources; and that which is from private sources comes subsidized by the investor or government (as noted above). The Calvert Foundation of the USA and Oikocredit of the Netherlands, for example, both require investors to accept interest rates on their investments which are below risk-adjusted market rates (between 0 and 3 percent). Few institutional investors who control literally unlimited funding are able to subsidize investment (save funding from charitable divisions), and as a result, very little of this kind of capital has made its way to MFIs. This, too, however, is slowly changing. BlueOrchard's securitization packages have attracted a modest amount of institutional funding. Other lenders such as PlaNet Finance have also attracted large institutional funds, in this case from Société Général.

Regardless of where the funding comes from, the bulk of it continues to go to larger, more mature institutions. In the 159 deals noted above in 2005–6, the total investment was $277 million from all sources. Of this, 38 deals of over $1 million accounted for over $162 million or 59 percent of the total. Normally an institution with under $5 million in portfolio assets (a large MFI by industry standards) cannot absorb a loan of $1 million: Obviously, larger institutions are receiving the bulk of MFI funding from friendly sources. This corresponds with findings of a 2004 survey by the Consultative Group to Assist the Poorest (CGAP), which showed 62 percent of all foreign funding going to larger MFIs (see Figure 7.2).

There are other reasons most new money will likely go to the top MFIs. Specialty funds typically promise commercial returns to stakeholders and investors, translating into rates that many MFIs (small and large alike) are unwilling or unable to pay. Layered over growing competition, price and term pressures from international financial institutions continue to distort loan markets negatively in some regions with generous terms or pricing. Moreover, it is the large, transformed, profit-focused institutions that are able to absorb larger volumes of capital. As noted, lending larger volumes is more cost effective to lenders, and thus, with the exception of Oikocredit, responsAbility, and RaboBank Foundation, most investors find only the larger MFIs suitable targets.

Equity challenges

Private investors control fewer than 3 percent to 5 percent of all shares of the top 10 specialty MFIs in the world. There has been a good deal of private equity invested in MFIs around the world through specialty MFI investment funds such as Oikocredit, Triodos Doen, ShorCap, and multi-laterals such as FMO and IFC, but much of this is subsidized or comes from development agencies (an estimated 80 percent). Development agency capital should be thought of as the high risk, early stage investment capital for microfinance. Be it in the form of technical assistance, straight equity, or portfolio grants, development agencies are the "venture capitalists" – a highly significant role both in the creation of the microfinance movement and in the integration of microfinance products and services into the formal financial sector. This gives development agencies a very important role in the growth, creation and even sale of MFIs.

However, development agency "venture" capital is available and used at all stages of an MFI's life. Some MFIs use it even when they can access all the private capital they need. A recent CGAP survey, for example, found a majority of MFIs – many of which are profitable, regulated deposit institutions – still believe that development agency capital is the most appropriate form of capital. Whether this belief has any bearing on donor capital allocation decisions is arguable, but the pattern of distribution is clear: The sector's high risk capital continues to be concentrated in a few large MFIs. Available capital is concentrated at one end of the MFI life cycle, serving mature institutions to the great detriment of institutions that still need "risk" capital, or those in areas where capital is simply not available and/or where microfinance products still struggle for profitability (for example, rural areas).

Such investments send the sector the wrong signal. Mature institutions are not encouraged to forge private capital ties, because development agency capital is easily available. They also foul pricing signals to a range of fund suppliers, including international specialty funds, which can be crowded out of the market by lower-cost development agency capital. More dangerously, and as previously noted, the sum of all MFI "non-private sector" investments dampens normal market development dynamics, and has led to the thinking that creating a sector full of large financial institutions is the goal, as opposed to helping to catalyse new, fast growing MFIs that can be sold to larger financial institutions who will rapidly expand market penetration rates.

NGOs and development agency donors are motivated to protect the social mission of the institutions, but sometimes their continuing involvement with the sector conflicts with the mission of providing services to a massively larger market. Selling shares to a larger, more capable, institution intuitively makes sense if the goal is truly to increase financial services to the poor. If the restless drive of venture capital to maximize investment and move on to other opportunities is absent, both the institution and the "sector" suffer.

There is a relatively strong demand for new equity, either to meet regulations or to fund growth. The search for equity is often complex, due to the issues described above. As we have seen, some MFIs still reject private investors as "unsuitable".[6] At the same time, many MFIs that would be interesting to private investors go unnoticed or are disregarded because of the generally insular nature of microfinance. This is true despite some attractive ROEs which range between 10 percent and 50 percent annually for rapid growth MFIs (although the MicroBanking Bulletin average ROE is much lower – see Table 7.2). That MFIs seldom have long dividend histories or any share liquidity further decreases private capital interest.

At the international level, there is some interest and funding available for MFI investment from investors that MFIs do consider suitable. These

Table 7.2 Performance of for-profit vs. non-profit MFIs, in percent

Year	Adjusted return on assets	Adjusted return on equity
2003		
Not-for-profit	−0.3	0.5
For-profit	0.4	6.3
2001		
Not-for-profit	−6.4	−23.3
For-profit	−1.0	−2.3

Source: MicroBanking Bulletin, Issue 9, July 2003, and MicroBanking Bulletin, Issue 7, November 2001.

investors are the specialty funds noted above and some international financial institutions, primarily the IFC. International investors, however, are challenged by high transaction costs on relatively small deals. Like debt, deals tend to favor larger institutions (see Figure 7.3). The average deal reported in the MFCM during April 2005 and 2006, for example, was just under $1 million, with a median deal of around $800 000. With few prospects of dividends and uncertain exits, this makes monitoring and servicing investments very difficult, not only for their individual size, but also because with the exception of Oikocredit, specialty funds lack sufficient scale of operations to fund operations without large debt portfolios generating income.[7]

Local investors are also few in number, due to the same considerations affecting foreign investors and also some unique reasons. Local private investors ask a host of questions even before assessing liquidity and dividend questions. The first is: What is microfinance anyhow? The second: Are the poor really a reasonable credit risk? Market, regulatory, and growth questions – all commonly understood and answered by microfinance experts but typically unfamiliar to local investors – follow. Developing country capitalists are also highly wary of social activist NGOs as co-owners (owners who typically have control of majority shares). Like most investors, local investors tend to invest in things they know, such as local real estate, government bonds, international stock markets, or in their own businesses. Finally, most local private investors like to have majority control, something most MFIs, afraid of mission drift, or new ownership MFIs from low-income markets, are likely to be unable to grant. Underdeveloped share pricing and a paucity of deal experience makes equity investments all the more difficult.

The result of these challenges is that many MFIs remain owned by NGOs with some minority participation by specialty funds. Only about 10 percent of all MFI shares are estimated to be owned by pure private money. This is not the case in all countries and increasingly, albeit

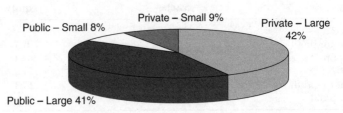

Figure 7.3   Foreign MFI equity funding
Note: Large MFIs as defined by the MicroBanking Bulletin.

slowly, the trend is toward private ownership. In Peru, for example, many of the *cajas rurales* are owned by purely private interests. Rural banks in the Philippines are typically owned by families. Indeed, there are limited examples of commercial bank ownership of MFIs around the world. Private ownership is increasing too. Of the 30 deals reported in the MFCM Update between April 2005 and April 2006, nine involved some private capital, for a total of $43 million. This compares with $17 million invested by specialty funds in 20 deals.

Again, the importance of specialty fund equity contrasts with its extremely limited availability – estimated at less than $20 million annually. With demand from the top 100 or so MFIs above $100 million in 2005, and forecast to be $250 million in 2009, there appears to be very limited suitable equity capital available to most MFIs. Clearly, investors are needed.

Challenging attitudes

Despite much "integration" rhetoric, MFIs remain, to varying degrees, outside the formal financial sector due to their social development origins, which have historically failed to inspire the confidence of private capital. The continued intervention of development agencies, support NGOs, foundations and the like, while essential at some level, reinforces the social movement image of microfinance for those unfamiliar with the commercial viability of microfinance products and services. So, even though NGO-born MFIs have proved the microfinance business case, much private financial capital continues to view the low-income market as "unbankable".

The best performing MFIs provide near venture capital returns at risk levels far below that of conventional venture capital. On the big capital playing field, however, a good ROE is just a start. There are many other requirements that must be met before MFIs become attractive to conventional investors. Institutional investors looking to place debt, for example, need cost-effective and somewhat liquid instruments such as bonds or securitizations. Unfortunately, few MFIs have managed to achieve the commercial ratings required by institutional investors. This limits MFIs pretty much to private investors for equity and commercial banks for debt.

Turning to equity we see a challenge that is at once more simple and more complex. It is a simple problem because few NGO MFIs are for sale or selling shares. It is complex because the few that are, tend only to want to sell to "suitable investors", or those with a demonstrated affinity to poverty alleviation. This complicates matters greatly because the numbers of such investors in developing countries are few, to say the least.

Even if more MFIs were selling, there are a number of disincentives for private investors to invest. Foremost among them, is that most NGO-born MFIs guard their majority positions and are not willing to sell volumes of shares approaching super minority, let alone majority. By contrast, most developing country investors tend to prefer majority control. Once bought, MFIs shares are particularly illiquid. Even when placed on domestic stock exchanges, shares seldom trade hands – witness the single movement of BancoSol shares on the Bolivian stock exchange over the last five years or so. Like most investors, private investors want the option of moving capital from one investment to another as competing offers arise. MFI investments historically have not responded to this need. Liquidity is complicated by a tendency among MFIs not to pay dividends. Private investors prefer to be compensated for the risk their capital takes and are naturally wary of owners that restrict income and share liquidity.

Commercial banks as owners of MFIs, or as providers of microfinance products and services, are more promising. According to a recent CGAP survey there are some 200 commercial banks with significant involvement in microfinance. Many of these are transformed NGO MFIs, but some are private commercial banks or non-bank financial service providers. But as recent research shows, commercial bank participation is still quite limited, either as wholesalers of capital to MFIs or as providers themselves. The trouble is, most commercial banks that offer or want to offer microfinance products have had to develop their own products and services, an unfortunately inefficient and often ineffective strategy. Corporate culture and traditional commercial corporate client markets make it difficult for commercial banks to downscale to microfinance.

In conventional, profit-oriented markets, large commercial businesses simply buy smaller innovative companies. They are bought for a variety of reasons – their innovative nature, their market intelligence, new market penetration potential or the things bigger businesses often have difficulty doing well on their own. It is very often a successful strategy. Consider the power of HSBC buying Compartamos in Mexico, the outcome of a merger between EBS and Centenary in Eastern Africa, or all *cajas rurales* in Peru forming a single business.

Commercial bankers should not be condemned for their conservative worldview and it may be too much to expect them to charge head-on into a still relatively small market. But other owners of capital exist. Wealthy entrepreneurs, established commercial groups, and family business owners have all shown interest or have invested in microfinance – albeit in a limited way, but enough to understand that microfinance institutions represent an investment option for private capital in emerging markets.

Unfortunately, the same barriers to investment noted above apply. They are exacerbated by a market dynamic that does not attract investors, despite the fact that the market for buying MFI shares has the characteristics of new, innovative fields that should attract investment. For myriad reasons, a rationalized process governing the buying and selling of MFI shares simply does not exist. In developing countries, for example, businesses are not bought and sold as a matter of course, as they are in developed countries. As a result, the regulations, pricing and transfer experience necessary for the sale of shares in any business, let alone in the highly regulated financial sector, is not widespread. As noted earlier, too, the single largest barrier to the buying and selling of institutions may be the reluctance of microfinance leaders born of social development roots to sell to anyone but a very small world of established development investors. This is a shame because a more dynamic market leads to more competition, client-driven products and services, lower prices, and greater market penetration.

If the goal is to serve billions, not merely millions, the idea of "proving the product" remains strategically sound, but proof is insufficient if private capital cannot easily move into the marketplace. Given the volume of capital required and the need for dynamic and competitive markets, the creation of an alternative sector with specialized institutions is a short-term strategy: In the long term, integrating microfinance products and services into the formal financial sector should be the goal.

Conclusions

The transition to private capital in microfinance is evolving, albeit at a slower pace than many expected. This is particularly true of deposits, but also of debt, where international supply is growing quickly but is still not equal to more than a modest fraction of demand. In equity, MFIs have defined a very small possible universe of suitable investors. At the same time, most investors remain typically uninformed and or wary of investments that have not historically returned cash to investors.

As a result, local investors certainly are not stepping forward in the numbers required, and specialty funds, and to a lesser extent development agencies, remain critical players in the transition to private capital. A key part of their work is to conscientiously aid MFIs in expanding their notion of suitable investors, keep MFIs focused on low-income markets and exit strategically from their investments. This will take some work because even while the need for and capacity to mobilize private funding has dramatically increased among all MFIs, almost 70 percent of over

100 leading MFIs still believe donor capital is the most appropriate form of investment for them to receive.

Notes

1   Some of the findings in this chapter have been inspired by work undertaken by Enterprising Solutions for clients, including the United States International Development Agency, the Ford Foundation, the International Development Research Centre (Canada), Triodos International Fund Management, and many others. The opinions in this chapter and any errors or omissions remain those of the author.
2   See P. Hawkins, A. Lovins and L. Hunter Lovins, *Natural Capitalism: Creating the Next Industrial Revolution* (New York: Little, Brown and Company, 1999).
3   B. Stephens, "Bulletin Highlights – Microfinance Institutions", *MicroBanking Bulletin,* 11, published by the Mix Market available at www.themixmbb.org.
4   It should be noted that not all deals are reported in the MFCM and that there may be a bias towards MFIs specialty fund reporting over private sector funding. This said, at least three larger such specialty funds do not consistently report. On balance, we believe that findings are order of magnitude (percentage and absolute) indicative of deal flow within the sector.
5   Importantly, too, most international lenders have underdeveloped currency protection and have yet to weather significant economic or financial system crisis.
6   This phrase was coined by Elisabeth Rhyne of ACCION International.
7   Common wisdom estimates that a fund of $60 million approaches operational self-sufficiency. Only three funds have this scale and only two do equity.

8
A Real Business Case on its Way

Michael Hölz

The Business Case: Microfinance in the spotlight

Microfinance is generally regarded as facilitating access to capital for micro-entrepreneurs worldwide. Microfinance has been shown to be a highly effective tool in combating poverty. Providing access to capital for micro-entrepreneurs via in-country intermediaries (microfinance institutions) can lift entire families out of poverty, break cycles of dependency and transform local communities.

The long-term success of microfinance is not least due to the fact that it offers a good risk–return profile to banks and investors. Industry growth is estimated at between 25 percent and 30 percent.[1] In addition, McKinsey & Co. projects that the total borrowing needs of 20 percent of the target market (or double the current market served) will exceed $9 billion. Additionally, many microfinance institutions are successful business organizations in their own right, frequently boasting returns on equity on excess of 30 percent and returns on assets over 10 percent. Finally, microfinance institutions boast historically low delinquency rates. Using PAR 90 as a benchmark for defaults, MFIs experience default rates of around 1.5 percent,[2] which compare favorably with a 4 percent default rate for US "A" rated issuers[3] and a rate of 5.3 percent for US high-yield issuers (also known as "junk bonds").[4]

Deutsche Bank aims to broaden the scope of people who understand the benefits of microfinance as it is felt that it is not enough to engage only those who are already involved in microfinance. It is more important to bring the message to those not yet included: Charity usually comes to an end while business as a matter of fact is infinite – these are the teachings of Muhammad Yunus, who first developed the concept of microcredits and founded the Grameen Bank.

Deutsche Bank embraces microfinance as a specialized investment banking business with the dual objective of profitability and social return. The goal of Deutsche Bank's global efforts and activities in the field of microfinance includes introducing microfinance as an investible asset class to private and public interest groups as well as educating the general public of the Business Case for microfinance. Deutsche Bank ultimately aims to demonstrate the industry's potential for both investment profitability and poverty reduction through a business-like approach. In doing so, Deutsche Bank actively supports the Millennium Development Goals worked out by the United Nations in fighting poverty. The critical endeavor is to integrate private money in addition to public money, thus amplifying the amount of financial resources.

Currently the most successful banks are those that have proved themselves agile in periods of change. Given the momentum behind microfinance as a tool for sustainable and ultimately profitable poverty alleviation, now is the perfect time to put the subject "investing private capital in micro- and small business finance" on the bank's agenda. This, in turn, will create real business opportunities for Deutsche Bank and at the same time show that the bank is a leader in promoting sustainable banking practices that generate long-term poverty alleviation opportunities.

Deutsche Bank can harness the full potential of microfinance by building and deepening connections between private banking and microfinance institutions. In so doing the Bank will be strengthening microfinance as the vehicle that provides access to capital for the working poor, thereby channeling money into markets which lack financial means, and at the same time generate good profits.

Microfinance and risk management: New dimensions and well-known risks

But why has microfinance not won the recognition it deserves within the private sector so far? Why has microfinance not yet reached the point of being truly acknowledged as a Business Case?

One explanation might be the risks inherent in microfinance. Generally, there are primarily four risk categories in the finance area, which need to be managed and kept in mind when evaluating the business case of microfinance:

- Traditional credit risks.
- Industry risks which are connected to the microfinance market.
- Country related risks.
- Foreign exchange risks.

First of all, there are the rather traditional credit risks (common in every kind of credit business managed and handled at banks).

The industry risks are connected to the microfinance market as well. These depend on the different regions although there is much evidence to suggest that the microfinance industry is contra-systemic. As such, MFI portfolios have shown promising signs of resilience in the face of economic turmoil in the wider economies in which they operate. For example, leading Indonesian MFI Bank Rakyat's PAR 30 peaked at only 6.08 percent during the Asian financial crisis in the mid-1990s.[5]

The third risk category, the country-related risks, consists of political, financial, economical and infrastructural risk components and seems to be inherent in the emerging markets and developing countries, with the caveat that there is evidence, as described above, that microfinance institutions outperform the national economy during periods of turmoil.

This inevitably entails the fourth category: the foreign exchange risk. The currency risk is probably the main reason – a powerful scaremonger – for people to hold back from investing sufficient amounts of money in these markets. Changing currency back and forth imports the risk of sudden exchange losses.

As a player in the international banking arena, Deutsche Bank has to handle all four risk categories, using innovative processes to integrate and manage loans. Since microfinance has a rather different background, it is important to adjust the international risk management structures to the requisites of microfinance in order to master it. One approach is to combine the knowledge of local retail banks with the expertise of international investment banks. Non-governmental organizations and microfinance institutions complement the commercial banks.

Deutsche Bank strongly believes that the time is right to open this investment opportunity to individuals to invest private capital and to come up with new models to accrue private money in this market. The greatest challenges are to develop strategies to avoid the aforementioned risks, to create new means and models of investment.

An important element to keep in mind is that opportunities and profits outweigh the risk factors by far.

Act in concert: NGOs and commercial banks – Improving the relationship between all parties

Historically, the idea of the founders of microfinance was to exclude commercial banks from planning, implementing and finally doing business. However, in order to improve their funding and financial means, many powerful microfinance institutions decided over time to work more closely with commercial banks. Even though the organizations at the grassroots still oppose this cooperation, it is demonstrably clear that the financial sector looks back on decades of investing mostly public money into the sector of microfinance: Investments were usually made from public money; supported by governments, supported by non-government organizations. This is not enough by far. By degrees, the microfinance institutions and NGOs started to consider cooperation with commercial banks. And it appears that they match.

The overall goal is not only to improve funding, but also to foster the institution as a whole. Building microfinance institutions and strengthening them is an important factor in the development of the Business Case. Effective, goal-oriented teamwork is an essential feature for the rising recognition and success of the microfinance institutions. Commercial banks tend to further the cooperation with the traditional microfinance institutions, which in some cases still oppose the collaboration with the international banks. If we want to go far, teamwork is vital.

Another factor is management knowledge – the management skills are being increased by cooperating with each other. Looking at the situation objectively, it is a typical win–win situation for all partners.

A real sustainable Business Case: Best practice, benchmark and challenges

Sustainability, the triad of environmental, social and economical aspects, is what Deutsche Bank subscribes to. The Business Case for microfinance belongs right in this category. Microfinance involves a long-term commitment; the duration of an investment usually lies between five and eight years. This commitment increases the chances of development for the poorest of the poor in society and safeguards opportunities for them.

The paradigm is also a guideline for positive development and behavior of Deutsche Bank's management. This again plays into the way and style in which microfinance is managed by Deutsche Bank. It is a great challenge, per se for Deutsche Bank but generally for commercial banks. New concepts, new ideas and new ways of handling need to be invented.

Microfinance is at the same time a best practice example, the best documentation of sustainability: Small amounts of money are lent over a long period of time to ensure a livelihood to whole families in the developing and emerging markets countries. People in those areas often need only a few dollars to establish their own businesses – this shows what microfinance really is: The opportunity for financially deprived people to help themselves. This resonates with Deutsche Bank's thinking on sustainability.

Nevertheless, the idea of integrating microfinance/investing private capital into the common bank business has not yet reached the mainstream. We believe in microfinance, not only because it is a Business Case which has the potential to generate rates and returns as high as – or even higher than – many of the traditional banks and financial institutions. At the same time, Deutsche Bank is certain that microfinance is a seminal concept, which will improve over time when everybody – commercial banks and microfinance institutions – act sufficiently and efficiently together.

Concluding statement: Management summary

The idea of microfinance has to be anchored in the daily banking workflow – with emphasis on the returns yielded by such investments. We are facing – or are already in the midst of – this period of opportunity, and only those who are actively taking part in these modifications help to improve the situations of many individuals while making profitable business, thus staying ahead in the race. Simultaneously we have to concentrate on ensuring that the idea is finally established within the mindset of investors – and this has to happen on an international basis.

Microfinancing and Deutsche Bank

A revolutionary force in fighting poverty: The pioneering Deutsche Bank Microfinance Funds provide capital to microfinance institutions, which make very small loans to the self-employed poor across the globe to make their businesses grow:

- **Deutsche Bank Microcredit Development Fund**
  As of 31 December 2005, the Deutsche Bank Microcredit Development Fund had an outstanding portfolio of $2.98 million, lending to 27 MFIs who serve more than 1.6 million clients worldwide. Since inception, the DB MDF has invested $4.2 million in loans to 40 microfinance institutions (MFIs) in 25 countries with a cumulative impact of approximately $55 million.
- **Global Commercial Microfinance Consortium**
  In 2005 the Global Commercial Microfinance Consortium was the landmark of our social accomplishments: A groundbreaking $80 million multi-tiered commercial fund that

provides local currency financing for up to five years to Microfinance institutions globally.

"This Consortium is an example of how working together, we can more effectively provide economic empowerment for poor communities, and it's a great example of the concrete action inspired by the Clinton Global Initiative," said former President William Jefferson Clinton, who spoke at the fund's closing ceremony in New York. "We need to give people in the developing world access to markets and the chance to provide for themselves. Microfinance programs like this one are vital to our common goal of alleviating global poverty."

Sustainable development projects that help poor communities prosper are a cornerstone of our corporate citizenship activities. In a year that the United Nations has designated the International Year of Microcredit and in response to the most devastating natural disaster known to man, Deutsche Bank pledges to continue and expand its innovative work in the field of microfinance.

Notes

1 S. Daley-Harris et al., *State of the Microcredit Summit Campaign Report 2002* Microcredit Summit Campaign, Washington, D.C. (2002).
2 Average data for complete sample size of 124 MFIs are reported in the *MicroBanking Bulletin*, Issue 9 (July 2003).
3 *Moody's Corporate Bond Defaults*, 1970–1992.
4 Data are for high-yield or so-called "junk bonds" monitored by *Standard and Poors* for the period 1981–2003, as reported by Reuters news agency on 7 June, 2004.
5 Deborah Drake and Elisabeth Rhyne, *The Commercialization of Microfinance* (Bloomfield, CT: Kumarian Press, 2002), p. 9.

Part IV
Structural Factors in Microfinance

Previous Parts established the substantial need for private capital in microfinance, matched by an increasing appetite within private capital for microfinance. We would therefore expect to see private capital continuing to flow into the sector and, as it does so, continuous changes in the industry. What will remain intact is the core purpose of microfinance, providing financial services to the less privileged. Microfinance will therefore continue to play a critical role in helping countries build the inclusive financial sectors that are fundamental to economic growth. In this part, Kathryn Imboden highlights the importance of financial inclusion, sets out a vision of an inclusive financial sector – independent of national differences – and describes the key considerations for designing a sound policy environment.

9
Building Inclusive Financial Sectors for Development: The Policy Framework*

Kathryn Imboden

Introduction

In most countries of the world, financial services are available only to a small percentage of the population and the vast majority of "bankable"[1] people in the world do not yet have access to financial services. While financial sectors are expanding in terms of growth of financial assets, these assets are concentrated in the hands of a few. Various constraints hamper or block the inclusion of different population groups needing access to financial services, notably women.

Yet we know that access to well functioning and efficient financial services can empower individuals economically and socially, allowing them to better integrate into the country's economy and actively contribute to economic growth. Heads of state and government, meeting in September 2005 at the World Summit at the United Nations, concluded that this is a problem warranting greater attention: "We recognize the need for access to financial services, in particular for the poor, including through microfinance and microcredit" (United Nations, 2005, paragraph 23i).

The potential of domestic financial markets as drivers of growth and of poverty reduction over the long term is demonstrated. There is a compelling case, and urgent need, for looking at financial sector development differently, placing greater value and emphasis on the access to financial services by poor households and enterprises. In this context, microfinance, often treated as a social measure, distinct from the mainstream financial sectors, needs to be taken out of a microfinance "ghetto" and become fully integrated into the financial sector in attitudes, mindsets and financial transactions. This requires vision, establishing the necessary preconditions, tackling constraints at multiple levels, assuring a favorable policy environment, and forging partnerships across the range of domestic and international financial sector stakeholders.

An "inclusive" financial sector would provide access to every woman and man in each of these main customer groups. An inclusive financial sector does not require everyone to use these services, but it does require that people should be able to use them if desired. This chapter addresses the importance of financial inclusion, lays out a vision of an inclusive financial sector and proposes a set of key issues for consideration in establishing a sound policy environment.

The starting point for discussion

Mainstream for-profit financial institutions have largely ignored the lower segment of the market, which includes small and medium-sized enterprises (SMEs) – often called the "missing middle" – as well as the smallest micro-entrepreneurs and poorest households. Governments and civil society organizations in both developed and developing countries have long sought to overcome this condition and broaden access to financial services. Government-owned banks and postal banks extended financial services to under-served populations.

Worldwide, important initiatives took place outside the government sector such as savings and credit societies and credit unions. Microfinance operations in many developing countries emerged more recently and focused specifically on providing financial services to poor and low-income people. Commercial financial institutions have begun to provide certain services to this market and some banks have opened full-service microfinance operations. Most developing countries have a range of these retail financial service providers with different ownership structures and legal charters that provide financial services to a portion of the low-income strata of the population.

Taking all the institutions together there is evidence that financial services are being supplied to a large number of people, but only a fraction of the target population for inclusive finance. Estimates from available data suggest that several hundred million people have savings accounts in the developing world and that over 100 million people are borrowers from an alternative financial institution of some sort that serves the poor, as shown in Figure 9.1. State-owned institutions have a dominant role, which reflects the fact that over half the accounts and loans in the figure are for customers in two countries with large state activities in financial services, China and India (which also account for over half the world's poor people).

Another striking feature that can be seen in the figure is the significance of microfinance institutions or MFIs. Unlike the state financial

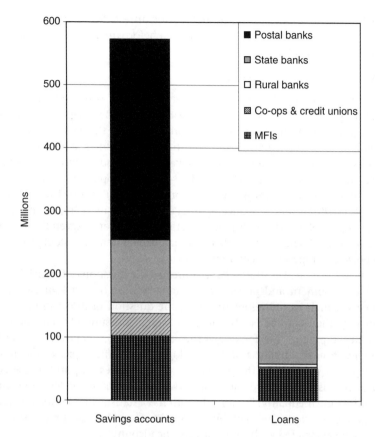

Figure 9.1 Alternative financial institution activity in developing countries
Source: Data (includes economies in transition) from CGAP (2004).

institutions, MFIs barcly existed 20 years ago. The Microcredit Summit Campaign reported that at the end of 2003, there were 2813 MFIs in developing countries serving over 80 million clients, of whom almost 55 million were classified as among the "poorest" people, of which 45 million were women.[2]

Despite these service levels, the number of people who do not use formal financial services is very large. Six percent or more of the population is estimated to have used credit from some alternative financial institution in only five of 119 countries on which data were collected;[3] over 70 countries had less than one percent coverage.[4] The situation is somewhat better on the savings side, where deposits in alternative institutions were held by over 8 percent of the population in a third of the countries. Clearly, much work has to be undertaken before financial sectors can be called "inclusive".

Why inclusive finance matters

There is substantial evidence that financial sector deepening and economic growth are mutually reinforcing. Several excellent papers describing the empirical studies that have been produced over the years lay out this evidence in a convincing way.[5] The studies underline the bi-directional linkages between financial sector development and growth. The more recent studies confirm that financial sector development exerts a large positive effect on economic growth, one in particular showing that the impact of financial sector development on growth is more important than the impact of growth on financial sector development.[6] Overall, there is increasing evidence that an efficient broad-based financial system provides a powerful impetus for economic growth.[7]

In addition, newer studies have addressed the question of financial sector development and poverty reduction. Because of a lack of data on access, which would allow analysing the question of direct impact on poverty, these studies use the more traditional measures of financial sector development, thus looking at the indirect impact on poverty. Recent studies show that financial sector development benefits disproportionately the poorer segments of the population. These studies support the theory that there is a negative relationship between financial sector development and income inequality: "financial depth has a statistically significant and negative association with income inequality"[8] and "deeper financial systems are associated with lower poverty headcount".[9]

Additionally, financial systems could do even better in helping overcome poverty through direct interaction with the poor. Microfinance – safe savings, different types of loans, and other financial services to poor people – is an effective way of helping poor people help themselves build income and assets, manage risk, and try to work their way out of poverty. Access to financial services increases incomes and helps build assets, thus meeting the needs of a much greater proportion of a country's population. For the poor, access to financial services means not only increased production, but also protection as the financial sector serves as a cushion in times of crisis. There is clear value in promoting inclusion, whose relative value (direct access as opposed to financial sector development overall) depends on the country context.

In sum, more developed domestic markets fuelled by domestic savings reach out more over time to the poorer segments of the population, or to those segments of the economy, which in turn most affect the lives of the poor.

A vision of inclusive finance

A vision of inclusive finance can be widely shared, while appreciating that the variety of approaches, the richness of diverse experiences and the policies of countries will differ. The vision begins with a goal: Each country has a set of financial institutions that, together, offer appropriate services to all segments of the population. This is characterized by:

a) Access of all bankable households and enterprises to a full range of financial services, including savings, short and long-term credit, mortgages, insurance, pensions, payments, local money transfers, international remittances, leasing and factoring.
b) Soundness of institutions through performance monitoring by stakeholders and, where required, sound prudential regulation.
c) Financial and institutional sustainability as a means of providing access to financial services over time.
d) Multiple providers of financial services, wherever feasible, to bring cost-effective alternatives to customers, including any number of sound private, non-profit and public providers.

To achieve this goal, financial services for poor and low-income people are viewed as an important and integral component of the financial sector and as an emerging business across institutional models. Inclusive finance should be part of any financial sector development strategy.

A number of other conditions complement this vision. First, the individual in his or her society should enjoy the right to fair treatment. This requires policies and practices that do not tolerate discrimination by gender, ethnicity or other characteristics that should be seen as irrelevant. It requires protection of customers' rights and enforcement of that protection, recognizing that financial market abuses of customers have been common. Promoting financial literacy increases awareness of the opportunities and the dangers of using financial services. Financial literacy increases access as well as the ability of clients to get the financial services they need on appropriate terms.

Second, historically some government or civic intervention has typically been required to foster organizations that open access to poor and low-income people. The variety of legal models for financial institutions of different sizes and forms requires recognition. Diversity can be accommodated, as sound private, non-profit and public financial service providers may very well coexist in competitive economies. Public/private partnerships are also possible.

Third, financial policy interventions, like those for every other sector, should be transparent. These measures should be adopted as conscious policy, whether they provide incentives or remove disincentives. Subsidies and fiscal incentives should find transparent expression in annual government budgets, where they may be judged against alternative uses of public funds. Policy should be the result of informed domestic debate among stakeholders. It should be openly monitored against commitments and revised as the need becomes apparent.

Fourth, other broad policy factors affect financial inclusiveness. Public sector governance and the proper functioning of the legal system are pre-conditions. Macroeconomic stability and pro-poor growth policies, including public expenditure programs supporting physical infrastructure and investments in education, health and nutrition, and adequate personal security, underpin inclusive financial sector development. Competition policies frame the degree of openness of the economy.

Finally, the dynamic and eclectic reality of financial sector development needs to be appreciated. New forms of service provision regularly emerge from technological and financial innovation. A strategy for building inclusive financial sectors should welcome them, especially when they hold out the promise of further breaking down the impediments to access to financial services of under-served people. Regulation and supervision of financial institutions should make room for financial entrepreneurs to innovate to enhance access, so long as it does not impede the fundamental imperatives of financial institution soundness and financial sector stability. Policy makers and the financial industry should be alert to changing opportunities and constraints. In other words, the vision requires being open to progress.

In many countries, a change in attitudes of official and private stakeholders may be required, along with a greater appreciation of what inclusive financial sectors can deliver for development.

There is a compelling case to look at financial sector development inclusively, placing greater emphasis on access by poor households and enterprises to financial services.

The policy framework: Issues and options

Government has an important role to play in building a pro-poor, pro-inclusive finance environment. It requires a policy strategy, a corresponding regulatory framework, and a set of legal structures that encourage responsive financial services for poor and low-income households and for micro, small and medium-sized enterprises. The overall government stance sets the tone, which derives from the political process. At the heart of the "enabling policy environment", there needs to be a clear vision of the possible roles of public sector and private sector stakeholders in bringing about an inclusive financial sector for development. Realizing the vision requires a better understanding of what impedes achieving it and how both state and market can be best mobilized in any particular national setting.

This section addresses a range of policy issues: from the importance of vision and a resulting policy stance, openness and competition in relation to financial inclusion, to current debates on deregulation and government intervention, regulation and supervision. We do this by presenting a set of issues for considerations for policy makers and other stakeholders.

A selection of policy issues and strategic options

Government policies, laws and regulations can constrain the building of inclusive financial sectors, or they can serve to re-engineer the financial sector, with a focus on sustainable inclusion. The question of the government role is not "whether" but "what". That question stirs much controversy and little consensus.

There is consensus that most countries have taken a fragmented approach to developing a financial sector that increases access of all people to appropriate financial services. There is rarely a clear articulation of how social (outreach) and prudential (stability) objectives should address each other. Microfinance, in particular, has been seen primarily as part of social policy for poverty reduction, when its essence lies in financial sector development. A leader from an international network observed, "It's our own fault, as we looked for allies [in the social sectors]." Across regions, stakeholders call for governments to adopt comprehensive and inclusive financial sector development strategies, with microfinance as an integral part, and without the misuse of microfinance for narrow political gain.

Government intervention in the market for financial services – how much intervention, what kind, where and when?

Governments have been widely concerned that access to financial services is not equitable and have attempted to shape the market with the aim of improving the way it functions. These policies aim to increase access to financial services to poor and low-income people, sectors of the economy, or geographical areas that are generally thought to be of little interest to commercial providers of financial services, due to perceived risk and low profitability. It is possible to increase financial inclusion successfully through a policy approach that relies on a high degree of government involvement in the financial sector, as with a policy approach that has a low level of involvement. This option set discusses the range of policy instruments governments have used with varying degrees of success.

Policy makers can opt to...

...remove barriers to entry of firms that serve this market. Concerns about creating a competitive environment suggest lowering barriers to entry. Barriers to entry promote some types of firms and discourage others, keeping prices artificially high, allowing price coordination or preventing geographic or market segment expansion. Barriers to entry often extend to ownership structure for reasons other than safety and soundness. In addition, they can reduce innovations in product design. At the same time, it is reasonable to limit market entry to assure quality of market participants (mission, sound governance, viable models) and to assure adequate supervision.

...level playing fields or allow for preferential treatment. Equal conditions presume developed markets, competition and scale. In accordance with policy goals, the playing field may be tilted towards increasing access to financial services for poor and low-income people, or on the contrary, towards protecting certain firms. Some organizations get preferential treatment while others may be burdened by special rules and practices. Preferable treatment in relation to access can include a wide range of measures, including tax measures, allowing for limited experimentation, for example.

...consider carefully which subsidies are valuable and which are counterproductive. Most financial systems have some sort of subsidies – whether they are transparent or hidden, or temporary or permanent. This policy option involves an examination of who gets subsidies and whether they are efficient and sustainable. Transparent expression of subsidies within the retail institution is important for determining its financial health. "Smart", or valuable, subsidies seed new retail or wholesale institutions, support research and development, support innovation, build capacity and promote access to financial markets (such as guarantee funds). Counterproductive subsidies are inefficient, weaken risk management and weigh on government budgets. When subsidies find transparent expression within the national budget they can be judged against alternative uses of public funds.

...*intervene in financial markets through mandates or allow the market to work.* Government mandates affect retail financial institutions and the financial sector at large. These mandates include interest rate ceilings, portfolio quotas and directed lending programs. Products designed as policy tools may respond to customer preferences, but they may not. The question is whether these mandates have their intended effect to serve and protect the consumer and encourage financial institutions to provide these services over the long term.

...*engage directly in financial service provision.* There are many state-owned banking institutions involved in retail services. Some are extensively engaged in serving the lower segment of the market and are net contributors to national budgets. Others contribute to government deficits but they have failed to increase access. The question is, what makes one succeed and another fail?

Financial sectors evolve – sometimes slowly, sometimes rapidly as advances in experience and technology pave the way for new innovations. Policy decisions about market entry, a competitive environment, and choices between market-based and government interventions are critical for developing increased access within the financial system. Incentives and disincentives for retail financial institutions can encourage innovation in financial technologies needed to increase access, or encumber it. Most of the reasons retail financial institutions serve the market come from within the retail institution. The balancing act for policy comes in freeing such institutions from disincentives or providing incentives that do not have unintended effects on national budgets, the health of the financial system, its retail institutions and their customers.

Getting the incentives right in the broader financial system and the willingness to review and correct those that do not function as originally intended are important for the evolution an inclusive financial sector.

How can we achieve affordable and sustainable interest rates?

Interest rates are among the most sensitive prices in any economy, but there is no global consensus on what constitutes reasonable and fair interest rates. There is however solid evidence that low interest rate ceilings, while politically popular, tend to support rationing of credit to better-off segments of the population. There is solid evidence that interest rate ceilings do not achieve the intended policy goal of providing sustainable access to credit at lower costs; they push clients into the high cost unregulated informal market for credit as financial institutions limit their operations and curtail expansion. At the same time, the call for deregulation of interest rates embodies optimism that the forces of competition will serve to lower interest rates within a reasonable timeframe.

The basic question is whether it is preferable to support a decline in interest rate levels directly and/or indirectly. Policy makers emphasize how difficult it is *not* to impose interest rate ceilings. Some countries that removed controls later re-imposed them. Other countries have repealed or avoided imposing interest rate ceilings in favor of a set of measures designed to increase competition, increase transparency or lower interest rates through driving down costs of service delivery. Others have chosen to subsidize interest rates in ways that are more indirect, such as through tax deductions for the individual, or lowering the cost of funds or allowing tax credits for institutions.

Policy makers can opt to…

… liberalize interest rates. The basic argument opposing interest rate ceilings is that the higher cost of offering microloans (operating costs, cost of funds, provisioning and the constitution of reserves) warrants a higher interest rate for lending and that borrowers would willingly pay the higher interest because it is lower than informal markets and credit is in fact available. The liberalization of interest rates presupposes that competition from new entrants will drive down costs, and thereby, interest rates. Putting into place the conditions and actions to realize this "optimistic" scenario, requires a more complex set of measures than issuing one single directive.

…take an indirect approach. The indirect approach presupposes an efficient tax registration and administration system that makes rebates and tax credits possible for the institution or individual.

…push for greater transparency of interest rates and fees and for reporting on the efficiency of the operations of financial institutions. Truth in lending laws allows customers to appreciate the full cost of borrowing, reinforcing their bargaining positions. Reporting on the efficiency of operations permits comparison and benchmarking among institutions, reinforcing the incentive to lower operating costs.

…recognize that a complex set of measures are required, interrelated to other policy options: Addressing issues of competition (market entry and regulations), of access to funds (financial market development), and of increasing efficiency at the institutional level, as well as reinforcing the financial

literacy of customers. This can entail supporting the lowering of costs (refinancing, costs of investment and innovation) through "smart" subsidies for the institution, or credits and rebates administered through the tax system.

Policy makers need to assess carefully the trade-offs between the understandably appealing short-term solution of interest rate controls (and the possible perverse effects of this policy) and decontrol, with the challenge of lowering interest rates through increasing efficiency and lowering costs of funds.

How can governments promote consumer protection?

Fair treatment entails honest dealing and transparency between the service provider and the customer. Governments and financial services providers are concerned about over-indebtedness, unscrupulous lending practices, and non-transparent charges on financial transactions including savings accounts, insurance policies, remittance charges and exchange rates on international payments.

Pro-consumer policies focus on both sides of the market – the buyer and the seller – and seek to foster a more equal relationship. They seek a balance between consumer education, protection, rights and obligations and the impact these have on price, competition and continued expansion of financial services to the unbanked. Policy options focus on financial literacy initiatives as well as regulating the relationship between the buyer and seller to differing degrees.

Policy makers can opt to…

…*"let the buyer beware"*. This minimalist option is often considered anticonsumer. It has little affect on consumer protection unless combined with effective and widespread financial literacy initiatives, as "poor consumer understanding of financial services means that competitive forces alone will not ensure fair treatment or adequate consumer protection".[10]

…*establish a truth in lending law* or transparency standards for publishing prices. This option requires policy makers to set the standards for transparent pricing, but not the prices themselves.

…*invest in financial literacy initiatives*. The ability of individuals and enterprises to do business with financial institutions depends on their degree of financial literacy. Financially literate customers are in a stronger position to access financial services at better terms and to protect against abuse.

...examine carefully the effects of interest rate ceilings. Interest rate ceilings are a politically popular measure, ostensibly for consumer protection. They tend to have an adverse effect on transparency within the lending institution, limiting the effect on consumer protection. They can also have an unintended negative effect on consumer protection, if borrowers are pushed into the informal sector where prices are higher and abuses more common.

...insist financial institutions sign a pledge and follow their own pro-consumer codes of conduct and practices or those developed by an industry association. Policy makers can be instrumental in setting standards for such pledges through dialogue with financial institutions and their associations.

...establish an independent third party rating agency that monitors, reviews, publishes and makes widely available annual ratings of financial institution good business practices, consumer complaints and redress, for example.

...require financial institutions to create an industry ombudsman to censure practices that violate the industry code, and/or add a dispute settlement mechanism within a trade association.

...establish an ombudsman independent of the financial services industry, within or linked to the regulatory authority that actively promotes consumer education, protection and redress.

The choices about the level of consumer education and protection within the financial sector are important because they make markets work better, or undermine them; they can encourage abusive practices or work to eliminate them; they can build consumer confidence in the financial system or restore it. Effective policies are those that require transparency in the relationship between the buyer and the seller; they provide customers with the information and the understanding to take responsibility for their own decisions. When promises of fair treatment are made to consumers, it is important that they be backed by credible and unbiased enforcement.

How many financial institutions of what types should governments promote?

The diversity in types of financial institutions increases access to "unbanked" populations and gives alternatives to customers. Diversity contributes to competition in terms of service and pricing, and increases the variety and quality of products available. Owing to their different operating modalities and risks, a diverse universe of financial institutions can be a cushion against the volatility of financial markets, and part of a strategy to promote financial-sector resilience. At the same time, a pro-diversity policy can result in a proliferation of the number and type of organizations, resulting in a chaotic financial sector and may exceed supervisory capacity.

Policy makers can opt to...

...expand the number of institutions and service outlets permitted to operate legally within the financial sector. This option requires policy makers to examine minimum capital and ownership requirements as well as branch expansion restrictions on existing providers. An example of this option is the expansion of small rural banks that increase access in com-munities, but may exceed supervisory capacity. An assessment of current supervisory capacity and provisions to shore it up become necessary when expanding the number and type of institutions.

...design new legal forms to increase outreach. One institutional model may not have the flexibility to respond to different market segments in dif-ferent locations. This option requires policy makers to examine existing legal frameworks (for example, for cooperatives, rural banks, credit-only organizations, avenues to transform NGOs, bank subsidiaries) to deter-mine whether the diversity of the organizations permitted by law ade-quately serves the market. This option requires an examination of tiered frameworks for licensing, regulations and supervisory requirements, where regulation and licensing requirement match the degree of risk engendered by the range of products offered.

...consolidate the number or type of institutions. Many countries have intro-duced requirements to consolidate the financial sector by requiring NGOs to become licensed and professional banking establishments or seek other aims and lines of business. In other countries, banking authorities have opted to close banks, reform them or privatize those that rely on gov-ernment budgets that grow smaller. The advantages of consolidation of banking sector are that it matches supervisory capacity, aims for safety and soundness and reduces government budget expenditures. The dis-advantages are that if one legal option is closed off, without putting another in place, it may decrease access; and if one bank is closed with-out others jumping into the breach it may decrease access.

It is important to keep the question of the appropriate diversity and number of institutions before policy makers. Just as the political and economic environment changes, the answer to the question may change over time. Periodic review and dialogue about the various institutional forms and their performance is part and parcel of the effort to increase access of poor people to financial services in a sustainable and safe manner.

What can regulators and supervisors do to foster financial inclusion?

Regulators and supervisors are challenged to determine if increasing access can be legitimately integrated as a goal of regulation and supervision along with the "traditional" considerations of protection of depositors, soundness of institutions and stability of the financial system.

Policy makers can opt to...

...seek to integrate access considerations into regulatory frameworks and supervisory practices. Regulators can ask all financial institutions for reporting on access data. They can choose to play a proactive role in increasing access over time, through an understanding of the impact of regulatory regimes and application of pro-inclusion regulatory parameters.

...change mindsets about financial services for the under-served and the institutions that seek to serve them. Regulators might rethink whether they understand the true risk profile of microfinance and small enterprise finance. On this basis, a mutual understanding between regulators and financial institutions paves the way for developing sound but flexible regulations and supervisory practices.

...treat microfinance as a business line across the full range of financial institutions and supervising microfinance as an emerging asset class. This means allowing the full range of financial institutions to offer microfinance services, treating microfinance portfolios as an asset class in terms of products allowed, risk categorization, reserves and provisioning requirements.

...differentiate between where flexibility can be introduced in regulatory frameworks and where regulations need to be tougher because of true risk. Increasing access entails introducing flexibility in regulations and supervisory practices while at the same time assuring the protection of depositors. Pro-access adjustments in the regulatory regime include expedient licensing procedures, lower minimum capital requirements, using portfolio quality to assess risk, flexible approval of new products and innovative delivery systems, simplified reporting requirements and branch approvals. Strict application of regulations in key areas is essential to ensure financial soundness: strict "fit and proper" tests, minimum capital requirements

reflecting the economic scale of institutions and the ability to supervise them, higher capital adequacy requirements, demonstration of solid performance in lending before permission to mobilize deposits, strict and early provisioning requirements, conservative requirements for liquidity and the extent of liabilities in foreign currency and rigorous internal and external audit procedures.

...adjust supervisory practices and reinforce supervisory capacity. Reporting requirements can be simplified to align with the methodologies of the financial institution, with audit procedures reflecting the nature of supervised institutions' financial structure. Supervisory capacity, weak overall in many countries, can be reinforced and supervisors' performance evaluated.

...exercise national prerogatives in applying international standards. Policy makers can opt to focus on what international standards can do to strengthen their financial sectors, working to apply the Basel Core Principles on Banking Supervision and adapting and implementing Basel II in their national context, while lobbying to make these standards more sensitive to concerns of financial inclusion.

Regulation and supervision affect the extent to which the financial system as a whole is "inclusive-friendly". With due consideration for fundamental stability and consumer protection objectives of regulatory processes, regulators and supervisors can adjust regulations and supervisory tools to take better account of their impact on financial inclusion. The stakes are high, because the regulatory framework has a proven effect on the degree of outreach of financial services to the unbanked and underbanked.

How can policy makers fashion financial infrastructure for inclusive finance?

The "financial infrastructure" is the set of services on which any country's financial system relies to hold itself together. It helps financial institutions to talk efficiently with each other (information/communication system), and pass money and financial instruments safely and quickly around the system (payments and settlement system). It reduces the risks of lending to the real sector (through credit bureaus and property registries) and from lending to each other (external audits and institutional credit ratings).

The importance of creating financial infrastructure support for inclusive finance is uncontested. The questions focus on: Who should provide it, what to build and how it should be financed.

Policy makers can opt to…

…leverage national budgets by investing in the "public good" of financial infrastructure. Investing in financial infrastructure may well be a better use of public funds than other interventions such as recapitalizing poorly performing financial institutions, providing subsidies that do not reach the intended group or designing products that serve political purposes and find little appeal in the market.

…give priority to those elements of the financial infrastructure that are essential in managing risk (for example, credit bureaus, or government guarantees for MFI lenders to borrow from domestic commercial banks), increasing transparency (for example, financial disclosure requirements), promoting efficiency (for example, standard reporting requirements or investment in information technology) and ensuring safety and soundness of the overall financial system (such as increasing supervisory capacity). Provide avenues for MFIs to link into the infrastructure serving the major financial institutions, such as the payments system, and credit bureaus. This opens an opportunity for joint public/private initiatives to upgrade information technology and adopt compatible systems that can communicate with each other.

…set the standards for service provision through the private sector or provide the service within the public sector. Owing to the range and nature of the infrastructure, some services are better provided by the public sector and others are more efficiently handled by the private sector or through private–public partnerships where private sector providers follow standards set by the government. Some may require on-going subsidy, particularly those that are considered "public goods," such as training and capacity building, or development of communications technology, and others can be quickly integrated on a fee for service basis, such as credit bureaus.

Most countries have yet to build the range of financial infrastructure required to underpin and render less risky and more efficient the support of financial institutions focused on increasing access of financial services to poor and low-income people. In this regard, a forward-looking strategy of providing the financial infrastructure would seek to include poor people's banks into the mainstream as well.

How can governments build "access" into financial sector policy?

The overall government stance about building an inclusive financial sector sets the tone for concrete financial sector measures. Experience has shown that consensus on a shared vision is likely to promote other supportive measures and practices within the financial sector and foster more responsive and accountable actions within the private sector and donor community. Governments may support and oversee strategy implementation through ministries with distinct interests.

Policy makers can opt to...

...establish a distinct national policy for microfinance bringing together all the microfinance and small-scale financing initiatives under the authority of one ministry most focused on economic development and poverty alleviation. This is common practice. The advantages of this approach are that it provides an opportunity for a focused political champion of inclusive finance to emerge in government while allowing for consolidation. The disadvantage is that it tends to isolate microfinance as a separate and not equal financial sector for poor and low-income people, distinct from the financial sector for everyone else.

...allow diverse financial sector strategies by encouraging various policy foci in government to promote in their respective sectors' finance initiatives (agriculture, industry, social services, housing/urban development ministries). This option often arises by default. While a decentralized approach may champion the program's clients and leave room for innovation, the disadvantage is that the financial landscape becomes cluttered with competing small financial institutions with overlapping customer bases and mandates, coordination is difficult and fragmented policy can result.

...develop a comprehensive financial sector development strategy, assigning responsibility for policy implementation to the ministry responsible for financial sector development. This option views microfinance as "finance" and credit and savings as banking activities. It is based on the idea that there is no strong case for financial institutions to be separated from the mainstream by the poverty of their clients. This option argues for strengthening the coherence in financial policy development. It has the disadvantage of diluting specific concerns related to microfinance and related poverty alleviation concerns.

Decisions regarding the overall policy stance are critical because they set the tone for the entire policy framework and what flows from it. Microfinance and inclusive finance are part of the financial sector and financial sector policy. While recognizing that the aims of improving access are centered on poverty reduction, strategies also need to recognize that inclusive finance, is after all finance.

Conclusion

> We reaffirm our commitment to eradicate poverty and promote sustained economic growth, sustainable development and global prosperity for all...
>
> We underline the need for urgent action on all sides, including more ambitious national development strategies and efforts backed by international support.
>
> 2005 World Summit Outcome[11]

Not only do developing countries need to design appropriate strategies for increasing access to financial services by all segments of the population, but they also must be able to turn their strategies into effective policy. This requires that governments and the private sector work together to design such strategies and determine the best ways to organize to implement them. It entails the cooperation of the range of financial institutions, civil society organizations and development partners to help realize this strategy. It requires that all stakeholders ensure that adequate attention is focused on financial inclusion today, tomorrow and the next day.

We believe the payoff to a focus on financial inclusion in developing countries is very high. It will enrich the overall financial sector development strategy. By increasing the economic opportunities of poor and low-income people, it will help make economic development itself more inclusive. Balanced and sustained economic growth helps support political sustainability and social progress. But most of all, inclusive development of the financial sector will increase incomes, build access, empower and enrich the lives of millions of households currently excluded from economic opportunity, who have the most at stake in this endeavor.

Notes

* This chapter is based on draft material for *Building Inclusive Financial Sectors for Development*, New York: Limited Nations, May 2006.
1 The term "bankable" refers to individuals and enterprises that are in a position to benefit from financial services (generate income to repay loans, to save, to build assets). The access to finance problem breaks down into two elements: (1) an increase in the bankable population (that is, making a larger

share of the population bankable) and (2) increase in access to the bankable population. This chapter addresses access of the bankable population.

2 S. Daley-Harris, "State of the Microcredit Summit Campaign Report 2004", Microcredit Summit Campaign, Washington, D.C. (November 2004).

3 "Alternative financial institutions" were defined to "include state-owned agricultural, development, and postal banks; member-owned savings and loan institutions; other savings banks; low-capital local and/or rural banks; and specialized microfinance institutions and programs (MFIs) of varying types. Historically, almost all of these institutions were set up with an explicit objective of reaching clients who did not have access to services from commercial banks and finance companies" (see Other key references section – CGAP, 2004, p. 2).

4 P. Honohan, Financial Sector Policy and the Poor: Selected Findings and Issues", World Bank, Washington, (March 2004) p. 21.

5 See S. Peachey and A. Roe "The Importance of Financial Sector Development for Growth and Poverty Reduction", UK Department for International Development, London, Policy Division Working Paper (August 2004); and David Porteous, "Making Financial Markets Work for the Poor", FinMark Trust, October 2004.

6 C. Calderon and L. Liu, "The Direction of Causality between Financial Development and Economic Growth", *Journal of Development Economics*, 72 (1) (2003) pp. 321–34, cited in Ellis (UK Department for International Development), "The Importance of Financial Sector Development for Growth and Poverty Reduction", Policy Division Working Paper, London, August 2004, p. 14.

7 S. Peachey and A. Roe, "Access to Finance: A Study for the World Savings Banks Institute", Oxford: Oxford Policy Management (October 2004) pp. 10–12.

8 H. Li, L. Squire and H. Zou, quoted in G. Westley, "Can Financial Market Policies Reduce Income Inequality?", Inter-American Development Bank, Washington, Technical Paper Series (2001).

9 P. Honohan, *Financial Development, Growth and Poverty: How Close are the Links?* (Washington D.C.: World Bank, January 2004).

10 FSA (FSA, Consumer Protection Panel, "Treating Customers Fairly", 2004, pp. 8–14).

11 United Nations (2005), "2005 World Summit Outcome." General Assembly (A/60/L.1).

Other key references

Asian Development Bank, "The Changing Face of the Microfinance Industry: Building Inclusive Financial Systems for the Poor", Asian Development Bank, Technical Paper No. 14 (2005).

Barry, R.A. "Finance and Pro-Poor Growth. DAI and Institute for Developing Economies" (March 2004).

Beck, T., A. Demirguc-Kant, and R. Levine. "Finance, Inequality and Poverty: Cross-Country Evidence". World Bank Working Paper Number 3338 (June 2004).

CGAP, "Financial Institutions with a 'Double Bottom Line': Implications for the Future of Microfinance", Consultative Group to Assist the Poor, Washington, D.C., Occasional Paper No. 8 (July 2004).

CGAP, "Building Inclusive Financial Systems: Donor Guidelines on Good Practice in Microfinance", Consultative Group to Assist the Poor, Washington, D.C. (December 2004).

CGAP, "Key Principles of Microfinance", Washington D.C. (2004).

Claessens, S., "Access to Financial Services: A Review of Issues and Public Policy Objectives", World Bank, Washington (July 2005).

Ellis, K., "The Importance of Financial Sector for Growth and Poverty Reduction", London: Department for International Development (October 2004).

Holden, P. and V. Prokopenko, "Financial Development and Poverty Allevation: Issues and Policy Implications for Developing and Transition Countries", IMF Working Paper (2001).

Honohan, P., "Financial Sector Policy and the Poor: Selected Findings and Issues", Working Paper No. 43, World Bank, Washington, D.C. (2004).

Imboden, K., "Building Inclusive Financial Sectors: Widening Access, Enhancing Growth, Alleviating Poverty", *Columbia Journal of International Affairs*, Spring (2005).

Morduch, J., *The Economics of Microfinance* (Cambridge: MIT Press, 2005).

Peachy, S., and Roe, A.; "Access to Finance: Measuring the Contributions of Savings Banks", World Savings Banks Institute, Brussels (September 2005).

Raghuram, R.G., and Zingales, L. *Saving Capitalism from the Capitalists: Unleashing the Power of Financial Markets to Create Wealth and Spread Opportunity* (New York: Crown Business, 2003).

Robinson, M., *The Microfinance Revolution: Sustainable Finance for the Poor* (Washington: World Bank, 2001).

United Nations, "Report of the International Conference on Financing for Development", Monterrey, Mexico, 18–22 March 2002. General Assembly (A/CONF.198/11).

Westley, G., "Can Financial Market Policies Reduce Income Inequality?", Inter-American Development Bank, Washington, Technical Paper Series (2001).

Women's World Banking, "Building Domestic Financial Systems that Work for the Majority", Women's World Banking, New York (April, 2005).

Part V
Assessing Microfinance Institutions

Thus far, this volume has demonstrated the already large, and fast-growing, demand for private capital in micro and small business finance. We have also considered the sources of that private capital and highlighted some of today's leading investment vehicles and business models for attracting capital into microfinance. But as we have seen, demand has met supply in a capacity bottleneck – there are simply not enough institutions capable of absorbing all the funds and the market today is squeezed for good opportunities. With too much money chasing too few opportunities, potential investors in microfinance need all the help they can get to make sound investment decisions. In this final part, we investigate how to measure the performance, and profitability of microfinance institutions. Von Stauffenberg and Sinha, from two of the world's leading microfinance rating agencies, provide some insight into the industry's key measurement metrics, and review specific examples from Latin America, Africa and Asia.

10

Rating Microfinance Institutions in Latin America and Africa

Damian von Stauffenberg

Introduction

Established in 1997, MicroRate was the first rating agency to specialize in microfinance. Since then, the agency has analysed over 200 microfinance institutions (MFIs) in Latin America and Africa. At the time of its launch, MFIs were far less sophisticated than today, and they often attracted funding by using stirring images of their work at the grassroots level, rather than hard financial information on their operations and performance. Yet microfinance is financial intermediation, just as is commercial banking, using specific techniques and measurable with appropriate metrics. Hence, both operations and performance can be assessed and measured. Because MicroRate has analysed so many MFIs it has a unique basis of practical experience and performance data. This is captured in an industry database, which is used to determine trends and performance benchmarks.

The agency's ratings are not credit ratings. A credit rating is an evaluation of an issuer's ability to repay principal and interest on its debt. In other words, a credit rating tells you how likely it is that you will not get your money back. It measures only that. A performance rating on the other hand assesses, "How good is this institution at what it is doing that is, providing microcredit?". MicroRate rates the performance of MFIs and benchmarks them against one another.

Credit ratings vs. performance ratings

There is a difference between a credit rating and a performance rating, and this can be seen from recent results from parallel ratings. Often, where the same company has been rated by both MicroRate and a credit rating agency, the results have differed. Why? Because credit raters are sometimes seduced by the characteristic numbers of MFIs.

Microfinance institutions are nearly always very liquid. Their portfolio quality is very good compared with commercial banks in the same countries. In addition, leverage is low – meaning that, compared with commercial banks, they have little debt on their books. To top it all off, MFIs tend to be much more profitable than banks. To the credit rater, this translates into a low degree of repayment risk and the MFI is therefore assigned a high grade. However, MicroRate focuses much more on how the institution carries out its business. For example, our analysts will talk to the loan officers to determine how they make loans.

The essence of microfinance is the ability to distinguish, among the poor, those who can use a loan productively. Those MFIs that have developed this ability will be successful; those who haven't, will not. Irrespective of how much money an MFI has, and no matter how creditworthy it may be at the moment, if it fails at this essential task it will not make it in the long run if it cannot identify borrowers who will use a loan to create wealth, rather than to increase consumption. Quite often, MFIs, even some of the best-known names, are not particularly good at this critical task. Conventional analysis of a MFIs finances will not reveal this.

Measurement metrics for MFIs

MFIs are growing fast. In a sample of 38 Latin American MFIs that have been rated by MicroRate over the past five years, portfolio growth in 2004 was just under 50 percent. Over the full five years, growth was about 30 percent. And this was profitable growth. The sample of 38 institutions had an adjusted[1] return on equity of 16.4 percent.

The most important characteristic of an MFI is the quality of its loan portfolio, generally measured by its portfolio-at-risk, or PAR. This, and not the repayment rate, is the preferred measure of portfolio quality in microfinance today. It is currently the most conservative measure available as it considers the entire loan amount to be at risk, even if only one dollar of the loan is in arrears. PAR > 30 – that is, the percentage of the portfolio affected by arrears of more than 30 days – is now largely the standard measurement. For this sample of 38 MFIs in Latin America, portfolio quality was excellent across the board, with PAR > 30 at about five percent: The figure was about the same in Africa.

Since the portfolio-at-risk figures can be improved by writing off bad loans, it is important also to consider the write-off rate. Among these MFIs, the write-off rate was found to be about 1 percent, a surprisingly low number, confirming the high quality of their portfolios.

Portfolio-at-risk can also be improved by simply refinancing bad loans. Hence, in assessing MFIs, MicroRate examines whether, and if so how, loans have been refinanced. When rating an institution, the agency typically spends approximately a week (three to five days) with the company, during which it will inspect the loan files, take a random sample of loans and check whether any have been refinanced. MicroRate also reviews the institution's refinancing policies.

Efficiency can be expressed as: "How much does it cost to put out one dollar of lending and get it back?" In this sample, the highest spent one dollar and one cent to get out one dollar of loan. Clearly, if it costs a dollar to lend a dollar, then there is something about which to worry. However, operating expenses are usually very closely correlated to loan size. This is to be expected because where a loan is extremely small, it will cost proportionally more to process that loan. A good example of an extreme case is that of village banking MFIs, which are in a category apart. Here, loan sizes tend to be extremely small and operating expenses are therefore very high. For average MFIs, operating expenses can reach about 30 percent of the average loan portfolio. But where loans are very small, that percentage can increase to 70–80 percent. Interestingly, however, the level of operating expenses is governed as much by competition as by average loan size. Where competition among MFIs heats up, lending rates drop, which in turn forces the institutions to cut their expenses if they want to remain profitable. Highly efficient MFIs in competitive markets will have operating expenses of about 10 percent. Ten percent seems to be a kind of sound barrier. Only very rarely have we seen MFIs with operating expense ratios below 10 percent.

There is an increasingly strong trend towards formalization – that is, NGOs transforming into supervised financial institutions. One might well ask why, given that supervision brings with it the requirement to pay taxes and more stringent reporting requirements. The answer is funding: It is harder to raise funding as an NGO than as a supervised, formal financial institution. Lenders, understandably, are more comfortable with supervised institutions, believing they must abide by certain rules that they already know. Not so with NGOs.

This is reflected in debt/equity (d/e) ratios. Rarely will an NGO exceed a D/E ratio of about 3:1; indeed 2:1 is already relatively high. A supervised financial institution, on the other hand, can easily go up to 5:1, and in some cases 6:1 – however, MFIs have so far not reached the level of indebtedness of commercial banks where d/e ratios of 10:1 or even 11:1 are common.

Growth may bring its own problems

As we have seen above, and as Mahajan and de Sousa Shields graphically illustrate in earlier chapters, this is an industry that is growing fast in response to the vast unmet demand. Microfinance has, as yet, only scratched the surface of the potential market; huge growth opportunities remain. The 50 percent growth rates seen in this Latin American sample may not continue. Long term, growth seems to be closer to 30 percent. But even at that rate, stresses will develop within MFIs. It is very difficult for an organization to grow rapidly year after year and to do so smoothly, without experiencing increasing stress. In tectonic terms, one speaks of stresses being adjusted through earthquakes; in some microfinance institutions, adjustment may mean trouble.

Doubtless, microfinance will go through cycles. But it remains unclear how MFIs will react to economic cycles. We have seen only a few cases so far, where a microfinance sector has gone through economic turmoil. Indonesia in the late 90s and Bolivia in 1999–01 are examples. In those cases, microfinance did extremely well. So well in fact, that one is tempted to conclude that microfinance is counter-cyclical. On the other hand it is too early to reach firm conclusions. Six or eight years ago, microfinance was still less developed and there was less competition among MFIs. It remains to be seen whether today's more highly leveraged MFIs, operating in a much more competitive environment will weather economic shocks equally well.

Another worrying sign is that at the moment there appears to be too much money chasing too few good investments. There is, it seems, a proliferation of funds. There is no doubt that funds are great. Indeed, this is one of the glories of microfinance – that the private sector has responded magnificently and is channeling funding (mostly loan financing) to microfinance through these private funds. If things continue at their current pace there probably will be too much of a good thing. Some funds will find that they have made loans where they shouldn't have and we will begin to see defaults in a sector that has so far been free of them.

This is all the more so because of the donor community and the international financial institutions (IFIs) such as the International Finance Corporation (IFC), the Inter-American Development Bank (IDB), the Asian Development Bank (ADB) are competing vigorously with the private funds. Since private funds can simply not compete with development institutions that are backed by government funding, development money is crowding out private funds. In a curious reversal of roles, private funds are now concentrating on smaller, riskier MFIs, whereas development money is concentrated in the strongest microfinance institutions.

So the market is being squeezed for good investment opportunities. A market that is already not very large. With too much money chasing too few opportunities, mistakes will be made as caution is thrown to the wind.

Another worrying development is the creation of so-called captive funds, which are funds that are managed by microfinance networks. In other words, a microfinance network – an owner of MFIs – sets up a fund into which it captures funding, which is then channeled to its own MFIs. This raises a question of conflict of interest. Objectivity in the allocation of funds to investments is a basic principle of investment funds. The fund manager's interests must be aligned with those of the investors, not the investee company. Where the fund manager is also the owner of the investment, this principle is being violated.

Conclusion

Notwithstanding the challenges ahead, it is encouraging to see the growth in the market, and important to remember that sound microfinance institutions far outweigh bad ones. Also, so far, the funds have done, and continue to do, an excellent job of feeding much-needed financing into the sector. Care is simply needed in order not to overburden a market that is still not very large.

Note

1　The returns were adjusted for accounting differences, with the main adjustment being inflation adjustment. Many MFIs do not use inflation accounting, whereas MicroRate adjusts for inflation. In addition, MicroRate standardizes all loan loss provisions.

11
Rating Microfinance Institutions in Asia

Sanjay Sinha

Introduction

[As] microfinance rating agencies, our role is to add a good layer of rationality onto the exuberance which pervades microfinance today.[1]

Rating agencies provide sound assessments of microfinance institutions (MFIs), giving investors the tools by which they can better appraise potential investments. Micro-Credit Ratings International (M-CRIL) is one of the world's leading raters of MFIs. Established in 1998, just after MicroRate, by June 2006 M-CRIL had undertaken 360 ratings covering 208 microfinance institutions in 15 Asian countries; from Azerbaijan in the Caucasus to the Philippines in South-East Asia. Most of these were in India, but a significant number elsewhere. These numbers are slightly higher than those for Latin America, and considerably higher than those for Africa. This is, of course, partly a reflection of the size of the continent. However, the overall performance of microfinance in Asia is well behind that in Latin America. Little wonder therefore that while a substantial proportion of international funds are flowing to Latin America, only a very small amount – something of the order of five to seven percent – comes to Asia.

Financing opportunities in Asia

Observing financing flows, one might be forgiven for thinking that any irrational exuberance was being directed to Latin America, while on the other hand, excessive rationality was being applied to Asia. In spite of the availability of a reasonable number of sustainable MFIs in Asia, and other potential new investments, far more funding is flowing to Latin America than is appropriate at this time.

Yet even in Asia, there appears to be – as shown in Latin America in the previous chapter – too much money chasing too few good investments. And that, of course, applies to what might be called the "tier one" MFIs – the leading MFIs in the region. There are perhaps eight to 10 such in India, and a handful in each of the other countries.

Now we consider some specific countries. With regard to investment, Bangladesh is not attractive as there is an excess of subsidized funding available. There are a few good investments in Cambodia, the Philippines and maybe a handful in Indonesia. Note, however, that Indonesia has a difficult regulatory environment. Other countries present significant political risks. For example, the ongoing political problems in Nepal; and in Pakistan, some political instability and a military government with which some investors are uncomfortable. There are some opportunities however – in India, Cambodia and the Philippines. Indonesia offers some investment opportunities for those able to deal with the regulatory issues, and Vietnam will become increasingly attractive over the next three to four years.

Rating MFIs in Asia

As does MicroRate, M-CRIL also examines the performance of MFIs, which it considers the most important aspect of the institution. Although both agencies have largely similar rating methodologies, there are some differences. The main difference is that M-CRIL ratings are also credit ratings; the agency does, in fact, give an opinion on whether or not an institution will be able to repay a certain amount of money within a given amount of time.

In addition to the factors enumerated by von Stauffenberg in Chapter 10, several others – particularly relevant to Asia – must also be considered when assessing MFIs. The biggest, yet most-overlooked, is management risk. One of the greatest difficulties for Asian microfinance today is the dominance, within the institutions, of "messianic leaders". The risk is that in spite of the increasing commercialization of MFIs, some still rely heavily on one key individual. It is therefore critical to look closely at the governance of the institution and the strength of its board. And beyond the strength of the board, at how active an interest board members take in the affairs of the institution. It follows that management succession is a very important aspect of assessing a microfinance institution. What does the second tier of management look like? How capable are they? What is the possibility that they will be able, in due course, to assume the leadership of the institution?

Another aspect that has lately reared its head in the course of the past couple of years is fraud. This, of course, affects all financial institutions. But MFIs, particularly those only just evolving beyond NGOs, find it difficult to introduce the kind of discipline and systems necessary to guard against fraud. This is therefore an aspect closely examined when M-CRIL evaluates the performance of an MFI, that is, the internal control systems, internal audits and so on.

The quality of external audits can be variable, so numbers presented should be treated with caution. For example, in Nepal, the agency recently uncovered discrepancies in entries for inter-branch transfers in a leading MFI. From head office to the branch, such transfers were registered as expenses, while the same flow of funds from the branch to head office was shown as income. In any case, the sums did not match. Eventually, it emerged that the MFI branch was being forced to pay this as protection money in order to be able to operate in the area. Yet these sums were shown in accounts to be already signed off by an external auditor.

Another aspect to consider is country risk. This is sometimes overplayed, evoking the specter of economic meltdown or currency devaluation. Economic meltdown does not necessarily mean meltdown of the microeconomies of relatively poor people. In fact, it is quite often the opposite. As people lose their jobs in the formal sector, they become microentrepreneurs, or at any rate they become people who demand the goods and services of microenterprises.

Conclusion

As we have seen, even though Asia attracts far less funding than Latin America, the region too suffers from a shortage of good investment opportunities. Nevertheless, opportunities do exist in some countries for investors prepared to invest the necessary effort to examine each prospect closely, paying particular attention to management capability and internal controls. Here the rating agencies can play a very important role.

Note

1   Sanjay Sinha, Address: Critical Factors for Private Investment in Micro and Small Business Finance Session, CASIN/GFC Private Capital Symposium, Geneva, 11 October 2005.

Appendix 1: The Geneva Private Capital Symposium: Speakers' and Chairs' Organizations

ABN AMRO

ABN AMRO is a prominent international bank ranking 11th in Europe and 20th in the world based on tier 1 capital, with over 3000 branches in more than 60 countries and total assets of EUR 855.7 billion (as of 30 June 2005). With European roots and a clear focus on consumer and commercial banking, ABN AMRO's business mix provides it with a competitive edge in its markets and client segments.

ABN AMRO is active in three principal customer segments: Consumer & Commercial Clients, Wholesale Clients and Private Clients & Asset Management. www.abnamro.com

ACCION International

ACCION International is a private, non-profit organization with the mission of providing people with the financial tools they need to overcome poverty. A world pioneer in microfinance, ACCION issued the first microloan in 1973 in Brazil. ACCION International's partner microfinance institutions today are providing loans as low as $100 to poor women and men entrepreneurs in 20 countries throughout many regions in the world. In fact, since 1992, ACCION and its partners have disbursed $7.6 billion in microloans to more than 4.7 million borrowers.

ACCION was awarded the 2005 Social Capitalist Award by Fast Company magazine for "using business excellence to engineer social change". www.accion.org

affentranger associates sa

Incorporated in 2002, affentranger associates (aa sa) is a business platform focused on the theme of value creation. As principal investor, aa sa aims to achieve sustainable long-term returns by investing a combination of labour and capital in companies which are in a transition phase. A business unit of aa sa, aa sa corporate finance aims to create value for its clients through strategic advisory work and execution of transactions. www.affentrangerassociates.com

AXA Investment Managers (AXA-IM)

As a dedicated global asset management company, AXA Investment Managers' assets under management of EUR 382.3 billion are invested in every major market and across a broad range of asset classes. AXA-IM is a core part of the AXA Group, a leader in financial protection and wealth management. Along with core fixed income and UK and pan-European equities capabilities, AXA-IM also offers specialist fixed income, structured and alternative products, private equity, real estate and multimanagement.
www.axa.com

Bank of Israel

The Bank of Israel's main functions include:

- Supporting financial stability in the economy;
- Aiding the government in promoting economic reforms;
- Undertaking economic and social research;
- Managing Israel's foreign exchange reserves;
- Acting as the government's and the banks' sole banker;
- Serving as the government's fiscal agent;
- Representing Israel in international financial institutions – IMF, the World Bank, the EBRD and the Bank for International Settlements (BIS).

The Governor of the Bank of Israel serves as the government's economic adviser.
www.bankisrael.gov.il

Banque Degroof/Debroof Bank

Banque Degroof was founded in 1873 by Franz Philippson, arguably one of Belgium's, and indeed Europe's, most eminent financiers. The bank claims that its success is based on its traditions and the personal relations that it maintains with a select clientele. During its development the bank has successfully enlarged the scope of its activities and developed specialized services and a regional presence. Today Banque Degroof operates under the independent Degroof Group label, under the control of its management and employees.
www.degroof.be

BASIX

BASIX is geared towards providing multiple services to rural poor households in India, including providing micro financial, livelihood promotion and institutional development services. It provides integrated financial services and technical assistance and strives to yield a competitive rate of return to its investors. With over 1300 employees, BASIX has more than 243 000 microfinance clients and 97.5% performing assets, and has supported over 37 000 clients with business development services.
www.basixindia.com

BHP – Brugger and Partners Ltd.

BHP – Brugger and Partners offers strategic consultancy to private and public organizations. Building on their broad academic and professional experience

gained in different cultural environments, the company provides expertise in evaluating and analysing the performance of companies and organizations, and helps them understand the implications of the analyses. BHP is actively engaged in several initiatives promoting financial services to micro and small enterprises in emerging markets, and in 2005 successfully organized an international symposium on microfinance for kick-starting mutually beneficial partnerships to mainstream this sector.
www.bruggerconsulting.ch

BlueOrchard Finance SA

BlueOrchard Finance SA was the first commercially financed group to invest in MFIs. It makes loans in 21 countries with over 50 MFI clients, and manages US$ 150 million. BlueOrchard intends to continue its role as a pioneer in linking private capital to the growing microfinance industry.
www.blueorchard.ch

Centre for Applied Studies in International Negotiations (CASIN)

The Centre for Applied Studies in International Negotiations, a Capacity Building Think and Do Tank is an independent Swiss non-profit foundation. CASIN organizes activities to support dialogue in areas such as national and international governance, sustainable development, conflict resolution, international trade and globalization. It also conducts research, scenario-building and coaching to assist policy makers, negotiators and senior managers in their search for policy options, aiming at improving both the government and the governance of national societies and the international system.
www.casin.ch

Citigroup Microfinance Group (CMG)

CMG has brought together microfinance sector expertise and experience across Citigroup to address the needs of individuals who are not served or are under-served by formal financial institutions. CMG's business includes individual and institutional lending, capital markets funding and provision of transaction services.
www.citigroup.com

Clearstream International

Clearstream is the premier international settlement and custody organization offering a comprehensive service covering both domestic and internationally traded bonds and equities. In 2005, Global Custodian magazine awarded Clearstream a top-rated ranking for the second consecutive year. In the same year it was named as the best Tri-partite Services provider and received a top-rated ranking for the fourth consecutive year.
www.clearstream.com

Consultative Group to Assist the Poor (CGAP)

The Consultative Group to Assist the Poor (CGAP) is a consortium of 30 public and private development agencies working together to expand access to financial services for the poor in developing countries. CGAP incubates and supports new

ideas, innovative products, cutting-edge technology, novel mechanisms for delivering financial services, and concrete solutions to the challenges of expanding microfinance, whilst serving development agencies, financial institutions including MFIs, government policy makers and regulators, and other service providers such as auditors and rating agencies.
www.cgap.org

Credit Suisse Group

Credit Suisse Group is a leading global financial services company providing private clients and small and medium-sized companies with private banking and financial advisory services, and pension and insurance solutions. In the area of investment banking, it serves global institutional, corporate, government and individual clients in its role as a financial intermediary. As of 30 June 2005, it reported assets under management of CHF 1341.2 billion.
www.credit-suisse.com

de Pury, Pictet, Turrettini & Co. (PPT)

A leading independent financial advisory firm, de Pury Pictet Turrettini & Cie SA offers services in asset management, family office, private equity, corporate finance and strategic advice. PPT is among the founders of BlueOrchard Finance SA, representing positive relationships between the Geneva financial center and the United Nations family.
www.ppt.ch

Deutsche Bank Microcredit Development Fund

Deutsche Bank has a long-standing tradition to promote and facilitate trade relations between Germany, other European countries and overseas markets. Its status as the largest private sector bank in Germany and an internationally recognized financial services provider has put it in the public limelight. Deutsche Bank sustains a considerable involvement in both cultural and social matters, e.g. education, music, art and sustainability. One of these engagements is the Deutsche Bank Microcredit Development Fund (DBMDF). Since inception in 1998, the DBMDF has invested $3.4 million in loans to 35 microfinance institutions in 21 countries with a cumulative impact of nearly $47 million.
www.community.db.com

Developing World Markets (DWM)

Developing World Markets helps microfinance and other socially motivated organizations in the developing world gain access to capital markets through innovative financial solutions. In 2004 DWM partnered with BlueOrchard Finance of Geneva as a sponsor and successfully completed the world's first securitization of cross-border loans to microfinance institutions. In two closings, the instrument channelled approximately US$ 87 million of US investor funds to low-income microentrepreneurs in various regions around the world: the largest single fundraising event in microfinance. Additional projects are now under way which aim to increase the financial resources available to microfinance institutions and other socially motivated enterprises to carry out their missions.
www.dwmarkets.com

Dexia Asset Management

Dexia Asset Management is a leading European asset manager providing investment solutions to institutional and private clients. Next to its competence in equity, bonds, money markets and global balanced mandates, Dexia Asset Management is a major actor in alternative management offering a complete range of strategies. We believe that "Money does not perform, people do" summarizes the reasons behind our success.
www.dexia-am.com

Enterprising Solutions

Enterprising Solutions provides management consulting, knowledge development and access to capital services in the areas of microfinance, small and medium-sized enterprises (MSME) in developing countries. ES also works to bring new capital resources to the sector through improved access to conventional markets as well as social investment financial markets. ES has extensive experience throughout the developing world but particularly in Africa and Latin America.
www.esglobal.com

Equity Bank Limited (EBL)

Equity Bank Limited started its operation as Equity Building Society. The initial focus was to offer mortgage services but in the early 1990s Equity Building Society changed its focus to microfinance services. EBS grew to become a leading micro-finance institution providing a wide range of products and services, and in 2004 was converted to Equity Bank Limited. EBL delivers quality financial services to the medium and low-income segments of the population.
www.ebsafrica.com

ethos Investment Foundation

The ethos Investment Foundation invests with an approach that integrates sustainable development to facilitate the responsible exercise of shareholder voting rights and to promote constructive dialogue with companies. ethos also participated in the launch of the microfinance fund responsAbility Global Microfinance Fund. Together with Centre Info, the company ethos services set up a Sustainable Governance Association to develop corporate governance services and represent Switzerland in the European Corporate Governance Service, the largest European corporate governance network.
www.ethosfund.ch

European Bank for Reconstruction and Development (EBRD)

The EBRD is the largest single investor in central Europe to central Asia and mobilizes significant FDI beyond its own financing. It provides project financing for banks, industries and businesses, both new ventures and investments in existing companies. It also works with publicly-owned companies, to support privatization, restructuring state-owned firms and improvement of municipal services. It promotes policies that will help bolster the business environment. The mandate of the EBRD stipulates that it must only work in countries that are committed to

democratic principles. Respect for the environment is part of the strong corporate governance attached to all EBRD investments.
www.ebrd.com

Financiera Compartamos

Financiera Compartamos is a regulated microfinance (MF) company that provides financial services for low-income clients through a network of 144 branches in rural and urban Mexico. Compartamos started as a pilot project in a local NGO and later converted into a formal financial institution. In its 15-year history, Compartamos has disbursed more than 2 million loans averaging US$ 300, primarily in rural areas. Compartamos is the largest microfinance institution in Latin America, serving 370 000 microentrepreneurs, most of them women, with a portfolio of just over US$ 140 million. With more than 2000 employees, it has been steadily growing at rates higher than 50 percent for the past few years. Compartamos is a private company with institutional investors such as the IFC, and Accion International, as well as young private investors. Compartamos was the world's first microfinance institution to issue debt on the public market and currently funds most of its operations through local markets and international lines of credit. The company is rated by S&P as an mxA+.
www.compartamos.com

Global Microfinance Group

Global Microfinance Group is a private, for-profit platform for funding, building and managing nascent micro and small business banks. GMG seeks growth opportunities in the microfinance industry through start-up investments and acquisitions. The GMG team combines a rich track record in microfinance with general management, technology and finance expertise. A proven credit methodology and operating model, as demonstrated in the first operational entity set up in Argentina in 2004 (Argentina Microfinanzas SA), provide a basis for replication and expansion in other geographical markets. GMG brings together private capital and microfinance market opportunities through a hands-on approach, thus providing investors with attractive returns, and invested institutions with the necessary ingredients (capital, know-how and management) for sustainable growth.
www.globalmicrofinancegroup.com (under construction) /
www.argentinamicrofinance.com

Gray Ghost Microfinance Fund

The Gray Ghost Microfinance Fund is a portfolio of fund investments from two sources aimed at connecting private social investors with microfinance. For the industry to grow in a healthy way, the fund believes that private social investors must constitute a key element of microfinance funding by 2008. These investors combine a commitment to a social purpose with business experience, creativity, discipline and financial resources, especially as a bridge to commercial capital. The personal commitment of social investors ensures that microfinance will support the ultimate goal of enriching lives, both financially and spiritually, on both sides of the investment relationship.
www.rockdalefdn.org

Housing MicroFinance, LLC

HMF was founded to develop, originate and manage housing microfinance funds. The long-term, local currency financing will enable their clients to borrow funds for home improvement, home acquisition, home construction and land acquisition. HMF expects that the fund's multilateral credit guarantees and standardisation will enhance its appeal to both capital markets and borrowers alike. By developing standardized lending products aimed at creating housing finance market development, the company's mission is to make housing microfinance available to 100 million new customers by 2010.

ICICI Bank Limited

ICICI is India's largest private bank and the second largest bank overall. It offers a wide range of retail, corporate and rural banking products. The ICICI Group offers a variety of financial services in the areas of investment banking, life and non-life insurance, venture capital and asset management. ICICI has a comprehensive strategy for rural, micro-banking and agribusiness with the twin objectives of meeting the needs of the rural economy and building a sustainable business model. The ICICI Group supports the communities in which it operates through a diverse range of social projects in primary education, healthcare and microfinance. ICICI Bank has been named "Best Bank in India" by Business India and "India's Most Customer-Friendly Bank" by Outlook Money, among other awards. It has also received numerous international awards.
www.icicibank.com

Institute for Management Development (IMD)

IMD was founded as a result of the merger of IMI Geneva (1946) and IMEDE Lausanne (1957). IMD's roots in industry have contributed greatly to its pragmatic approach to management education, in close partnership with many of the world's top companies. IMD is truly international. Every year 5500 executives, representing over 70 nationalities, attend more than 20 open enrollment Executive Development Programs (including an intensive MBA program) as well as company-specific Partnership Programs. Some 1000 executives also attend our Discovery Events from our Partner and Business Associate companies. IMD currently has over 50 000 IMD Alumni from 140 countries worldwide and 40 IMD Alumni Clubs in 30 countries. Faculty members divide their time between teaching, carrying out research and acting as consultants to major companies in many industries. This approach ensures that they remain firmly on top of the latest developments in management practice.
www.imd.ch

International Finance Corporation (IFC)

The International Finance Corporation promotes sustainable private sector investment in developing countries as a way of reducing poverty and improving people's lives. Like all other World Bank Groups, IFC aims to improve the quality of the lives of people in its developing member countries. It promotes sustainable private sector development primarily by: financing private sector projects located in the developing world; helping private companies in the developing world mobilize

financing in international financial markets; and providing advice and technical assistance to businesses and governments.
www.ifc.org

Internationale Projekt Consult GmbH (IPC)

Internationale Projekt Consult GmbH is a consulting firm that focuses exclusively on issues and projects in the field of international development cooperation, providing micro, small and medium-sized enterprises (MSMEs) in developing countries and transition economies with access to financial services at fair and affordable terms and conditions. Today IPC acts as a manager of long-term consultancy projects, a manager of microfinance banks and a provider of research-oriented short-term consultancy services.
www.ipcgmbh.com

Investor & Partner for Development (I&P)

I&P is a private investment company which invests in developing countries, especially in Africa, both in micro-finance institutions and in medium-size businesses, within relationships of durable partnership with management. I&P always associates investment to active partnership. It aims to contribute towards generating strong and professional entrepreneurs and sustainably performing businesses.
www.ip-dev.com

KMB Bank

KMB Bank ranks among the Top 10 Russian SME lenders and focuses on becoming the leading provider of financial and other banking services to Russia's individual entrepreneurs and small and medium-size businesses by offering high-quality customer service, a wide range of products and access to a countrywide network. The Association of Russian Banks described it as "the foreign-owned bank that contributed the most to the development of the national economy in 2003". KMB Bank's credit ratings from Moody's and Interfax reflect its high creditworthiness relative to other Russian borrowers/borrowings and extremely high creditworthiness under short-term obligations.
www.kmb.ru/english

La Compagnie Financière Edmond de Rothschild Banque

La Compagnie Financière Edmond de Rothschild Banque is a specialist bank with expertise in asset management including private banking and fund management, specializing in equities, fixed-income, structured products, multi-manager funds, alternative management and private equity. Its investment products have for many years been ranked among the world's top performers.
www.lcf-rothschild.fr

Lombard Odier Darier Hentsch

The Lombard Odier Darier Hentsch Group is the oldest firm of private bankers in Geneva and one of the largest in Switzerland and Europe. The company helps clients to preserve and grow the assets they have entrusted to it, and to pass these assets on to future generations.
www.lodh.com

McKinsey & Co.

Global consulting company McKinsey & Co's experience in microfinance includes pulling in new players into the sector, building capacity in under-served geographies, improving the performance of existing MFIs, expanding product ranges, refining existing models to go downstream, developing required industry, developing required industry infrastructure, improving linkages to capital markets, and assisting in the revamping of legislative and regulatory environments. McKinsey has acquired this expertise through projects with central banks, commercial banks, and international institutions spanning the globe.
www.mckinsey.com

Mennonite Economic Development Associates (MEDA)

MEDA is a private investment company with a focus on investing in businesses in poor communities in developing economies and a goal of benefit for the poor. The membership association is composed of Christian business people in USA and Canada, which owns a group of non-profit and for-profit companies working in international economic development. Since its inception, MEDA has, among other things, promoted investment-based development, injecting capital into the production processes that benefit poor communities.
www.meda.org

Michael & Susan Dell Foundation

The Michael & Susan Dell Foundation's mission is to fund initiatives that foster active minds, healthy bodies and a safe environment where children can thrive. The Foundation works as a catalyst for enduring, systemic change. Using a collaborative approach, existing programs and organizations are sought that will serve as links to address unmet needs in the focus areas of health and education in the US in major urban areas and internationally in select countries.
www.msdf.org

Micro Service Consult (MSC)

Micro Service Consult is a consulting firm and think tank for microfinance and small business development, providing services in the areas of strategy development and implementation, catering in particular to financial institutions and the public sector. MSC focuses on corporate strategy, public policy, competitiveness, and micro and small business finance. Moreover, MSC builds up and strengthens links between MFIs and private capital or international organizations by providing project cycle services, such as due diligence, feasibility studies, project design and evaluation.

Micro-Credit Ratings International Ltd (M-CRIL)

M-CRIL undertakes microfinance assessments and research. Its activities are based on the belief that a greater flow of reliable information and credible judgment by an institution with knowledge and experience of the functioning of MFIs is needed for the formal financial sector to increase the provision of wholesale/bulk finance for on-lending by MFIs to low-income clients. Towards this end M-CRIL launched a credit rating product. M-CRIL's positioning as a social enterprise has also led to

the development of a social rating product launched in 2005. In line with its mission, M-CRIL also undertakes sectoral research on aspects like benchmarks and standards, best practices, markets and means of expanding the scope and outreach of microfinance services through regional and commercial banks.
www.m-cril.com

MicroRate

MicroRate rates microfinance institutions (MFIs). Its objectives are to evaluate risk for potential investors, link MFIs with domestic and international capital markets, and thereby help make credit available to those who can use it productively. MicroRate is a fully independent company, dedicated to the single purpose of evaluating risk in microfinance companies.
www.microrate.com

MicroVest Capital Management LLC

MicroVest was co-founded by MEDA Investments Inc and CARE USA in order to bridge the capital gap between private North American investors and microfinance clients in developing economies. Both loans and equity investments are being made in MFIs around the world.
www.microvestfund.com

Moody's Investor Service

Moody's Investor Service is among the world's most respected, widely utilized sources for credit ratings, research and risk analysis. Credit ratings and research help investors analyse the credit risks associated with fixed-income securities. Such independent credit ratings and research also contribute to efficiencies in fixed-income markets and other obligations, such as insurance policies and derivative transactions, by providing credible and independent assessments of credit risk. Customers include a wide range of corporate and governmental issuers of securities as well as institutional investors, depositors, creditors, investment banks, commercial banks, and other financial intermediaries.
www.moodys.com

Omtrix Inc.

Omtrix Inc. is a financial consulting company with strong expertise in the development and management of capital funds and special purpose vehicles, the promotion, appraisal and supervision of investments and loans of bilateral and multilateral institutions, and in diagnostics and strengthening of microfinance institutions.
www.omtrixinc.com

The Positive Investment Initiative

The "Positive Investment Initiative" was created to contribute to eradicating poverty. Composed of entrepreneurs, banking, investment and industry professionals, the association aims at linking investors who wish to join forces to influence positively the future of the planet. The association wants to contribute to

improving life conditions on Earth, by directing investment towards activities that respond to the most essential needs.
www.positive-investment.org

Pictet & Cie

Pictet & Cie is one of Switzerland's largest private banks, and one of the premier independent asset management specialists in Europe. The Pictet Group is an asset management specialist focusing mainly on the following areas of expertise: private and institutional asset management, fund administration and management, global custody and Family Office services.
www.pictet.com

responsAbility Social Investment Services (rAGMF)

responsAbility provides Social Investment services and products with a specific focus on developing countries. While aiming at an economic return, responsAbility always strives for clearly defined social benefits as well. rAGMF makes highly diversified investments in microfinance debt and equity throughout the world.
www.responsability.ch

Schwab Foundation for Social Entrepreneurship

The Schwab Foundation for Social Entrepreneurship is the second organization founded by Klaus Schwab, after the World Economic Forum. The Foundation works from the bottom up. It identifies leaders who have discovered practical solutions to social, economic and environmental problems at the local level, innovative solutions that transform people's lives and that can be adapted to solve similar problems elsewhere. It provides accomplished social entrepreneurs with unprecedented opportunities by giving access to usually inaccessible networks, thereby mobilizing resources that enable them to further their causes. Together with these facilitating structural supports, the micro-level innovations can improve the state of the world and the state of the people in it. Every year, the Foundation selects 10 to 15 social entrepreneurs from approximately 250 nominees. The Foundation ensures that it selects only the most accomplished, innovative and ethical social entrepreneurs. This year, for the first time, the Foundation is partnering with media companies in 25 countries to search and select the leading social entrepreneurs.
www.schwabfound.org

Share Microfin Limited

Share Microfin Limited (SML) is one of the leading and largest MFIs in India. Its main aim is to provide financial and support facilities to the rural poor women living below the poverty line thus enabling them to use their skills in any income-generating activity.
www.sharemicrofin.com

State Street Corporation

State Street is one of the world's leading providers of services to institutional Investors, providing investment management, investment research and trading,

and investment servicing to some of the industry's largest and most sophisticated investment portfolios. The company's focus on the institutional marketplace ensures that its clients stay ahead of investment trends, benefit from research and technology advances, and have access to the latest products and services. Through its longstanding commitment to innovation, State Street has become a recognized leader across its capabilities, including a broad array of investment strategies, transition management, global market services, securities lending, and performance measurement and analytics.
www.statestreet.com

Swiss Investment Fund for Emerging Markets (SIFEM)

SIFEM is a spin-off of the Swiss State Secretariat for Economic Affairs (seco) managing its investment portfolio in developing and transitional countries. It advises seco on new investment opportunities and provides, on its behalf, long-term capital for private small and medium-sized enterprises and infrastructure projects in Africa, Asia, Latin America and transitional countries. Investments are done either directly in businesses of all sectors or indirectly through financial intermediaries (private equity funds, local banks or microfinance institutions) by providing private equity, quasi-equity and loans. The company co-finances projects together with European development finance institutions, international finance institutions and private local or international investors.
www.sifem.ch

The Economist

The Economist is written for a global audience of senior business, political and financial decision-makers that value *The Economist* for the accuracy of its incisive writing, its international outlook and lack of partisanship. Hugely influential, *The Economist's* contributors includes many impressive names from among the world's opinion leaders.
www.economist.com

UBS Philanthropy Services

To respond to the need for a professional approach in philanthropy, UBS has designed a unique platform providing a one-stop access to cutting-edge expertise and implementation solutions in the "jungle" of civil society and the charity sector. UBS Philanthropy Services is designed to add value throughout the entire philanthropy lifecycle. The philanthropic service offering is designed to:

- Help you translate your philanthropic aspirations into an actionable program that truly meets your expectations and creates high impact on the ground, establishing proper indicators and exit options.
- Identify and design the optimal legal vehicle and governance structure to support your engagement efficiently.
- Align the asset management strategy with your philanthropic values and budgetary requirements.

www.ubs.com

United Nations Capital Development Fund (UNCDF)

UNCDF's principal goal is to help reduce poverty, by investing with the poor, building the productive capacity and self-reliance of poor communities by increasing their access to essential local infrastructure and services. The Fund also works to strengthen these communities' influence over economic and social investments that directly affect their lives and livelihoods. Investing with the poor implies close partnership and emphasizes participation, engagement and dialogue. This approach places firm value on the creative and productive potential of the communities the Fund serves. This is why UNCDF-sponsored investments are planned, implemented and monitored with broad local leadership and popular participation. This is also why UNCDF focuses sharply on promoting transparent and accountable local governing institutions that can take on the responsibility of managing civic assets in the common interest. The Fund derives its resources from voluntary contributions made by member states, and from co-financing by governments, international organizations and the private sector.
www.uncdf.org

United Nations International Year of Microcredit 2005

The United Nations' International Year of Microcredit 2005 raised awareness of the financial needs of poor and low-income people. Celebrities including Princess Mathilde of and Princess Maxima of the Netherlands, government officials, bankers, students and current and potential clients created a dialog on how to best provide those financial services, and countries are taking action to try to meet this challenge.
www.yearofmicrocredit.org

Unitus

Unitus is a global microfinance accelerator, acting as a social venture capital investor for the microfinance industry. It identifies the highest-potential microfinance institutions in developing countries and helps accelerate their growth through capital investments and capacity-building consulting, thus empowering them to help exponentially more poor people worldwide. In doing so, Unitus aims to demonstrate that MFIs can be run as profitable, large-scale, poverty-focused businesses with links to local capital markets.
www.unitus.com

Vantage Point (VP)

VP is an independent not-for-profit organization dedicated to promote sustainable investing in emerging markets. Based on its long experience in sustainable finance, VP's main objective to build the capacity for delivering the services required by investors interested in sustainable financing. VP's purpose is to support organizations and companies in emerging markets that have the skills, knowledge and experience to provide the services and products needed to favour and promote sustainable investment in emerging markets.
www.vantagep.org

Women's World Banking (WWB) Foundation, Cali

The WWB Foundation Colombia is an NGO specialized in microcredit provision. The Foundation's main client groups are low-income microentrepreneurs in remote areas. The Foundation's lines of credit are targeted at increasing an enterprise's working capital or fixed assets. The Foundation has received numerous national and international prizes for its activities.

www.fwwbcol.org

Appendix 2: Common Financial Ratios for Assessing Microfinance Institutions

In Part V, von Stauffenberg and Sinha discuss the assessment of microfinance institutions, in particular how to measure portfolio quality and performance. The following section gives an overview of some commonly used ratios in the microfinance industry used to evaluate MFIs. This list is by no means exhaustive. Some ratios have been included because they are common, while others are included because of ambiguity in their use.

Introduction

The evolution of the microfinance industry has led to a greater focus on the financial viability of microfinance institutions (MFIs). A variety of measurements have been used to measure MFI performance, many of which have been recognized as standard indicators. On closer examination, it is evident that these standard indicators are being calculated and applied in many different ways. This has led to confusion among practitioners and analysts, as well as to considerable distortions when comparing MFIs. The industry recognizes this deficiency and agrees that developing standard definitions of financial terms and some common indicators is an important next step in its development. This step would make comparisons between MFIs more meaningful and promote more transparency in MFI reporting. Transparency is increasingly important in the industry as mature MFIs look to commercial funding sources and investors to support their growth.

The following list of terms is based on the results of a project initiated by Damian von Stauffenberg of MicroRate. Contributors to the project included Frank Abate of MicroRate, Tillman Bruett of Alternative Credit Technologies and the SEEP Network, Isabelle Barres of the MicroBanking Bulletin, Robert Christen and Richard Rosenberg of Consultative Group to Assist the Poorest (CGAP), Dana de Kanter of the SEEP Network, Tor Jansson of the InterAmerican Development Bank (IDB), Barry Lennon of the US Agency for International Development (USAID), Alice Negre of Planet Finance, Sanjay Sinha of M-CRIL, and the Financial Services Working Group of the SEEP Network. Intended as a first step towards creating a standard terminology for some financial terms and ratios within the international microfinance industry, the project eventually led to the development of SEEP's *Measuring Performance of Microfinance Institutions*, the Framework, and the FRAME tool, an Excel workbook – a set of complementary instruments to be used in conjunction with one another. FRAME is intended to serve as a tool by which the industry can achieve global microfinance performance standards. Further information can be found at: http://www.seepnetwork.org/section/frame/.

The terms and ratios presented here mostly include those that the authors believed were not only commonly used, but also the subject of some confusion. This list assumes some basic familiarity with accounting terms, financial statements and microfinance institutions. It should be noted that not all micro-credit providers can use the same accounting standards and chart of accounts, as these are frequently dictated by local practices and internal needs. The definitions here are not intended as a substitute for a chart of accounts or accounting policies. Nor are they to be taken as a financial analysis guide, as analysts will normally use other financial indicators and information beyond what is contained here.

Financial ratios

The following list defines the formulae and purposes of key ratios, and highlights some of the key issues related to each ratio, including some general calculation issues. The ratios are divided into four categories, namely:

- Sustainability/Profitability
- Asset/Liability Management
- Portfolio Quality
- Efficiency/Productivity

It should be noted that some MFIs may use definitions or formulae that differ from those provided. However, the definitions given here may serve as a reference point for comparing such alternatives. For each ratio, there is a reference code, a formula and an explanation of its purpose.

Calculation issues
Annualizing

Unless otherwise indicated, it is assumed that all revenue and expense accounts used in indicators are stated on an annual or annualized basis. When calculating financial ratios in Part III, it is assumed that the income statement represents one year. If not, then income statement figures must first be annualized before they can be compared with previous years or against other MFIs.

To annualize a number, the formula is: $AA = [A \times (12/M)]$

Where: AA 191= annualized amount
A = amount for the period
M = number of months in the period.

Averaging

Many financial ratios require an average for a balance sheet account, such as the net loan portfolio outstanding. Averages for a period (such as a year) can be calculated simply by adding a beginning amount and an end amount and dividing the result by two:

$$Pavg = [(P^0 + P^1)/2]$$

Unfortunately, such simple average calculations often provide a distorted number. This distortion is particularly true for institutions whose loan portfolios are growing quickly or for institutions that experience significant seasonal fluctuations in lending activities. Period averages are much more meaningful when they are computed on a monthly or at least a quarterly basis. When using such sub-period averages, the numerator is the opening balance plus the sum of the balance at the end of each sub-period, while the denominator is the number of sub-periods plus one. As an example, a quarterly average would be calculated as:

$$\text{Pavg} = \frac{(P^0 + P^1 + P^2 + P^3 + P^4)}{(4 + 1)}$$

Sustainability/profitability

R1	Return on equity (ROE)	$$\dfrac{\text{Net operating income + taxes}}{\text{Average equity}}$$	Calculates the rate of return on the average equity for the period. Because the numerator does not include non-operating items such as donations, the ratio is a frequently used proxy for commercial viability. Usually, ROE calculations are net of profit or revenue taxes. MFIs that are not using average equity as the denominator should indicate if it is based on equity at the beginning of the period or the end.
	Adjusted return on equity (AROE)	$$\dfrac{\text{Adjusted net operating income + taxes}}{\text{Average equity}}$$	This ratio may be calculated on an adjusted basis to address the effects of subsidies, inflation, loan loss provisioning and other items that are not normally included in an MFI's net operating income.
R2	Return on assets (ROA)	$$\dfrac{\text{Net operating income + taxes}}{\text{Average assets}}$$	Measures how well the MFI uses its total assets to generate returns.
	Adjusted return on assets (AROA)	$$\dfrac{\text{Net adjusted operating income + taxes}}{\text{Average assets}}$$	This ratio may also be calculated on an adjusted basis to address the effects of subsidies, inflation, loan loss provisioning, and other items that are not normally included in an MFI's net operating income.

R3	Operational self-sufficiency	$$\frac{\text{Operating revenue}}{(\text{Financial expense} + \text{Loan loss provision expense} + \text{Operating expense})}$$	Measures how well an MFI can cover its costs through operating revenues. In addition to operating expenses, it is recommended that financial expense and loan loss provision expenses be included in this calculation as they are a normal (and significant) cost of operating.
R4	Profit margin	$$\frac{\text{Net operating income}}{\text{Operating revenue}}$$	Measures what percentage of operating revenue remains after all financial, loan loss provision and operating expenses are paid.
R5	Financial self-sufficiency	$$\frac{\text{Adjusted operating revenue}}{\text{Financial expense} + \text{Loan loss provision expense} + \text{Adjusted operating expense}}$$	Measures how well an MFI can cover its costs taking into account a number of adjustments to operating revenues and expenses. The purpose of most of these adjustments is to model how well the MFI could cover its costs if its operations were unsubsidized and it was funding its expansion with commercial-cost liabilities.

Assets/liability management

R6	Yield on gross portfolio	$$\dfrac{\text{Cash financial revenue from loan portfolio}}{\text{Average gross loan portfolio}}$$	Indicates the gross loan portfolio's ability to generate cash financial revenue from interest, fees and commissions. It does not include any revenues that have been accrued but not paid in cash, or any non-cash revenues in the form of post-dated checks, seized but unsold collateral, etc.
R7	Current ratio	$$\dfrac{\text{Short-term assets}}{\text{Short-term liabilities}}$$	Measures how well the MFI matches the maturities of its assets and liabilities. Short-term are assets or liabilities or any portion of the same that have a due date, maturity date, or may be readily converted into cash within 12 months.
R8	Yield gap	100% minus	Compares revenue actually received in cash with revenue expected under the terms of the loan contracts. While a small gap is common, a substantial yield gap (>10%) may indicate significant past due payments (arrears), fraud, inefficiency or accounting error.

		$\dfrac{\text{Yield on net portfolio}}{\text{Expected annual yield}}$	In this formula, "expected annual yield" means the loan contracts' effective interest rate (the declining-balance-equivalent rate) for a single payment period, multiplied by the number of periods in a year.
R9	Funding expense ratio	$\dfrac{\text{Interest and fee expenses on funding liabilities}}{\text{Average gross loan portfolio}}$	Shows the blended interest rate the MFI is paying to fund its financial assets. This ratio can be compared with yield on gross portfolio to determine the interest margin.
R10	Cost of funds ratio	$\dfrac{\text{Interest and fee expense on funding liabilities}}{\text{Average funding liabilities}}$	The ratio gives a blended interest rate for all of the MFI's funding liabilities. Funding liabilities do not include interest payable or interest on loans to finance fixed assets.

Portfolio quality

R11	PAR ratio	$\dfrac{\text{Portfolio at risk (X days)}}{\text{Gross loan portfolio}}$	The most accepted measure of portfolio quality. Portfolio at risk is the outstanding principle amount of all loans that have one or more installments of principal past due by a certain number of days.
			When referring to PAR, the MFI should always specify the number of days.
			MFIs should indicate whether restructured loans are included in their calculation. Some MFIs automatically include restructured loans in their portfolio at risk. This practice reflects the belief that restructured loans have higher risk than those than current loans.
R12	Write-off ratio	$\dfrac{\text{Value of loans written-off}}{\text{Average gross loan portfolio}}$	Represents the percentage of the MFI's loans that have been removed from the balance of the gross loan portfolio because they are unlikely to be repaid. A high ratio may indicate a problem in the MFI's collection efforts. However, MFI's write-off policies vary, which makes comparisons difficult. As a result, analysts may present this ratio on an adjusted basis to provide for uniform treatment of write-offs.
	Adjusted write-off ratio	$\dfrac{\text{Adjusted value of loans written-off}}{\text{Average gross loan portfolio}}$	
R13	Risk coverage ratio	$\dfrac{\text{Loan loss reserve}}{\text{Portfolio at risk} > \text{X days}}$	Shows how much of the portfolio at risk is covered by the MFI's loan loss reserve. It is a rough indicator of how prepared an institution is to absorb loan losses in the worst-case scenario. MFIs should provision according to the aging of their portfolio at risk: the older the delinquent loan, the higher the loan loss reserve.
			For example, a ratio for PAR > 90 days may be close to 100%, whereas the ratio for PAR > 30 days is likely to be significantly less. Thus, a risk coverage ratio of 100% is not

R14	Loan officer productivity	$$\frac{\text{Number of active borrowers}}{\text{Number of loan officers}}$$	Measures the average caseload of each loan officer, as defined in Part II. This is a common ratio, but is difficult to compare among MFIs when their definitions of loan officer vary. MFIs may also substitute (1) number of loans outstanding as a surrogate for number of active borrowers; and (2) number of financial services officers for loan officers. Regardless, MFIs should explain their definition of the numerator and denominator.
R15	Personnel productivity	$$\frac{\text{Number of active borrowers}}{\text{Number of personnel}}$$ $$\frac{\text{Number of active clients}}{\text{Number of personnel}}$$	Measures the overall productivity of the MFI's total human resources in managing clients who have an outstanding loan balance and are thereby contributing to the financial revenue of the MFI. Alternatively, the MFI may wish to measure the overall productivity of the MFI's personnel in terms of managing clients, including borrowers, savers, and other clients. This ratio is the most useful ratio for comparing MFIs.
R16	Average disbursed loan size	$$\frac{\text{Value of loans disbursed}}{\text{Total number of loans disbursed during period}}$$	Measures the average loan size that is disbursed to clients. MFIs should be careful to distinguish between disbursed loan size and outstanding loan size (see R17).
R17	Average outstanding loan size	$$\frac{\text{Gross loan portfolio}}{\text{Number of loans outstanding}}$$	Measures the average outstanding loan balance by client, which may be significantly less than the average disbursed loan size. It is frequently compared to per capita GDP to determine how well an MFI is targeting very low-income clients.

R18	Operating expense ratio	$$\frac{\text{Operating expense}}{\text{Average gross loan portfolio*}}$$	Includes all administrative and personnel expense, and is the most commonly used efficiency indicator. Care must be taken when using this ratio to compare MFIs. Smaller MFIs or those that provide smaller loans will compare unfavorably to others, even though they may be serving their target market efficiently. Likewise, MFIs that offer savings and other services will also compare unfavorably to those that do not if gross loan portfolio is used as the denominator.
R19	Cost per borrower	$$\frac{\text{Operating expense}}{\text{Average number of active borrowers}}$$	Provides a meaningful measure of efficiency for an MFI, allowing them it to determine the average cost of maintaining an active borrower or client. MFIs may choose to substitute number of active loans as the denominator to see cost per active loan outstanding. It is also useful when to compare to GNP per capita to assess the MFI's efficiency in the local context. Because they count clients rather than amounts, these indicators have the advantage that they do not prejudice MFIs who offer smaller loans and savings accounts.
	Cost per client	$$\frac{\text{Operating expense}}{\text{Average number of clients}}$$	
R20	Other expense ratios	$$\frac{\text{Any expense}}{\text{Average gross loan portfolio*}}$$	Expense ratios can be created for nearly any expense account on the income statement. The purpose is to allow the MFI or analyst to track the growth or decline of particular expense over time or across a group.

Efficiency/Productivity

These indicators reflect how efficiently an MFI is using its resources, particularly its assets and its personnel. MFIs use many different efficiency and productivity indicators, tailoring them to reflect their own organizational structure, product lines and monitoring priorities. In calculating these indicators, MFIs need to select which denominator they will use. The most common denominators related to assets are (1) gross loan portfolio, (2) performing assets and (3) average total assets. Most MFIs choose to use the average gross loan portfolio because they calculate other ratios using this same denominator. However, there are strong arguments for using performing assets, which is the standard for the commercial banking industry, or average total assets, which is the most easily measured of the three. Using average total assets as the denominator for efficiency/productivity ratios is more relevant for MFIs that manage deposit and/or share accounts in addition to loans. Regardless, the MFI should be consistent in its use of denominator. For the sake of simplifying the presentation, the gross loan portfolio is used below; however, the asterisk (*) in the denominator of several ratios indicates that average total assets could be used.

MFIs must also decide if they wish to use the number of personnel or number of loan officers as their benchmark for human resources. The purpose for considering loan officers as a separate category is that they are usually involved directly in revenue generating tasks and income (i.e. making and collecting loans), whereas other personnel are not. However, there is a trend toward using total personnel in productivity calculations, recognizing that loan officers' tasks may overlap with the tasks of administrative staff.

Note

1   Compounding is not used. Thus, if the effective monthly rate is 3%, then the expected annual yield is (3% × 12 months) = 36%, not $1.03^{12} - 1 = 42.58\%$.

Appendix 3: Comments on the Geneva Private Capital Symposium, 2005

Congratulations on an excellent event that has had not only touched on that most critical of crossroads between private capital and microfinance, but has also reinforced most significantly the image of Switzerland and Geneva in the world of microfinance and economic development. The entire symposium, both in terms of speakers, contributions, breakout sessions and – of course – networking was an unqualified success.

Dinos Constantinou, Global Microfinance Group

The Symposium was able to bring forward the different players and views of the microfinance world. The complexity and growth potential of this field was dealt with professionally, and at the top level.

Coming to this symposium from both a private banking and investor vantage point, I was extremely impressed. Bravo and thank you for your diligent work.

Brigitte Reverdin, MARKETrends, Geneva

I am looking back to two excellent days at the Geneva Private Capital Symposium. It was a highly inspiring event, and I think the mixture of plenary and breakout sessions were well balanced.

Maximilian Martin, Wealth Management, Head, Philanthropy Services, UBS

I honestly believe it was the best conference on microfinance that I have attended, partially because it was the first one I have been to that included a large number of participants from the private sector. The topics discussed and the list of attendees and speakers made the conference, in my opinion, a huge success.

Rosalind Copisarow, ACCION

It brought together a much wider range of interested parties than most conferences and will result in some concrete outcomes.

Bob Annibale, Global Director, Microfinance Group, Citigroup

Allow me to congratulate you for the success of the Microfinance Symposium, which I attended with a lot of interest. I have not only learned from it but also could establish fruitful contacts with a series of extraordinary experts and visionaries involved in the microfinance world that you successfully assembled for this Symposium. The lessons taken from this event will allow us to better define ICRC's policy in what regards the support to microfinance institutions in post-conflict regions.

Gilles Carbonnier, Economic Counselor, International Committee of the Red Cross (ICRC)

I have rarely learned as much as in such a short period of time. Rarely as well, so many questions have been raised constituting challenges to be solved. The value of these contacts will be revealed during the following weeks, and the following months. I am pleased with this Symposium and I am already looking forward to the next one. Personally, I think that the values created in this Symposium should be kept within a foundation based in Geneva. The database, the cumulated experiences, the support given by all interventions should be kept for the history of microfinance. We are only at its beginning! I congratulate you once again for the success of this enormous presentation.

Philine Read, credit link ligne de crédit, Genève

Organization and logistics were impeccable and the content/quality of speakers of a very high level. Congratulations from my part for the great job.

Isabel Guggisberg, BHP – Brugger und Partner AG

You did a very fine job. Did not expect to take away so much.

Arthur Vayloyan, Member of the Executive Board, and Head, Private Banking, Credit Suisse, Switzerland

Masterful organization!

Elizabeth Littlefield, CEO, CGAP

Congratulations for the flagrant success of this microfinance symposium. Much appreciated its depth and the strong feeling of need for further exchanges and openings on the theme.

Henry Morgan, de Pury Pictet Turrettini & Cie S.A

I very much enjoyed the event because of its many rich discussions. It was interesting to see the different points of view of the portfolio managers and social actors. Mr Damian von Stauffenberg's intervention on the critical issues of private and commercial investment in the MFI seemed just right to me. The discussion within the "Funds of funds" breakout session was vivacious and turned out as a true debate between the social and the purely commercial issues. The question on the harmonization between multilateral/bilateral and private actors is an ongoing debate that has not finished yet. Finally, I congratulate you for the high quality "speakers" that you successfully invited and for the diversified audience that was very interested in the subject. It was a pleasure to attend this event; I congratulate you for the excellent organization, which implied a lot of work and compromise from the entire CASIN team.

Rita Schmid, Project Manager UN Year of Microcredit 2005, Swiss Agency for Development and Cooperation

Index